P9-EAX-983

.....THE LAST

NAVIGATOR

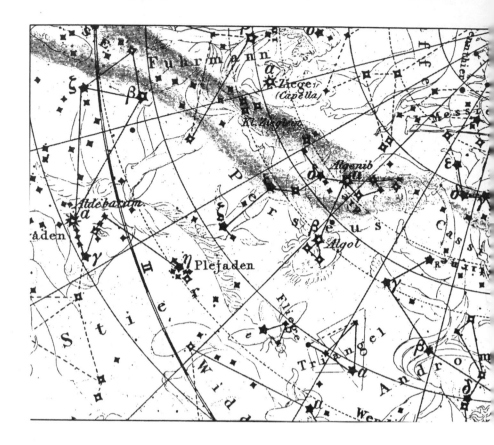

Steve Thomas

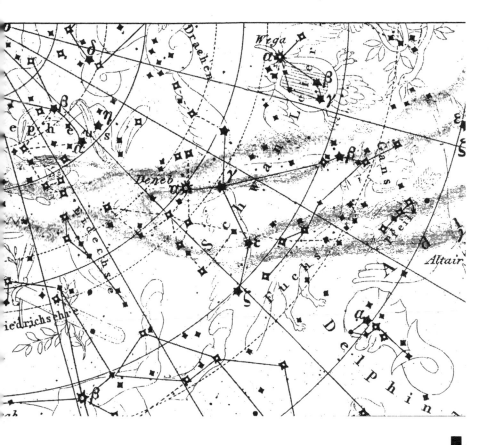

A Young Man,

THE LAST

An Ancient Mariner,

NAVIGATOR

The Secrets of the Sea

International marine
Camden, Maine

FOR EVY . . . AND SAM

International Marine/
Ragged Mountain Press

A Division of The McGraw-Hill Companies

10   9   8   7   6   5   4   3

Copyright © Steve Thomas

All rights reserved, including the right to reproduce this book or portions thereof in any form. The name "International Marine" and the International Marine logo are trademarks of The McGraw-Hill Companies. Printed in the United States of America.

First published in hardcover by Henry Holt, 1987. First paperback edition Ballantine Books, 1988.

"This Old House" is a copyright of the WGBH Educational Foundation and is used with permission.

Library of Congress Cataloging-in-Publication Data

Thomas, Stephen D.
 The last navigator : a young man, an ancient mariner, the secrets of
the sea / Steve Thomas.
  p. cm.
 Originally published: New York : H. Holt, c1987.
 Includes index.
 ISBN 0-07-064574-4 (acid-free paper)
 1. Navigation—Caroline Islands. 2. Piailug, Mau. 3. Ethnology—
Caroline Islands. 4. Micronesians—Social life and customs.
5. Thomas, Stephen D. 6. Ethnology—Caroline Islands—Field work.
I. Title.
GN671.C3T48 1997
996.6—dc21   97-20220
                 CIP

Questions regarding the ordering of this book should be addressed to:

The McGraw-Hill Companies
Customer Service Department
P.O. Box 547
Blacklick, OH 43004
Retail customers: 1-800-262-4729
Bookstores: 1-800-233-4726

This book is printed on 60-pound Renew Opaque Vellum, an acid-free paper which contains 50 percent recycled waste paper (preconsumer) and 10 percent postconsumer waste paper.

Printed by R.R. Donnelley, Indianapolis, IN

Design by University Graphics, Inc.
Production by University Graphics, Inc.

Acknowledgments

I wish here to thank: Peter Fetchko and the Peabody Museum of Salem, Epel Ilon, Jesse Marehalau, Dr. Peter Ochs, Sheila Bernard, Lee Van Gemert and John Clayton at Hood Yacht Systems, Dick Pinn, Norman Marquis, Herb Lison and Data Tree Inc., Dr. Patrick Kirch, Jesse Tamel Gajdusek, Dr. Don Rubenstein, Francis X. Hezel, S.J., Ben Fitial, Mark Skinner, Ron and Dianne Strong, the Honorable John Mangafel, Hillary Tacheliol, Francis Defngin, Russ and Verna Curtis, Jesse Raglmar, Mike and Angie McCoy, ham-radio operators Gus McFeeley and Leo Dellarosa.

Special thanks are due to Dr. Sanford Low, René D. Varrin, Esq., Dr. Carlton Gajdusek, Dr. Ward Goodenough, Andrea Simpson, Phil Kinnicut, Bill Acker, the Honorable Tosiwo Nakayama, and to the chiefs and the people of Satawal Island.

Major funding for this project was provided by Pacific Resources, Inc., with additional funding from The Wenner-Gren Foundation for Anthropological Research and Continental Air Lines.

PREFACE

In July of 1989, I was offered the chance to host Public Television's premiere home-renovation program, "This Old House." It was a once-in-a-lifetime opportunity, and I took it. It may seem an unlikely eventuality for a yachtsman who had spent nearly a decade researching and writing a book about non-instrumental navigation, but there is a certain haphazard logic to my career that I shall endeavor to explain.

I bought my first sailboat when I was 13. After college I crewed on a yacht racing out to Hawaii, sailed the boat back to Seattle, and was hooked—I wanted to be at sea. The next year I became the first mate of a 103-foot schooner in the Mediterranean, and by the end of the year I was working for a boatbuilder in Antibes, in the South of France. The following year I delivered a 43-foot sloop from England to San Francisco via the Canaries, the Caribbean, Panama, the Galapagos, the Marquesas, and Hawaii. I met my future wife on that voyage, and to her more than anyone, I owe the existence of this book.

My other occupation, and the more profitable one, had been old houses: First painting them while in college, then working on them as a carpenter, and finally buying, renovating, and selling them. After that voyage, my wife and I bought a large house on Boston's North Shore, which we renovated. We had intended to sell it, purchase a cruising boat, and continue traveling around the world. Instead, I became inspired by an old dream to go to the Pacific islands and live among a seafaring people who were fully attuned to the sea's natural rhythms. This quest led me to Satawal, and Mau Piailug, the fully initiated navigator, or *palu*.

In 1983, after a year of preliminary research, I journeyed to Sata-wal. I stayed in Micronesia six months and returned in 1984 for five months. I spent the next two years writing the manuscript, and *The Last Navigator* was published in 1987.

Then, by chance, I met a British documentary film producer in a trattoria in Venice. We obtained backing from British and American educational television to shoot a film and in 1988 returned to Micronesia in a chartered sailboat. Using the 32-foot outrigger canoe *Aningana*, which I had helped build, I sailed with Piailug and his crew for six days from Satawal to Saipan, the longest passage his people have tradition-ally made. We had no radio, charts, compass, or other navigational equipment on board.

Finishing the film brought to a close the Satawal epoch in my life. After my son's birth, I went to the Alaskan Arctic, where my grand-father had been an Episcopal missionary early in this century and where my father was born. I made three field trips to research a book and, I hoped, a film on Eskimos, the oil industry, and my family's history in the Arctic village of Point Hope.

I returned from my last trip to the Arctic in 1989 to the realiza-tion that success as a writer and documentary filmmaker did not mean one could feed one's family. It was clear that I had to find a job with a steady paycheck and fit in the Arctic project when I could. My wife (rather generously) granted me a month or so to contemplate my fate, and while I did, I renovated my attic.

In the United States, *The Last Navigator* film had been part of PBS's Adventure series. While working in the attic, I received a tele-phone call from the series publicist, who also, it happened, worked for "This Old House." Offhandedly, she suggested I talk to the show's pro-ducers, who were deep into a national search for a new host; they had already passed over more than 400 candidates. I called them and ap-plied, never expecting to get the job. I was interviewed, screen-tested and, ten days after that chance telephone call, offered the position. Life has never been quite the same since—but that is another story.

Going to Satawal, and studying and voyaging with Piailug, was a great and romantic dream. I had the supreme good fortune to be able to realize that dream. Much of opportunity is timing; five years earlier I would not have had the maturity to undertake this journey; five years later and family responsibilities would have prevented me from doing so. It was a young man's quest, and I was able to undertake it as a young man.

Then too, my arrival on Satawal coincided with a window in Piailug's schedule. He had been fully involved in the Hokule'a project in Hawaii before I arrived, and returned to Hawaii after I left. Had this timing been different, it may well have been impossible for me to study with Piailug at all.

There is also the matter of the age of the wise elders. By 1983, the old men were beginning to realize that unless they bequeathed their knowledge to someone, it would die with their mortal frames. Indeed, our "father" Pwitack, who I call Maanusuuk in the narrative, died between my first and second field trips. Aeoweiung, who I call Mwaramai, was very old when I worked with him and knew he had not many years to live. Chief Otolig, Rewena in the narrative, died on the field ship en route from the hospital on Yap back to Satawal.

Micronesia's is an oral tradition. As the old navigators have passed away, so has any opportunity to learn the Talk of the Sea, and the highly secret Talk of Light. I was indeed fortunate to go to Satawal when I did.

It has been nearly fifteen years since I first met Piailug. In that time I have been blessed with relative fame and prosperity—an eventuality, by the way, that Piailug foretold to me. As I look back, I am impressed now by the twin qualities in the man that impressed me then: his generosity and his courage. Piailug took me into his family, assumed responsibility for my material and political well-being, and taught me his navigation without reserve. The knowledge he gave me about navigation is considered priceless in his culture. The knowledge he gave me about myself, I have come to see, is priceless as well. I often think of Piailug, and the fierceness and determination with which he defends a way of life he knows will die as the wise elders died. He has the courage to live and teach and voyage in spite of the certain knowledge that his struggle can never stem the tide of Westernization, which will change the character of his archipelago and may well eliminate the very role of the navigator as steward of his island's sustenance and keeper of the flame of cultural knowledge.

This is what makes Piailug a hero, both to me individually, and to all of us as Westerners. The core of his teaching is heroic. Piailug delivered it to me late at night and late in my stay with him and not until I was reviewing my tape recordings months later did I realize how important his words really were:

"To be a *palu* you must have three qualities: fierceness, strength, and wisdom. . . . The knowledge of navigation brings all three. Fierceness, strength, and wisdom, Steve: That is a navigator, and a navigator is a man."

CONTENTS

PART I   *Re Metau*: The People of the Sea   1
PART II   The Talk of Our Fathers   63
PART III   The Canoe of Palulap   133

APPENDICES   237

   1   Stars and Planets   239
   2   Subdivision of the *Etak* of Sighting   243
   3   *Itimetau*   245
   4   *Pwipwimetau*   247
   5   *Aruruwow*   250
   6   *Pookof*   252
   7   *Wofanu*   261
   8   The Fighting of Stars   268
   9   *Kapesani Serak:* The Talk of Sailing   272
  10   *Fu Taur*   286

GLOSSARY   291

INDEX   299

· *The Pacific Ocean* ·

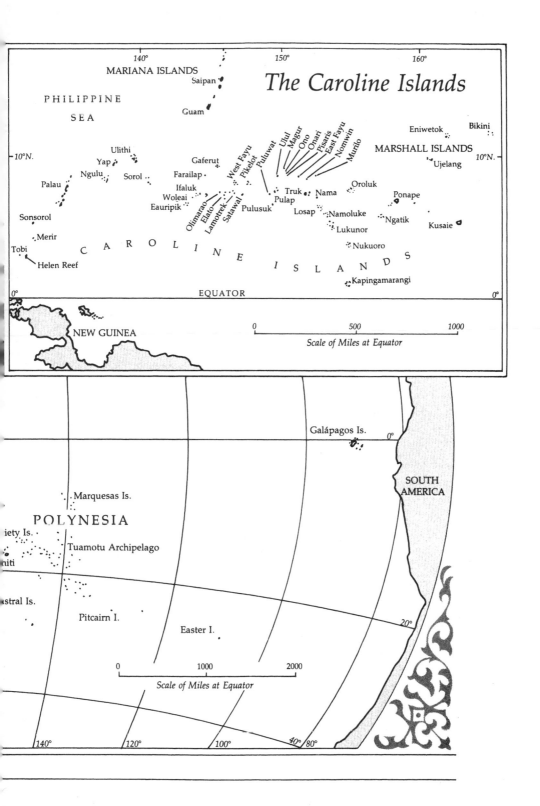

The Caroline Islands

140°   150°   160°

MARIANA ISLANDS

Saipan

PHILIPPINE

SEA

Guam

−10°N.

Ulithi

Yap

Ngulu   Sorol

Palau

Gaferut

West Fayu   Pikelot   Puluwat

Ulul   Magur   Ono   Onari   Pisaris   East Fayu   Nomwin   Murilo

Eniwetok   Bikini

MARSHALL ISLANDS

10°N.

Ujelang

Frailap

Ifaluk

Woleai

Eauripik

Olimarao   Elato   Lamotrek   Satawal   Pulusuk

Truk   Nama

Pulap

Losap

Oroluk

Ponape

Namoluke

Ngatik

Kusaie

Sonsorol

Merir

Tobi

Helen Reef

C A R O L I N E   I S L A N D S

Lukunor

Nukuoro

Kapingamarangi

0°   EQUATOR   0°

NEW GUINEA

0   500   1000

Scale of Miles at Equator

Galápagos Is.   0°

SOUTH
AMERICA

Marquesas Is.

POLYNESIA

Society Is.

Tuamotu Archipelago

Tahiti

Austral Is.

Pitcairn I.

Easter I.

20°

0   1000   2000

Scale of Miles at Equator

140°   120°   100°   40° 80°

PART I

Re Metau: The People of the Sea

1

The plane seemed to hover in the pink cumulus clouds as the first sunlight spilled over the Koolau mountains and down the green slopes to lap against the hotels and office buildings of Honolulu. Already the lei shops, tourist catamarans, and all-you-can-eat Polynesian dinner boats were preparing to sell, for another day, their piece of old Oceania. The plane climbed, then rolled away to the southwest and out over the sea. Two hours later we landed at tiny Johnston Atoll, dropped off fresh milk and eggs for the U.S. naval outpost there, refueled, and took off again. From there, the flight would hop four thousand miles through Micronesia's Marshall and Caroline islands to its final destination, Guam. I would go on, flying south to Yap, where I would board a small freighter for a two-week voyage to Satawal, one of the most remote islands in the Carolines. I hoped to study there with a man named Piailug, one of a dying breed of navigators who used only natural signs—stars, ocean swells, and birds—to guide their outrigger sailing canoes across hundreds, even thousands of miles of open ocean. I was in search of my own piece of old Oceania.

Long before Columbus and Magellan, before Europeans had even dared to venture beyond sight of land, a nation of seafarers had already discovered and colonized the vast expanse of Pacific islands. Some six thousand years ago seafarers left islands in eastern Indonesia and the Philippines to branch into the western Pacific. Archeologists trace their migrations by a distinctive style of cultural materials—shell hooks, coral files, and bone tattooing needles—found in sites from the Bismarck Archipelago, near New Guinea, all the way out to the Solomons, New Hebrides, Fiji, Tonga, and Samoa. Scientists call these early seafarers the Lapita people. In the ruins of their settlements have been found adzes and other cutting tools chipped from obsidian, or volcanic glass, which spectrographic analysis suggests was quarried on New Britain's Talasea Peninsula. Obsidian was evidently one commodity in an extensive network of trade that connected Lapita islands until the dispersal of the culture in 500 B.C. It is astonishing that, at a time when the Greeks were making short hops between intervisible islands in the Aegean, Lapita navigators were guiding long blue-water passages without charts, compass, or instruments.

Beginning about 1300 B.C., Lapita navigators left the northern New Hebrides to voyage a thousand miles north to the Marshall, Gilbert, and Caroline islands. Lapita material has been unearthed in sites on Ponape and Truk, and more finds are expected. Over time, these settlers developed a unique set of languages and culture traits, which today distinguish Micronesia from Polynesia and Melanesia, the two other cultural areas of Oceania.

On Tonga and Samoa, the Lapita people developed a distinct Polynesian language and culture. At about the time of Christ, they voyaged into the eastern Pacific, making the eighteen-hundred-mile windward passage to the Marquesas. Later, perhaps following the migratory flight paths of the golden plover and the long-tailed cuckoo, they fanned out to discover and colonize Tahiti, Hawaii, New Zealand, and tiny Easter Island, a feat of seafaring as great as Columbus's discovery of America or Magellan's first circumnavigation. Thus all of Oceania, an area nearly a quarter of the earth, was populated by a single race. Navigators using just the stars, the ocean swells, and the flight paths of birds were making epic ocean voyages in hand-hewn sailing canoes while Europeans still lived in rude huts scattered across a land of primeval forests.

Upon discovering the Hawaiian (then Sandwich) Islands in 1778, the redoubtable Captain James Cook marveled: "How shall we account for this Nation spreading itself over this Vast ocean? We find them from New Zealand to the South, to these islands to the North and from Easter Island to the Hebrides." Cook had discovered the Polynesians. At that time, the indigenous navigating tradition was still very much alive in Oceania. In Tahiti, Cook took on board with him a chief and navigator named Tupia who enumerated the range and bearings of 130 islands around Tahiti and, on his subsequent voyages with Cook, always knew the direction back to his home. Yet in the following years of European exploration and trade, these navigators disappeared. Now, throughout Polynesia and in much of Micronesia, the tradition is forgotten, swept aside in the rapid adoption of Western culture. The central Carolines is one of the few places where traditional navigation is still practiced. Here the "talk of the sea" has been kept alive in the frail vessel of human memory, passed from father to son in a shining braid of talk.

Approaching Kwajalein Atoll in the Marshall Islands, the airplane banked into a shallow dive and sliced through the clouds. Beneath us a fishing vessel lolled in the swells—a Russian trawler, the pilot announced over the intercom, spying on the U.S. missile-testing range on "Kwaj," as the atoll is nicknamed. ICBMs launched from California's Vandenberg Air Force Base are tested for accuracy as they drop into Kwajalein's lagoon. The plane circled the vessel, landed on the long, narrow island, debarked several military people, and quickly took off again.

During World War II, Kwajalein was the principal Japanese naval base in the Marshalls. As the airplane banked and headed toward its next stop, Ponape, I remembered, as a child, watching *Victory at Sea* on television with my father. The images of the fierce contest for the Pacific islands had wedged in my mind: fighter planes screaming through the clouds, gun-camera footage of the tracers rushing to straddle a helpless vessel, bullets finding their mark, Japanese sailors scattering on deck before the pilot pulled the nose up and wriggled away. The film would cut to a long shot of a ship blowing up, then a bow or stern section sliding beneath the waves.

My father had served in the Pacific during the war. In Hong Kong he had had a plimsol mark tattooed high on his thigh. Curious, I used to run my fingers across the blue-green skin as I watched him shave in the morning. On Saturdays he would take me to his office in San Francisco and, for our lunch, would buy ham-and-cheese sandwiches at the Chinese grocery on the waterfront. We would eat them by the docks, watching the squealing cranes unload from the freighters' holds goods from the far shores of the Pacific. My father's ship had plied the same sea routes over which I was now flying, from San Francisco to Hawaii, Guam, Saipan, the South China Sea. He had found his manhood in these waters. It was not by accident that I gravitated here.

The plane set down at Ponape, capital of the Federated States of Micronesia, the government of the Caroline Islands. Because of the outer islands' small size and fragile subsistence economies, access to them is severely restricted. Tourists are not even allowed to board the ship that services them. Six months before, I had begun the difficult process of obtaining a research visa, submitting my project prospectus, a vita, police reports attesting to my good character, and letters of recommendation. I had gone to Washington to present myself to the liaison officers there. Now, on Ponape, I met with officials of the FSM government: President Tosiwo Nakayama, Vice President Petrus Tun, and Secretary of External Affairs Jesse Raglmar. All were men from the islands and all were related to navigators. They said they envied me, going off to learn navigation on Satawal, their most traditional island. They gave me their personal approval and their government's. Three days later I boarded the airplane again, headed for Guam.

The 727 banked hard and climbed off the runway at Ponape. Hydraulic pumps whined as the landing gear retracted; the well doors thumped closed. I pressed my nose to the plastic window to trace the serried fissures and channels through the broad reefs surrounding the island. A motorboat skimmed across water as smooth as the skin of a blue snake. Then we punched through the cloud deck and into the transparent blue of high altitude.

The thin light of the reclining sun skidded across the clouds, igniting their tops but never warming the white towers. Below the clouds were the islands, dull and purple in the fading light, and below the islands, reefs and channels and brilliantly colored reef fish. The earth seemed composed of nothing but huge, piled racks of cloud, a few islands, and reefs. I remembered an evening over five years before, leaving the Galápagos to sail to the Marquesas, three thousand miles away. The clouds, the sun, and the islands were all this same color as they slipped beneath the horizon and left me and a single crewman alone on the sea. I was taking a yacht from England to San Francisco via the Marquesas and Hawaii.

That particular ocean crossing was different from the other passages I had made. Sailing the Atlantic, I had felt the comfort of populated shores all around me. Even when, several years earlier, I had crewed on a racing yacht from Seattle to Hawaii, I'd felt the same assurance from the teeming continent at my back. But the Galápagos were an isolated outpost; the Marquesas an even more remote landfall. My boat had neither electronic navigation equipment nor a two-way radio. If something were to happen, no one could help me. I used to imagine that if the boat sank and I drowned, my body would drift slowly to the bottom of the sea and be eaten by fishes until it was gone. The wind and sea and stars would go on, hard and powerful, and my brief passage on earth would stand for nothing.

At sea I lived in a world of finite size and finite human acts. The habitable globe was the length and breadth of my small boat; the sphere of human action was everything I or my crewman did. All else was chance. Each act took on huge proportions: tying a knot in a line, plotting a sextant shot, resting for several hours before a night watch. Any act could set off a chain of events ending in death. All acts seemed bound together, like molecules aligned, as it were, by some intense magnetism of the sea. We saw no ships, no airplanes, not even satellites while we traversed that vast tract of ocean. The sea was an awesome field of waves that went on and on, was joined to the sky at the scar of the horizon, to flow past the moon and sun to the galaxies with such terrible beauty and profound indifference that, when I reached Hawaii several months and five thousand miles later, I had to get away from it. For two months I didn't go back aboard my boat.

I first learned about the native navigators of Oceania on that Seattle-Hawaii race. I was just out of college and, instead of going on to graduate school for advanced study in philosophy, as I'd intended, I was drawn unpremeditatedly onto a course similar to my father's: I went to sea.

On the return voyage to Seattle, the yacht's navigator taught me celestial navigation. Mastering the sextant was an easy pleasure to me, but I found the calculations cumbersome because of my mathematical ineptness. The navigator was reading *We, the Navigators*, a definitive survey of early and contemporary Oceanic navigation techniques written by David Lewis, a yachtsman and medical doctor. After a thorough examination of the pertinent anthropological and ethnographic literature, Lewis, in the early 1970s, sailed to remote corners of the Pacific to interview those navigators who still remembered the lore and practice of their forefathers. I was deeply impressed, for Lewis's teachers used only the stars, the ocean swells, cloud formations, and the flight paths of birds, yet made blue-water passages as difficult as ours. At home, I bought the book and reread it. Idly, I wished to sail to the Pacific as Lewis had and experience what was left of old Oceania.

Then, on that passage to the Marquesas, I lost the rotator to my taffrail log, a device that, by measuring mileage, allowed me to project the distance my boat had run over the course I had sailed, thus producing a "dead reckoning" of my position. I tried judging my boat's speed the way the Micronesian navigators did, by simply eying the water flowing past my boat's hull. I could check the accuracy of my estimates by sun or star sights with my sextant. After several days my estimates became surprisingly accurate. I was intrigued; was I capable of learning this ancient way of seafaring?

Navigating and keeping my boat at sea took all my time, skill, and concentration, even with the aid of a modern sextant, digital watches, and accurate charts and sailing directions. Hundreds of vessels had steered this course before me; I knew my landfall and position. Still, my experience of that wilderness was profound. It was as if the universe were divided into two unequal parts: the sea, immense, protean, awesome in its remove from the ken of man, and the tiny planet of my boat. To survive, I possessed the methodologies of navigation; they divided the sea into latitude and longitude, marked the passage of the sun, moon, and stars across its dome in seconds of Greenwich Mean Time, and drew imaginary lines, like fine wire spokes, from the center of the earth to the centers of all heavenly bodies. The point at which these spokes pierced the sea formed the first apex of a great triangle; the North or South Pole formed the second, and the eyepiece of my sextant formed the third. By measuring the angle between the heavenly body and the horizon, I could determine the distance to that body's sea point. By "shooting" a number of stars, or the sun and moon when both were present in the sky, I could get a "fix," a small cross on the chart locating me precisely in the vast waste. Without my charts, sextant, digital watches, almanac, and sight reduction tables, I was lost. My navigation threw up a gossamer cage that tamed and calmed the raw wild thing of the sea. Just as life without language would be a formless concatenation of unmediated perceptions, the sea without navigation would be a trackless waste of wind, waves, and stars, ferocious in its muteness and unapproachable in its illogic. Navigation was the language of the sea.

But what of the Oceanic navigator, I wondered. What was his experience? He had to deal with the same problems I did, establishing his initial heading to an objective, maintaining that direction at sea, determining speed and distance sailed and finding the displacement from his intended course by current and leeway. Yet he could use the stars and ocean swells like a compass and interpret the flight paths of birds for signs of land. The structure by which he imposed order on the events of a sea passage was quite different from mine. My navigation was based on mathematics and the refined technologies of cartography, instrument-making, and timekeeping. Micronesian navigation was nonmathematical and noninstrumental, based instead on the organization and memorization of a vast quantity of information about the rising and setting positions of the stars, seasonal variations in ocean currents, the properties of ocean swells, clouds, and the behavior of birds. If the language of my navigation imposed its own structure on the sea, wasn't this also true for the Oceanic navigator? If so, didn't the structural difference between our two systems imply a fundamental difference in world view? I wanted to learn this ancient language of navigation; I wanted to hear it describe an ocean I imagined to be vastly different from Western seas.

At least this was my stated epistemological interest; my true motives were far different. The navigator on that Hawaii race had helped me get a job as first mate on a 103-foot schooner plying the charter trade in Greece. I was twenty-three years old then, and nervous about the reaction this "unserious" escapade would elicit from my father. To my surprise, he wrote me a letter communicating his tremendous excitement and giving me his highest praise. It was as if he and I together could vicariously live in the world of his favorite author, Joseph Conrad: a world where men played out their drama on the clear sea, far from the tangled confusion of land, which, in the opening metaphor of Conrad's story "The Secret Sharer," resembled a fish weir: "a mysterious system of half-submerged bamboo fences, incomprehensible in its division . . . and crazy of aspect." I nurtured an idealized image of my father: through force of will he had succeeded in imposing the clarity of the sea on the confusion of land; he was the iron man at the helm of our family, strong and resolute. He had the qualities I sensed were in me, but were as yet untapped and unrealized.

I had taken my girlfriend with me to the Mediterranean. Over that year our relationship had disintegrated, based as it was on clinging need, and when we returned to the United States, she firmly ended it. I was heartbroken. At the same time, word came from a young man I had met in Europe who made his living buying and refurbishing classic yachts, then sailing them to the United States to sell at a profit. He asked me to be his partner. I borrowed enough money to buy a stake in the venture and flew to England to meet him.

Eventually, circumstances forced him to return home; I would command the boat alone. By then I was twenty-five and had never been the master of a vessel. I needed my strong, resolute father to help me across the lonely sea lanes, and in this, my image of him did not fail me. I came into my own on the sea. Sailing a forty-three-foot yacht halfway around the world was my first test of manhood, and I passed it. My heart healed and I met the woman who later became my wife. The young man who delivered the yacht to his anxious partner in San Francisco was different from the one who had sailed it away from England.

If, over the course of my voyage, my father actually lent me strength, it seemed to be at the expense of his own, as if a fixed quantity existed between us. Before I had left, it was clear my parents were having problems, and I had begged them to face their difficulties. But by the end of my voyage they had faced nothing, resolved nothing, and the marriage had crumbled.

But over time, this "failure" was less disheartening to me than a profound frustration I perceived in him. He once told me he had a recurrent dream in which he strained to hold a ship from hitting a dock, pushing against it with all his might. I knew that, when he was my age, he had wanted to be a writer. He had paid the hospital bill for my birth, he used to tell me, by selling a short story about conflict between men at sea. But after that he had written nothing more, becoming a businessman instead to support his growing family. He had shrunk back from the risk of writing, or so it seemed to me.

In my experience at sea, especially on those extreme wastes of the equatorial Pacific, the ghost of death whispered through every action. The fear of death, I felt, must be harnessed to drive life. The small totality of my acts should stand for something, should feed some ultimate life's goal. I felt now that my father had alerted me to the ghost, but had not heeded it himself.

Yes, skippering a yacht halfway around the world was my first test of manhood but after a time I sensed that although I had passed the test, I had mastered nothing, neither seamanship, nor navigation, nor myself.

Soon the airplane tracked north of Satawal, home of the navigator Piailug. Also known by his nickname "Mau," he was in his mid-fifties, yet was his island's youngest *palu*, or fully initiated navigator. In former times, one could not guide a canoe without receiving the power of Anumwerici, the spirit of navigation, in the sacred *pwo* ceremony. The most important event in a young navigator's life, it not only marked his passage into manhood, but also gained him entrance to a select and privileged class and gave him the right to learn secret, mystical, navigational lore. Piailug's had been the last *pwo* ceremony to be held on Satawal.

Once initiated, he had voyaged incessantly. In 1970, in violent weather, he led his crew on the nine-hundred-mile round-trip voyage from Satawal to Saipan in his twenty-seven-foot outrigger sailing canoe. Without charts or instruments, he helped to reopen one of his ancestors' trading routes, abandoned for generations. In 1976 he became a hero in Hawaii when he guided the *Hokule'a*, a replica of an ancient Polynesian voyaging canoe, from Maui to Tahiti. Again he navigated without charts or instruments. He had appeared in numerous magazine articles and a *National Geographic* documentary film about this voyage. (In fact, I first saw him in this film in Hawaii, after I had made the passage north from the Marquesas.) In 1980 he made the voyage a second time.

Piailug seemed to have stepped into the twentieth century from the seaways of old Oceania. I had wished I was part of his crew, for I imagined he could teach me a way of seafaring and of living that was fed by and linked to the sea, one older, wiser, and truer than my own.

Whereas Lewis's book, and other writings, discussed the techniques and feasibility of voyaging without instruments, I found myself hungering for insight into the navigators themselves: What kind of men were they? How did they relate to their skill? Was it, as in the West, simply a mechanism of commerce, a qualification that earned them membership in an elite class, or was it something more, a part of some broader conception of life, a discipline that gave them a focus and a center, similar to the way Western artists sometimes described their art? It seemed to me the existing literature had not touched these questions.

Over the next several years, I developed a plan: I would go to the Pacific and find a navigator. I would become his apprentice, live with him, learn his language and customs; I would hear his ghosts.

My first choice was Piailug. I was not sure why, but thought it was because he was the most famous of the *palu*. There was something in his face, some fusion of steely hardness and feminine softness, that drew me to him. Something in him resembled my father, the invitation to come and know mingled with the warning to keep distant.

By then it had been almost a decade since the first *Hokule' a* voyage; I didn't know if Piailug, or any of the *palu*, were still alive. I wrote letters of inquiry to anthropologists, but no one seemed to know; the last significant research had been done in the early seventies.

Chance led me to Dr. Carlton Gajdusek, who had done medical research in the Pacific for nearly forty years. Over that time he had adopted more than two dozen Micronesian and Melanesian children and brought them back to the United States. He had ties throughout the islands. When I visited him in Washington, he grilled me extensively about my proposed project, its philosophical underpinnings, my background, education, and sea experience. Then he announced that he knew of navigators on only five remote islands in the Carolines, but the most traditional were on Satawal. He took me under his wing, firing off cables to his friends in Micronesia. With him as an advocate, my credibility was vastly increased.

Chance further led me to a documentary-film producer, Sam Low. From an old Hawaiian family, he had long been fascinated with Oceanic seafaring. He had just returned from shooting a film on Satawal with Piailug. I became a consultant to the film, responsible for the accuracy of the sequences on navigation, for by then I had finished a thorough review of the anthropological literature. From the film's corporate sponsor I received funding for my first trip to Satawal. In exchange, I was to conduct some additional research for the film, shoot publicity photographs, and write all the promotional literature. I had written to

Piailug asking to be his student, but had gotten no reply. I doubted he had ever received the letter. Now, even as I journeyed to Satawal, I didn't know if he was there. And if he was, I wasn't certain that he, or anyone, would teach me skills still regarded as secret, passed only from father to son.

2

After a night's layover on Guam, I caught my flight to Yap, the port-of-entry for the outlying islands of the central Carolines. An hour after takeoff, the pilot banked steeply around the southern end of the island and lined up for his final approach. Brush fires smoldered in the dry hills. It was the worst drought on record, he announced, and Yap's municipal water system was shut down. There was no water to put out the fires. The landing strip was a short, narrow patchwork of asphalt, barely long enough for the fully laden 727. A few moments of suspense as the ground on either side rushed up to meet the belly of the plane, then a hard touchdown at the very end of the runway: screaming thrust reversers, hard brakes. A pair of Japanese "Zero" fighters rusted beside the field.

I waited in the crushing heat as a forklift unloaded the cargo and baggage from the plane. In the shade of the thatch-roofed terminal, a small crowd watched for their arriving friends and relatives. The Yapese are thin, with dark-olive skin and high, fine cheekbones. The women were dressed in skirts and the men in trousers and shirts. Every man, woman, and child chewed betel nut with an air of serene self-possession. The visitors from the outer islands, in contrast, waited patiently, respectfully; the short, powerfully built men dressed in loincloths and the fat, bare-breasted women in woven skirts called *turrh*. I was met by Halelegam, a state senator from the island of Eauripik, also dressed in a loincloth, who escorted me through Immigration. He helped me with my crates of sailcloth and fishing gear, research materials, cameras, film, and baggage, then put me on a bus to my hotel in Colonia, the capital of Yap state, which, with Truk and Ponape states, makes up the Federated States of Micronesia. The only other passengers were a handful of Japanese war veterans who returned every year for a reunion.

Yap is about ten miles long and three wide, large by Micronesian standards (after all, Micronesia means "small islands"). Yap usually enjoys abundant rainfall, which runs down its mountainous terrain in many streams. It is a rich island with plenty of land for the cultivation of taro, breadfruit, and coconut. The island is ringed by reefs that form numerous shallows and flats, on which fishermen have built large stone weirs. At low water, they merely have to stroll across the reef to spear the fish trapped by the receding tide.

Scientists believe the Yapese, like the inhabitants of the Marianas and Palau, originated in the Philippines and voyaged directly to their new homeland, in contrast to the atoll-dwellers who back-filtered to the west from ancestral landfalls in the eastern islands of Micronesia. Linguistic evidence supports this theory, for Yapese is a much different tongue from those of the atolls, which are closely related to one another and collectively termed "Carolinian."

Once the Yapese sailed hundreds of miles south to Palau to quarry huge disks of stone and freight them home in their outrigger canoes. The value of the coin lay in the dangers and hardships of the voyage. This stone money still decorates their men's houses and the chiefs' yards.

Yap has long had a highly stratified caste system. The highest members enjoy a near-imperial status, while the lowest are so low they cannot even fish the reef, banished instead to the muddy rivers. Only those in the highest castes may own land.

Yap is accustomed to its status as a capital, for in the past it was the head of a great empire that extended throughout the western Carolines, past Satawal to Namonuito. Here, too, a caste system was imposed: an island's status diminished with its distance from the head of the empire. Yearly tribute voyages were made, each island shipping its offerings by outrigger canoe to the island of next-higher status until the goods finally reached Yap. Satawal was low on the hierarchy, while Ulithi and Fais were the highest. To neglect Yap threatened grave consequences, for it was reputed to have the most powerful sorcerers, who would destroy the offending island with a typhoon or send spirits bearing disease.

The islands east of Satawal—Puluwat, Pulusuk, Pulap, and Namonuito—ceased to participate in the tribute voyages under the German administration (1889-1914), and the rest of the system atrophied under the Japanese administration's (1914-44) prohibition of long-distance voyaging. Yet the caste system is still in place. Each of the outer islands has a Yapese *saway*, or sponsor family, which offers them protection and allows them to harvest their coconut and breadfruit trees while on Yap. The *saway* parents regard the outer islanders as their children and hand down the responsibility for them to succeeding generations. When an outer islander comes to Yap, he will be taken to his *saway* father to offer gifts and seek his blessing and protection. The Satawalese, being of the lowest caste, are meek and subordinate on the island of their masters.

In 1528, the Spanish explorer Saavedra stumbled across Fais island; two days later he discovered Yap. His track was followed sixteen years later by Villalobos, who was astonished when the natives greeted him in Spanish. He pressed on to his unsuccessful mission to colonize the Philippines; Yap and the Carolines were of no interest to the Spanish, whose will was bent on acquiring the riches of the East.

It re-emerged in European awareness in the mid-1700s, when British East Indiamen bound for Canton began sailing up through Dampier Strait, off the northwest tip of New Guinea, to pass east of the Philippines, thus avoiding the strong monsoon headwinds in the South China Sea. Shipmasters following this route, known as the Inner Passage, made numcrous sightings of islands near Yap and Palau. By 1870, Yap was the area's major trading center for copra and *bêche-de-mer*, the dried sea slug considered a delicacy by the Chinese.

Curiously, the same factors that brought Yap into contact with the West protected Satawal and the surrounding islands. At the beginning of the nineteenth century, three trade routes crossed Micronesia. After dropping off their cargo of convicts and undesirables at Port Jackson in Australia, British ships curved up through the Marshalls and Gilberts (named for British captains), put in at Kusaie and Ponape for wood and water, and continued on their way to China. American China traders, some having taken on furs in the Pacific Northwest, crossed the Pacific in the tradewinds and also touched at Ponape and Kusaie for replenishment. Spanish traders fanned out from the Philippines seeking *bêche-de-mer*, mother-of-pearl, turtle shell, and edible bird's nests to sell to Chinese merchants. The ultimate object of all these voyages was to procure the East's silks, teas, and spices, so desired by Westerners. The tiny, isolated islands in the central Carolines could contribute little in the great enterprise of the China trade, neither rich in the commodities sought by Chinese, nor conveniently located as rest-and-refreshment stops for China-bound ships. Satawal, one mile long and one-half mile wide, with a narrow, wave-scoured, fringing reef and no lagoon in which to anchor, must have been particularly unappealing.

The natives of the central Carolines had a reputation for treachery and ferocity, which further disinclined shipmasters to venture into those waters. Maritime journals of the day warned that any vessel insufficiently armed and manned would be attacked. As late as the 1870s, even after the Marshalls had been laced with the outposts of German trading firms and Protestant missions, little was known about the area.

In 1890, Germany declared the Carolines, along with the Marshalls, Marianas, Bismarcks, and New Guinea, part of the Hohenzollern empire, only to lose them in 1914 to Japan. Yap, along with Palau, Guam, and Saipan, then became quite developed. Much of the island was tilled, and men from the outer islands were brought in to work the fields. But neither the German nor the Japanese colonial administration had sought to change the culture of the outer islands, being content to use them as a source of copra and labor and a market for modest trade.

World War II largely ignored the Carolines; the major battles were fought on Tarawa, Eniwetok, and Kwajalein to the east, on Peleliu to the west, and the Marianas to the north. Truk, one of the largest Japanese naval bases in the Pacific, was bombed by U.S. carrier-based aircraft, and its offshore waters patrolled by U.S. submarines, but never invaded. Ulithi, with its huge protected lagoon, became the U.S. Navy's main western-Pacific anchorage and supply depot. Some islets were turned into airfields for bomber and fighter aircraft, others into recreation centers for the men. Yet, for the most part, the small, strategically insignificant islands of the central Carolines were untouched.

After the war, the United Nations placed the Carolines, along with the Marshalls, Marianas, and Palau, under the trusteeship of the United States. Profound and rapid cultural change followed. Slowly and somewhat dilatorily, the American government has spun the territories off into independent governments according to the terms of its original U.N. charter. The Federated States of Micronesia recently voted to adopt a Compact of Free Association with the United States. It will act as an independent nation while still receiving American military protection, postal service, and aid.

The bus ground along the rutted dirt road from the airport into town, past Filipino laborers working desultorily on the accoutrements of progress, a new airport, paved roads, and a sewer system. Everything was covered in a thick skin of dust, the countryside, the construction machines, the work crews. The bus whined down a long grade, which leveled off at the terminus of the Blue Lagoon, a narrow tidal inlet whose shores were piled thick with red-and-white Budweiser cans. My hotel was perched on the edge of the lagoon. Other buildings included a new firehouse and police station, a Methodist church, a half-dozen tin-roofed shacks, and a few tin warehouses belonging to the Blue Lagoon Trading Company. Besides the Japanese war veterans, the hotel's only guests were two Palauan women selling industrial chemicals and a group of American construction workers installing an underwater sewer outfall.

On its seaward end, the lagoon communicated with the harbor through a narrow slit in a causeway. Along the harbor were the port facilities, more trading companies, Yap Memorial Hospital, an oil storage depot, and the offices of the state government. Across from the oil depot was a ramshackle shantytown called Madrich; there the people of the outer islands live while visiting Yap. On the afternoon of my arrival on Yap, Halelegam brought me there to present me to Thureng, one of the chiefs of Satawal.

He led me through the wide courtyard littered with rags, bits of tin, aluminum belly tanks salvaged from World War II fighter planes, and scraps of lumber. He explained that the two government-built cinderblock buildings rimming the courtyard were now so over-crowded that islanders had improvised tin-and-scrap-wood houses on stilts over the water. Thick smoke filled the air. We went down a narrow alleyway past women, squatting over their sputtering coconut-husk fires, who looked up at me fearfully. In the center of the Satawalese compound was a kitchen area. A filthy table built of castoff shipping pallets stood in the center; rusty oil drums provided wash water; mongrel dogs and piglets rooted in the filth and slime underfoot. Here more women squatted over coconut-husk fires. Others grated coconut and sliced the tough brown skin from taro, a staple resembling a cross between a sweet potato and particle board. One fat woman with sagging breasts called teasingly to Halelegam in a loud voice, waving her machete at me as she spoke. He responded with something that sent her into peals of laughter.

Then he opened a plywood door to an over-water shack, the men's house. Three men sat cross-legged on the floor: old Auhror, with tattooed arms and legs; Muanirik, who, with Piailug, is one of Satawal's most famous navigators; and Thureng, one of the three chiefs of Satawal. Thureng had brought his daughter to Yap to give birth to her first child at the hospital. Halelegam confused me by introducing all three men as chiefs.

"Are you the one who telegrammed us earlier asking to come to our island to study navigation?" the gray-haired Muanirik asked through Halelegam.

"Yes, I am the one," I answered, watching his brown eyes twinkling behind his wire-rim spectacles. "I have read about your voyage, Muanirik," I continued. "I have great respect for a man who can sail a small outrigger canoe hundreds of miles without instruments."

Two years before he had made the 450-mile open-sea voyage to Saipan without charts, compass, or instruments. He then continued north to Okinawa, where his canoe was put on permanent display in the municipal museum.

He asked me why I wanted to learn navigation and how long I wished to stay on Satawal. Then he discussed the arrangements for my visit. He advised me to bring my own food, for it was now winter, a time of little fish and no breadfruit on Satawal. In less than five minutes the meeting was over. Halelegam told me the chief wished to shake my hand, so I extended mine toward Muanirik, thinking that since he had done most of the talking he must be the highest authority.

The senator nudged me and motioned to Thureng, explaining in a low voice that *he* was the chief, who, in their custom, voices his will through a spokesman. Apologizing profusely, I shook Thureng's hand.

"We understand you are a captain who has sailed to many islands," Thureng said soberly. "It is good that you will go to our island, for you must be a very good navigator, very strong. But Satawal is small, no bigger than an American ship. Please make sure you don't sail it away!" His somber face cracked in a spasm of laughter. Muanirik giggled as he rocked back and forth. Auhror emitted a low, rasping laugh. I looked at all three in astonishment, because I had taken the meeting with the utmost seriousness. But they laughed all the harder at my consternation, so I laughed, too.

Before leaving, I gave each a carton of cigarettes. Thureng told me to return later that evening and to come every day so I could start to learn their language and their ways.

For the three weeks until the ship departed, I spent the mornings in my small hotel room poring over a grammar book for the language of Woleai Atoll, since none existed for Satawal's language. Yet although Satawalese and Woleaian are related dialects, they are not mutually intelligible, and in the afternoons I went to the men's house in Madrich, where the chief would have one of the younger men help me translate what I had learned of Woleaian into Satawalese.

I always tried to bring something from my own culture to show them. One afternoon I brought a copy of *Canoes of Oceania*, a classic study of watercraft from the whole Pacific. All the men, old and young, gathered to look at the pictures. "From which island is this canoe?" Auhror would ask, and when I answered he would nod and repeat the name of the place: "Ah, a canoe from New Guinea" (or Fiji, or Tahiti). Then everyone would crowd around the book to discuss the similarities and differences with their own.

Another afternoon I brought my charts, sextant, and sailing directions, which the three old men carefully examined. Muanirik asked the mileage from Satawal to Saipan and on to Okinawa. Then, scrutinizing a pilot chart, he asked the significance of the many symbols—green lines indicating the mean strength and direction of the current, isolines in red showing the area and frequency of gales, and wind roses, colored blue, showing the direction and strength of the prevailing winds. After this I demonstrated the use of the sextant, explaining how by adjusting the movable mirrors one brought the image of the sun down to appear to skim the horizon, thereby measuring the angle between one's eye, the horizon, and the sun. Taking the instrument, Muanirik made the sun appear to rest on Auhror's leg, which he thought very funny. Then he took the sextant into the overwater privy in search of a clear line-of-sight to the horizon. "Why does a famous navigator like you need a sextant to find a place to urinate?" I quipped, which, when translated, brought the house down.

When evening fell, some teen-age boys brought in bowls of steamed fish, taro, and rice. The chief urged me to squat in the circle with the rest of the men to eat. I was dubious about the cleanliness of the food and tried to select pieces not already fingered by the other diners. But the fish was fresh and delicious, and as the meal progressed I lost some of my squeamishness and felt joined to the people of Satawal.

We finished as the sun set, and soon the stars blazed overhead. As the men sat back to smoke their cigarettes, I asked the names of the stars. Castor and Pollux were Mongoisum, Aldebaran was Ul, Sirius was Maan.* A small star in the center of Cancer was evidently used in weather forecasting. Muanirik would say no more. Everyone suddenly seemed very nervous. I bade them good night and walked back to my hotel.

The next afternoon the young man who had been my translator took me aside to explain I had made a serious mistake in asking about secret navigational knowledge. He himself could never ask such questions. I cut short my visit and returned to my hotel feeling anxious and depressed, hopelessly over my head. I was a foreigner and always would be. If a young Micronesian could not get access to navigational teachings, how could I, an American, ever expect to do so? I spent the evening reading *The Sot Weed Factor* in my crate-strewn room, too sick with anxiety to do any work. The next day I gave the three older men each a carton of cigarettes and some fishing gear. Then, for several days, I avoided Madrich.

When I finally returned, Thureng protested that I had been neglecting them. I had had appointments with many government officials,

*A list of Satawalese star names can be found in Appendix 1.

I stammered. Perhaps there was no substance to the incident after all, I thought. Maybe the young man was mistaken, or my own state of nervous anticipation had made me read too much into his concern. Surely when I mastered the language I would have much freer access to navigation.

3

On boat day, I rose early, checked out of my hotel, and loaded my gear aboard the *Microspirit*. Cranes lifted pallets of lumber and cement into the small freighter's hold. Islanders tied squealing pigs to the ship's railing and staked out their places on deck with battered suitcases and coconut-frond baskets filled with taro and breadfruit. Wriggling burlap sacks contained grunting piglets. Government officials came aboard with their luggage, and the doctor and his assistant with their supplies. A copra buyer from the local trading firm carried a scale to weigh the bags of copra he would buy from the islanders. Storekeepers checked their manifests against the crates stowed in the ship's hold. In the late afternoon a great crowd jammed the quayside: outer islanders dressed in traditional garb, government officials in slacks and aloha shirts, Yapese dockworkers in heavy boots and yellow hardhats. A truck drove up and began pumping fresh water aboard the ship. The captain paced the bridge impatiently. When the water truck's noisy pumps fell silent, he blew the ship's whistle and ordered the lines cast off. People leapt from the quayside to the ship and from the ship into the water to swim back to land. Some threw baskets of food across the widening gulf between ship and shore as others shouted last-minute instructions and goodbyes. Finally, as the sun set, we slipped through the channel to the open sea.

Late that night I found Muanirik by the rail. "What is the name of that star?" I asked, pointing to Hadar. He waited until two young men passed and answered: "Annupo." Then he would say no more. He seemed to be withholding, but I attributed it to my poor knowledge of Satawalese.

Muanirik, like Auhror, was born into one of Satawal's three chiefly clans, which is why the senator introduced him as a chief. Had Muanirik's mother been older, he would have become the chief instead of Thureng, for title as well as land ownership descends matrilineally. I knew that Piailug was from a lowly clan. He was "of the people," and had earned his fame and stature by his achievements. In Madrich, I had never mentioned I hoped to study with him for fear of exciting the jealousy I had been warned could run strong between navigators. I had tried to sound out opinion about him by tactfully mentioning his name. Muanirik would look at me blankly as if to say: "Oh yes, Piailug, we know him." I sensed hostility toward him, and since the chiefs were the unquestioned authorities over the island, I wanted to remain neutral.

In the morning, the *Microspirit* anchored off the isolated atoll of Ngulu, stopped briefly, then continued. I had been told Piailug was on Ulithi, and the next day we reached that island. The ship anchored and immediately began unloading lumber and cement. Outboard skiffs buzzed around like flies. Drunken boys fell from the ship into the water. Shy high-school girls sat in clusters on the beach, giggling at the boys. Men came on board to transact their business. It was midafternoon and the hot sun blasted the color from the beach and waving palm trees and bleached the blue water to a pale, sparkling aqua.

I spotted Piailug immediately upon going ashore. He was seated in the back of an old pickup truck parked on the beach, holding a puppy in his lap. He looked no more than forty, his softly curled, short-cropped hair still black and shiny. He stroked the puppy gently but there was an almost savage intensity about him, his brow knitted up, glistening with sweat, half frowning, half squinting against the sun, his head swiveling back and forth to watch the activities. His face was cut in flat Oceanic angles, as if hacked swiftly and deftly from a chunk of obsidian, flat brow and nose, angled cheeks, a round, knobby chin.

Epan, a young outer-islander who worked for the state government and had received training from his navigator father, presented me to Piailug. I stepped forward to give him a carton of cigarettes as Epan told him in Carolinian who I was and why I had come. He listened attentively, head slightly cocked, eyes flashing from Epan to me. When all had been explained he faced me directly.

"Sam Low says hello," I said nervously, trying to establish contact through our mutual friend. He scrutinized me severely, then asked in broken English:

"What does Sam say? Hello?" He shook his head, holding me with his hard gaze until I grew uncomfortable and looked away.

"No!" he roared. "He says, *'Aloha!'* " He erupted in wild laughter but, when he saw my bewildered expression, reached out to put his hand on my shoulder. "Oh!" he sighed, still laughing. "It is good you have come to study with me." The top of his hand was almost black and the underside pink. His skin was tough and dry and hard, like old leather.

Piailug intended to return to Satawal. He came aboard the ship and immediately took me under his wing. I tried to downplay our budding relationship before Muanirik, for I had noticed the two navigators spoke only to exchange formalities.

The ship steamed from atoll to atoll: Fais, Sorol, Eauripik, Farailap. At each island Piailug would take me ashore. "Come, Steve," he would say and I would feel the soft pressure of his leathery hand in mine as he led me across the village to meet the chief. It struck me that Muanirik never went ashore.

On one island we entered the canoe house and sat before a wizened old man. Half blind, the chief peered at the world through rheumy eyes, watering and clouded over like tarnished silver. When Piailug spoke the chief seemed to recognize the voice and fixed his gaze in Piailug's direction. Piailug reached out to place his hand on the old man's bony knee. I gave the chief a small gift of cigarettes.

While they talked I inspected the canoe house. The structure itself was built of huge timbers mortised into massive uprights and lashed together with rough rope made from coconut fiber. Fat coils of black, tar-impregnated line salvaged from a wrecked Japanese fishing boat hung high in the rafters, along with canoe paddles, spars, sails, fishing nets, and lines. Other men sat in the corners, talking and smoking. Curious boys peered in through the doorways.

The canoe house, I knew from my preliminary research, was the men's social club, dormitory, and classroom; women were seldom allowed even to visit. A boy came here when he could first walk, to watch his father, uncles, and cousins build and repair canoes. Here he learned his first lessons in making rope and hewing the sculptured planks of a canoe. In the evenings, he would learn the elements of sailing and seamanship by listening to the men talk as they sat in a circle amid the wood shavings drinking tuba, the sweet, fermented palm toddy. He was lucky if his father was a navigator, for as he worked and fished with him by day and relaxed with him at night, he would learn the *kapesani lemetau*, the "talk of the sea." If he was intelligent and worked very hard, he would one day become a navigator himself, and when his own hair turned gray, his sons and nephews would gather at his feet.

As we continued on through the sparkling chain of atolls, Piailug questioned me carefully: Why did I want to learn his navigation? How would I use this knowledge? How long was I willing to study on Satawal? I answered each question and he considered my answers for a long time. Finally he announced I would be his student. If I truly wanted to learn he would take me as a brother. I would be part of his family and he would teach me everything. In return I would help provide those things his family needed: sailcloth, fishing gear, kerosene, perhaps a little money—whatever I could afford.

He told me there had been a meeting on Satawal to discuss my visit. The chiefs expected I would live with them and had drawn up a fee schedule for all my activities: meals, lodging, photography, and navigational instruction. Just to go sailing I would be required to pay the captain a hundred dollars, and each of the seven-to-ten-member crew fifty dollars!

"This is wrong," Piailug scoffed. "Do they want outsiders to think we are only interested in stealing their money? I don't know how it is with you, but in my family, if you are a navigator, you are like our brother."

"But what should I do about the chiefs?" I asked nervously. "If they want me to go with them, what can I do?"

"Did you come here for me?" he asked, watching me closely. I answered yes.

"Then I will tell the chiefs you came to see me," he said with finality.

He began instruction that afternoon in the ship's fo'c's'l, the only private place we could find, amid the coiled hausers, cans of paint, and outboard motors. I launched into a long list of questions from my preliminary research. He listened patiently, and carefully answered each question in simple English. When I paused to contemplate my notes, he took my pad and pencil, removed a plastic prescription bottle from his woven pandanus handbasket, and used it to trace a circle. Then, grasping the pencil as if for the first time, he painstakingly placed thirty-two dots around the circle.

"First we must learn the stars," he explained gently. "Do you know the stars in our language?"

I began with Mailap, the name for Altair, then managed Paiifung (Gamma Aquila), Ul (Aldebaran), Maragar (Pleiades), Egulig (Cassiopeia), and Mun (Vega) before I needed help.

"Where did you learn this?" he demanded in surprise.

"From you," I said factually. He gave me a sidelong glance—I had learned the names from the film footage. Then he helped me fill out the rest of the names of the stars in my notebook.

Micronesian navigators use the rising and setting positions of fifteen stars or constellations to define thirty-two points around the horizon. The stars' rising positions are indicated by the prefix *tan*, setting positions by the prefix *tubul*, both with an "a" suffixed to bridge two consonants. Since the stars keep their positions relative to one another as if painted on the underside of a vast dome, they always rise in the same place on the eastern horizon, follow the same arc through the heavens, and set in the same place on the western horizon. True, they rise four minutes earlier each evening, causing the night sky to change with the seasons, but they always rise and set in the same place. Micronesian navigators use the stars both to name the directions around the horizon and to maintain direction at sea, by pointing the bow of the canoe at the rising or setting star, or one that follows the same arc. This circular array of stars has been called the "sidereal compass" by Westerners.

"My grandfather Raangipi taught me the stars," Piailug commented as I scribbled the names in my notebook, "but I didn't write it down like you are doing. I kept everything in my head." He paused for a moment and concluded: "This is called *paafu*."*

---

*The *paafu* chart can be found on page 81.

Paafu, meaning "numbering the stars," is the young student's first lesson in navigation; in it he learns the principal navigational stars. Piailug began to learn *paafu* at age five, accompanying his grandfather while he worked or fished. Sometimes the old man simply had him repeat the names of the stars. Other times he would place thirty-two lumps of coral in a circle on a woven pandanus mat to help him visualize the star points. This is called *merek keiky*, or "unfolding the mat." Raangipi tied strands of banana fiber between the coral lumps representing the major axes—north-south, east-west, northwest-southeast, northeast-southwest—to help his grandson visualize the reciprocal relationships.

Piailug learned his next two lessons on the mat as well. For *amas*, or "facing," Raangipi constructed a small canoe of palm fronds, placed it in the center of the circle, and had Piailug name the stars that lay over the canoe's bow, stern, outrigger, and lee platform. At sea, if the guiding star is unavailable or obscured, the navigator can steer by a star over the stern, outrigger, or lee platform. In the second lesson, *aroom*, Raangipi pointed to each star in the circle and asked Piailug to name that star and its reciprocal or "partner" star, thus inculcating the reciprocal relationship between the star points—critical knowledge at sea.

When I had finished copying the names of all the stars in the *paafu* array, Piailug took back the pencil and notebook and drew lines to represent the coconut midribs.

"These are paths," he explained. "There are many of them. Paths connect rising Mailap with setting Mailap, rising Paiifung with setting Paiiur, rising Ul with setting Uliul—paths connect all the stars. You must always place yourself in the center of the paths. Do you understand this?"

I nodded yes. I understood that just as I, a Western navigator, projected my compass rose onto the world, placing myself in the center of a sunburst pattern of radians—north, south, east, and west—he mentally projected *paafu*.

Then he placed a dot in the center of the circle of stars, at the intersection of the paths.

"This is Satawal," he said. He pointed to the rising Uliul, Orion's Belt: "Pulusuk lies under this star. Truk lies under this star, Mailap." He glanced up to see if I was following. "Puluwat lies under rising Paiifung, Pulap under rising Ul, Pikelot under rising Wulego, West Fayu under setting Mailapellifung, Farailap under setting Maragar, Lamotrek under setting Paiifung. Do you see, Steve? We call this *wofanu, wofanu* for Satawal."

Wofanu means literally "to gaze at the island." It is the *palu's* chart case, for it delineates the star courses to all known points in his world. Just as a Western navigator cannot voyage without the right charts, a *palu* is helpless without *wofanu*; his voyaging range is as great or as limited as his knowledge of the star courses. Piailug later recorded the star courses to and from all the islands in the central Carolines, from Ponape and Kusaie in the east to Yap and the Philippines in the west and Saipan and Guam in the north. Then, to my astonishment, he recorded the courses from Satawal to Pikelot, then north to Hawaii; from Hawaii he delineated courses to North America, South America, Tahiti, the Marquesas, Samoa, and Japan. He told me he learned this *wofanu* from his grandfather.

The next day we resumed our lessons. Piailug seemed to teach me with urgency, immediately sensing what I understood from my own sea experience and previous study, and what was new to me.

I asked if he used the shape of the waves to tell which direction the current was setting his canoe, one of the most formidable problems for any navigator. I gestured with my hands to show the waves coming from the direction of the wind and the current flowing against them: "In this case," I said, "the waves would get bigger."

"Not bigger but steeper," he corrected me. "And what if the current goes *with* wind and wave?" he asked.

"The waves will be lower, smoother," I answered. He nodded.

"We use the waves to tell the current," he explained, "but first we do *fatonomuir* [literally: facing astern]. We look back at the island to see if it has moved." He sketched a map of Satawal and the surrounding islands on the back of an old envelope. When departing on a voyage, he explained, he sailed out to the point at which Satawal was about to dip beneath the horizon, then observed the effects of the current. If Satawal had moved north, he knew a current was pushing him south. If Satawal had moved south, the current was pushing him north. The procedure was nearly identical to Western practice, except that Piailug visualized the islands moving in the sea while the canoe remained rooted to the bottom.

"What if you are here, out of sight of all islands?" I asked, drawing an "x" on the envelope. "If the current changes, how do you know?"

I expected him to elaborate on the art of reading the current by its effects on the shape of ocean swells. But instead he studied the sketch for a long time. Then slowly, almost reverently, he placed some dots near the island of West Fayu.

"A bird stays here," he explained in a low, intense voice, "a dolphin stays here. Over here is a fish—I don't know what you call it in America, the kind we call *aiu* [jack crevelly]. When you see one you *know* you are not on the road to the island." Then he fell silent, the muscles in his jaw twitching and jerking.

"Are these birds and fishes there all the time?" I asked.

"Yes. I have seen them," he answered. "It is just special birds and fish. They do something special: fly close to the water, have special marks on their back or sides [slapping himself on the back and sides], swim a certain way in the water." He grew reflective: "I don't know; it is said that when they die another bird or fish will come to take their place. But I know the creatures live in their place for a long time." He was astonished when I told him we didn't use such signs.

This was *pookof*, one of the most intriguing elements of Micronesian navigation, a system which charts the range and star course to a ring of sea creatures around each island. That certain birds and fish returned to the same feeding grounds day in and day out seemed quite plausible to me. I had been captain of a yacht whose owner frequently treated his guests to whale-watching expeditions. We always found the humpbacks in the same spot on Stellwagen Bank, off Boston. But *pookof* seemed to be more than a catalogue of fauna. Micronesians I had talked to during my preliminary research referred to it guardedly, and looked surprised that I even knew of it. Once, in Washington, I spent the evening with an official of the FSM government, a young man my age, whose father was a navigator. With regrets, he had gone to college and entered government service, leaving his father without a son to take his place. After dinner and drinks, I asked about *pookof*. The young man avoided answering, but as the evening drew on I noticed he asked more and more penetrating questions about me and my research. When it was very late he told me quietly:

"My father taught me that the sea is full of signs. Let's say we leave on a voyage at sunset. At midnight the navigator listens for chirping birds. You and I don't hear them—we can't hear them. Only the *navigator* can hear them." I tried to get him to elaborate, but he demurred. "You must ask the *palu* you finally study with about these things," he said. "I really know nothing about it."

The borders between the natural and the supernatural seemed to be drawn differently in the Micronesian navigator's mind. If the *palu* actually believed *pookof* was imbued with spiritual significance, then he was some fusion of shaman and technician. As a Western navigator, I used sextant, charts, compass, Loran, and Satnav. The rules that guided my way of navigation—from the technical skills of reading a chart and plotting a line of position to the manual skills of using a sextant—constructed my navigational world. But *pookof* implied that for Piailug the rules were different: the appearance of birds, fishes, or dolphins could be a critical clue to his whereabouts. The *palu* had to master successfully the same sea conditions as I did with my charts and instruments. Therefore, I shared with him some common seafaring ground.

The ship continued on to Eauripik. At sunset I stood with Piailug at the rail, the raking light modeling the sharp folds of his frown, the squint of his eyes, and his high, full, almost sensual cheekbones. He watched the water intently, his hand resting lightly on the rail, his body seeming to merge with the rolling steel deck at his feet.

I asked where the current was coming from.

He pointed toward the setting sun and continued to watch the water. "From there," he said matter-of-factly, "from the west."

The pilot charts showed it was the time of year for the Equatorial Countercurrent to set in. During the winter months, when the North Pacific High—a vast area of high barometric pressure that dominates the weather patterns of the whole northern Pacific—moves south, the North Equatorial Current flows from east to west through the Caroline Islands. As winter shades into spring, the High migrates north, with the North Equatorial Current tagging along. During the summer and fall, the Equatorial Countercurrent flows through the Caroline Islands from west to east. For me to measure the current, I would have had to take bearings on an island—but we were out of sight of land—or take sextant observations of the sun, stars, or other heavenly bodies. Piailug had done neither; he had simply been watching the waves.

I knew from the literature and our earlier discussions that he could determine the current from the ocean swells. But this evening there were no swells, merely wavelets too small even to form whitecaps.

"How can you determine the current when there are no swells?" I asked.

"You look at the water and it is tight," he answered. "The small waves go like this [pushing in one direction] and then—how can I explain?" He extended both his hands and pulled them back as if stroking the keys of a piano. He claimed this sign was now present and that it indicated a weak current from the west, flowing against the light northeasterly wind. I had never read about such a sign in the literature and I pressed him for a more articulate description. He tried to get me to see a kind of "tightness" in the water—tiny ripples flowing on the surface, almost like the wrinkles on a weatherbeaten face. If I watched carefully enough, he said, I would perceive the ripples flowing against the wind and wavelets. I stared at the shimmering water until my eyes hurt, but could detect nothing, just the wavelets, glittering like a multitude of fishes caught up in the nets of the sea.

In the morning we anchored off Eauripik. I asked the captain the direction of the current during the night. He glanced at the ship's track penciled on the chart and at the sextant shots the first mate had plotted. It had been weak, he told me, from the west.

I had been told by other researchers not to expect anyone to discuss navigation for at least six months. But now, two days after I had met Piailug for the first time, he was freely discussing elements I understood to be secret. Just several days before, I had been tormented with doubt whether he would even accept me; now he was teaching me without restraint. Fleetingly, I wondered why. Perhaps it was because of the connection through Sam Low's film, I speculated; or because he and I had mutual acquaintances in Hawaii. I even flattered myself by thinking he accepted me as an American *palu* (since this is what I was called), and that there was some professional bond between us. The skeptic in me was fully aware of my own material value to whoever took care of me: I would be expected to provide cigarettes, coffee, sugar, fishing gear, and whatever else they felt they needed. Later, I would become another contact to be tapped in time of need, a kind of American *saway* brother. Still, I sensed in Piailug a commitment that went beyond material interest. He was so free in his answers, as if he trusted me to determine my part of the bargain and then uphold it like a man. Muanirik, in contrast, had watched the clock like an expensive lawyer, squeezing maximum trade value out of each piece of information and waiting for payment before releasing the next. But for now I didn't care what Piailug's motives were. I was with my teacher at long last, and he was teaching me the ancient talk of the sea.

On Woleai, he took me to drink tuba with his friends in canoe houses all around the atoll. We arrived at the first one about ten in the morning. He had me sit next to him in the circle of men. The watery palm sap had been collected before dawn and fermented all morning; now it bubbled and frothed in its bottles. A young man sat in the middle of the circle to serve us, his eyes already bloodshot from drink. He filled the coconut-husk cup and handed it to me. I sipped the sweet, warm stuff slowly. It tasted like cheap champagne mixed with coconut milk. When I finished he refilled the cup for Piailug, who quaffed it in a single gulp. Then he handed me a second cupful. Again I sipped it and again Piailug tossed his off. We had to drink five cups in a row, for we had arrived at the tuba circle late, and tradition demanded we catch up to the rest of the drinkers before the cup could resume its passage around the circle. Piailug told a long story that had the rest of the men laughing and hooting while I attended to the various gurgling noises in my stomach.

After an hour or two we took a boat across the lagoon so Piailug could visit a friend. The man had a scarred and weatherbeaten face, and most of his right hand had been blown off during the war, when the Japanese forced him, and many Carolinians, to dynamite fish to feed their troops. He plied us with cheap vodka mixed with instant coffee. Laughing, Piailug recounted how once the two of them had taken a motor launch from Yap to fish for the afternoon, run out of fuel, and drifted for five days in the Philippine Sea without food or water until they were picked up by a freighter. It was a testimony to his hardiness, but cast doubt on his prudence.

As the day wore on he got drunker and drunker, bragging in broken English to anyone who would listen, "This man is an American captain, but he follows me!" I had had enough to drink and refused more.

He took me to another islet to visit his uncle. In the middle of a long monologue, he broke down and wept bitterly. When he stopped, he explained that the jealous Muanirik had told him he could no longer be a navigator on Satawal.

I sank into despair. In our first days together Piailug had told me the ship would stop briefly at Satawal, continue overnight to one of the eastern islands, then return to pick up passengers for Yap. He would leave on that ship with his wife and young son Bonefacio to visit Halig, another son, who lived on Saipan. I would be cared for by his brother Uurupa until he returned on the next ship, in about a month.

I had ignored this when he first told me, so relieved was I to have found him and been accepted, but now the implications struck home. I had cast my lot with a man who seemed little more than a braggart and a drunk, and in so doing had incited the jealousy and anger of the chiefs, the authorities of Satawal. Soon Piailug would leave and could no longer teach me. I might have just cut myself off from the other navigators as well.

Two weeks out of Yap, the ship reached Lamotrek, last stop before Satawal. Again Piailug took me ashore to visit his relatives, including his second son, Mesailuke, who had married a Lamotrek girl and lived there with her family. I left when the men started to drink, took the first path I crossed, and followed it along the wide, calm, protected lagoon, past the ruins of a Japanese military outpost and on to the taro swamp. The taro's broad, heart-shaped leaves thrust out of the thick mud; the brown water exuded a rich, dank smell. The swamp was deserted and quiet, except for the cries of sea birds.

As I approached the exposed eastern shore, the salt smell grew stronger and the surf louder. The air was filled with a gauzelike light. I stepped gingerly onto the narrow coral foreshore as if entering some august chamber to which I had come uninvited. All around, the horizon sliced the belly of the ocean like a perfect surgical incision. Cumulus clouds rose in solitary towers, one here, one there, one, one. I suddenly felt the same pang of fear and loneliness as I had when sailing to the Marquesas: for thousands of miles around me, only the wind swept across the naked sea, only the wind.

Satawal hove up on the horizon the next dawn. Muanirik assured me he would take care of everything and told me to wait for him while he went ashore. Then a friend of Piailug's warned me that if I went with Muanirik the chiefs would make me live with them and would enforce their fee schedule. He advised me to go with Piailug and do exactly what he said. It seemed I had landed squarely in the middle of the conflict between navigators I had sought to avoid. Sick with anxiety, I waited on the ship with my crates of gear.

To starboard lay Satawal, first object of my quest, curled up like a child against the lash of the sea. The ship's whistle split the dome of morning silence. Cocks crowed in the village. The sun rose from behind a massive cumulo-nimbus, spraying white spikes across the eastern sky. I remembered making landfall in the Marquesas. It was a similar morning, with strong tradewinds, big cumulus clouds carving the sky into a ragged blue cloth, a torn-up feeling in my stomach. Those islands had also emerged mysteriously after a long passage, as if dropped accidentally by a negligent god.

As the sun rose higher, the whole settlement seemed to empty onto the beach. Crowds of women sat in the shade of the coconut groves while the men stood around with their stacks of bagged copra. The doctor and the government officials took the first boat to shore as naked children lined up in the waves shouting taunting singsongs at the ship. Boys paddled their little outrigger canoes through the breakers. Some scrambled aboard the ship to make nuisances of themselves with the storekeepers in the open hold; others simply dove off the ship's rail into the water, clambered back into their canoes, and orbited the ship. Men came out in larger, paddling canoes to buy fishing line, hooks, cigarettes, and rotgut vodka with the proceeds of their copra sales.

Suddenly Piailug appeared with his clansmen. He instructed them to load my gear into the ship's skiff and to me lightly said, "Come, Steve." He took charge as we pushed through the surf, telling the boatman when to speed up or slow down to avoid being dumped by a wave. In the shallows he hopped onto the reef to tow the skiff along the beach to a canoe house.

"You will stay at my brother's house," he commanded. I didn't know what had transpired between him and Muanirik, but I was incredibly relieved.

His clansmen lugged my gear across the beach, past the canoe house, and into the village, where they dumped it in the coral-rock courtyard of a small thatched hut, my new home. Piailug asked for cigarettes for his men. I handed him a carton and he broke it open, tossed a pack to everyone, and told me to save the remainder. He was clearly in command now; there was no question he was the leader. He was centered again, poised, speaking with the voice of a father. Gone was the rootless drunk of Woleai.

His third son, Inaiman, took me into the hut, where I theatrically exchanged my Western clothes for a red loincloth, my *thu*. Everyone looked up when I emerged; some applauded as they made room for me in their circle. Even though I was fit and tanned, I seemed soft and pale next to them. As we drank cheap vodka and Sprite from the hacked-off bottom of an aluminum can, I examined my new home with dismay. It seemed to be in the poorest section of the island. The courtyard was littered and my hut dirty and filled with junk.

That evening, all the islanders crowded into the large tin-roofed chapel to receive communion from the American Jesuit priest, pastor of Yap's outer-island parish, who was making his rounds on the ship. I sat on the cool cement floor in the rear of the church; Piailug squatted in the doorway, just outside. Everyone sang hymns. The high, nasal voices of the women rang piercingly from the left side of the church, while the deep voices of the men boomed contrapuntally from the right. The songs were Catholic, sung to the same God to whom I had sung as a Catholic schoolboy, but the words and melody were Satawalese. They seemed to echo from the lost world of Oceania, no longer exotic but, for the first time, haunting and utterly foreign to me. The song flowed back and forth like ocean waves. I was out of my culture now, on the fringe of the Western world. My home and my sense of myself all lay beyond some barrier that had closed as the growl of the ship's engines faded and was replaced by the cries of naked children and the low boom of the winter waves on the northern reef. The singing rolled and rolled and I could contain myself no longer: I put my head in my hands and wept.

4

It was late. The dogs had ceased barking in the village to the south, and the only sounds were the surf pounding on the distant reef and the wind ruffling the palm fronds overhead. Piailug had fallen silent, too, and sat cross-legged on his mat, staring off into the night. Huddled by the kerosene lantern in the courtyard, I scribbled notes quickly, hoping I could remember everything later, when he had gone. The weak light flickered on the jagged coral stones and flowed evenly across the smooth angles of his face before being sucked into the vast darkness that lay with the sea all around the island.

Traditionally, Piailug explained, the annual solar cycle was divided into two seasons or "years," each lasting six lunar cycles. *Lefung* concurs with our winter; it is "the impatience," the time of hunger. *Leraak*, approximately our summer, is "the year," the time of plenty. Certain stars, when forty-five degrees from the horizon at dawn, name the "moons" that wax and wane beneath them. There are twelve such star months, together constituting the two seasons. Knowledge of the star months, said Piailug, was common before the advent of the Western calendar; it was the only way to mark the rounding of the seasons. People didn't know their age; instead they compared their size to others. If two people were the same size they were said to have been born under the same star. During Japanese times, when the young men returned home from labor camps on Yap and Palau, they claimed there were twelve moons, not six, in a single year. "Liars!" hissed the old men. "Who taught you such a thing?"

For the navigator, there is an even more important set of stars. During each star month, certain stars will cause inclement weather when they hover just beneath the horizon at dawn or as they set into the sea at sunset. This lore, called the "fighting of stars," is exclusive to the *palu*; its mastery is an essential element of seamanship.

At least one storm star rules the weather of each star month, but in five months, two storm stars rule. There are seventeen fighting stars in all. In the months with only one, inclement weather will occur in the first five days of the moon's cycle—that is, when the sliver of the waxing moon appears in the western sky at sunset. In the months with two storm stars, there will be inclement weather for the last five days of the moon's cycle, when the dying crescent in the east fades with the sunrise.

Lefung begins in the first week of our November, their month of Sarapul, when the fighting star Arcturus has finished storming. The northeast tradewinds now return and build in strength through the next star month, Roe (Corona Borealis), our December.

By Tumur, when the star Arcturus stands halfway to the zenith at dawn, the winds are fierce, pinning the big voyaging canoes in their canoe houses. Breadfruit trees hiss overhead, empty of fruit. There is no rain, the wells are dry, the sun burns the palm leaves brown. People become skinny, for there is no fish, no breadfruit, just a little taro. *Tumur* means "empty," Piailug said; the old people believe the star itself sucks the juice from the coconuts.

But the next month, Mun (Vega) gives back some of what Tumur took away. There is rain, tuba, and taro, but still no fish. Two stars will fight this month: Sepie (Delphinus), when the moon is waning, and Ceuta (a star group in our constellation Equuleus), when the moon is waxing. This is an auspicious sign, Piailug said, for Ceuta means "to sweep": the star sends big waves all the way to the foot of the canoe houses to sweep the beach. Then the turtles will come to lay their eggs in the clean sand.

During our March, the month of Mailap (Altair), men who know the stars will listen for a single clap of thunder. "Ho! Na is finished!"

they will cry, for with the end of the storms of the fighting star Na (Alpheratz) comes the end of "the impatience" and the beginning of "the year." Na comes from the word *nana*, meaning "plenty." Breadfruit now form on branches; flowers blossom. Men troll the rich deep-sea reefs for tuna, voyage to West Fayu and Pikelot for fish and turtle, and sail down to Lamotrek to visit relatives.

In our June—the month of Cu, when the dolphin constellation dominates the morning sky—the winds grow feeble. Great, dark rain-squalls sweep across the sea and the trees and gardens drink deeply. The island holds the rain in its porous structure, the fresh water floating in the shape of a huge lens on the heavier water of the sea. The taro swamp is full, and even the shallowest wells offer cool water to drink or bathe in. Breadfruit hang thick in the trees; the coconuts are full of juice. People grow fat. At night, when the sea is smooth and the air hot and still, the men fish the shallow reef near shore in their paddling canoes. Two stars storm this month, Ul (Aldebaran) and Uliul (Orion's Belt), but they are weak and the inclement weather they generate is of no consequence.

Late in August, the Southern Cross sets with the sun. Soon the west wind will blow—and typhoons. Huge swells close the reef pass. Again the sailing canoes are trapped ashore. Men bottom-fish the face of Satawal's narrow, wave-scoured reef while the women harvest taro, now the only staple, since the breadfruit season is over. This is another period of hunger. The easterly winds that come again with the beginning of *lefung* offer a chance to voyage, but the wind is growing stronger all the time and the stars of hunger lie just beneath the horizon.

When I finished writing, I put down my notebook to watch the sky. Orion had ascended the dome of night and now poised above Piailug's shoulder, flickering in the gusty trades.

"The stars are like people," he said suddenly as if adding out loud to an unspoken train of thought. "When they try to swim to the top of the water they fight for air. They fight everything: islands, people, canoes."

For my race it was Orion the warrior, his legs spread wide to brace himself in his fight against Taurus the bull. On many nights at sea I had watched this warrior, for he tied me to my own people and our classical past. But here Orion's Belt was Uliul, a point on the horizon, a guide to the navigator, one of the "stars that fight." I tried to see the three stars only as Uliul, and to apprehend that since Anumwerici brought the talk of the sea to man, they had always been Uliul. For just an instant I succeeded; the constellation began to slip away. Then I panicked and the sensation was frightening; quickly, I searched for the familiar Betelgeuse and Rigel, the bright stars framing Orion's Belt, and embraced the formation as my own.

5

For some moments I drifted in the charmed haze of sleep; sights and sounds registered but were still unattached to their mantle of language. Sunlight filtering through the white canopy of mosquito netting, wind chattering in the palm fronds, the cries of children playing in the distance—everything blended into a single, whirling image.

A hollow pounding noise rang out from somewhere, like a broom beating a stiff rug. Footfalls crunched on the coral stones. Two young boys trod lightly past the open mat doors of my hut, one holding a thick brown coil of rope, the other a long forked pole. Then two older girls followed, carrying woven baskets of brilliant green breadfruit. Slim, with full, pendulant breasts, they stooped to look through the hut's low doors, then yelped and ran away giggling when they realized I was awake. Women hollered at one another like street vendors, in an unintelligible stream.

I rose quickly, adjusted my *thu* as best I could, and squeezed through the low door into the hard morning sunlight. A group of older women sat straight-legged on the ground by a rickety cooking shed. Each wielded a stone pestle with which she mashed breadfruit into thick yellow paste. The forest echoed with each blow. They stopped their palaver when they saw me.

"Good morning," I said in Trukese: "*Lessor anim.*" It was the only morning greeting I knew. The ladies looked at one another questioningly; then one understood.

"Oh! *Lessor anim, lessor anim*, Steve," they repeated, bobbing their heads respectfully. One hastily consulted with the others, then picked up a blackened sphere and waved it menacingly.

"Come and eat!" she commanded. It was a roasted breadfruit.

"I'm full, I'm full," I sang out in my newly minted Satawalese, gingerly patting my stomach. Another rummaged in a big blackened pot, pulled out a long, slimy thing, and shook it at me.

"Eat this. Eat octopus. Good!" she coaxed. But I refused again, still patting my stomach.

She tossed the creature back into the pot with dismay and began an animated discussion with the other ladies. One by one they glanced at me with concern.

"Not hungry yet," I managed. "I eat soon."

"Oh! Oh! You will eat soon," they repeated, bobbing their heads and smiling, looking much relieved.

My hut was wedged in amid many others of a similar design. It was about fifteen feet long and eight feet wide, with two doors in each of the long sides and one in the seaward end. The doorways were fitted with woven coconut-frond mats that slid closed on a piece of rope. The sidewalls, made of lumber salvaged from a wrecked fishing boat, were only about three feet high, but the steeply pitched thatched roof soared up fifteen feet. Most of the other houses were larger, with traditional woven-mat sidewalls, which, like the roofs, had turned light gray under the sun and rain. The settlement looked like a haphazard array of weathered haystacks.

Between the houses were small tobacco patches enclosed by mat fences to keep out the scrawny dogs, chickens, and pigs that roamed everywhere with impunity. Woven mats propped up on sticks shielded seedlings from the sun. In the next courtyard, a woman carefully removed the mats to water her plants from a bucket. "*Lessor anim*," I attempted. She smiled mysteriously and returned to her plants. An old crone sat in the shadows of a doorway watching me with glinting eyes.

This was the village called Asugulap. It belonged to the women of

MAP OF SATAWAL ISLAND

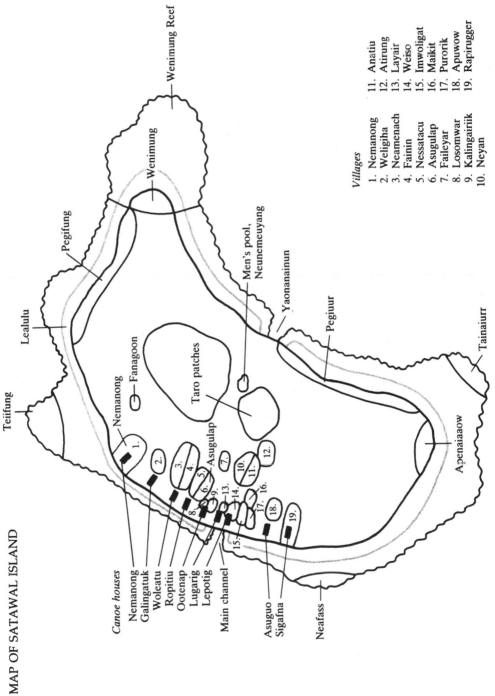

Teiifung

Lealulu

Pegifung

Wenimung

Wenimung Reef

Nemanong

Fanagoon

Taro patches

Men's pool, Neunemeuyang

Yaonanainun

Pegiuur

Asugulap

Apenaiaaow

Tainaiurr

Neafass

Canoe houses

Nemanong
Galingatuk
Woleatu
Ropitiu
Ootenap
Lugarig
Lepotig

Main channel

Asuguo
Sigafna

1.
2.
3.
4.
5.
6.
7.
8.
9.
10.
11.
12.
13.
14.
15.
16.
17.
18.
19.

Villages

1. Nemanong
2. Weligiha
3. Neamenach
4. Fainin
5. Nessatacu
6. Asugulap
7. Faileyar
8. Losomwar
9. Kalingairiik
10. Neyan
11. Anatiu
12. Atirung
13. Layair
14. Weiso
15. Imwoligat
16. Maikit
17. Purorik
18. Apuwow
19. Rapirugger

the Katamang clan, into which Piailug and Uurupa had both married. Piailug had placed me in his old house. The previous year he had built a new house on the site of an abandoned Katamang village called Nemanong, inhabited since the smallpox epidemic of Japanese times, the old people claimed, only by ghosts.

Nemanong was a five-minute walk north, past the last village and canoe house, through the dense growth along the beach. I found Piailug sitting cross-legged on a mat in his courtyard. He barked orders at three women pounding breadfruit by a cooking shed—his wife and two of his daughters, I recognized from our film footage. Two young boys jabbered to each other as they pranced naked through the courtyard. Each held an empty soy-sauce bottle to his eyes to look through the amber glass. A shout from one of the girls brought them scurrying to the cooking shed with the bottles they had been sent to retrieve.

Two dwellings, a small thatch-roofed hut and a larger one with a tin roof to catch drinking water, bordered the large, sun-dappled courtyard that rolled down a slight incline to the clean white sand. The courtyard had been paved with white-coral gravel laboriously gathered from the beach at low tide. Coconut trees laden with ripening nuts provided shade. There were few dogs and chickens. Nemanong had a restful, parklike atmosphere. It seemed a place of order, quiet, and plenty, removed from the dirt and squalor of the main settlement. As I looked around I wished that Piailug were not leaving and I could stay here with him.

"Sit, Steve," he said in a soft voice. I sat on the coral stones, taking coffee, sugar, creamer, and cigarettes from a paper bag. He fired off another string of unintelligible words, which ended with "Steve." His wife, Nemoito, thin with high cheekbones, came across the courtyard, bending at the waist. She placed a coconut-frond mat next to me, patting it with her hand to indicate where I should sit, and laughed softly when I tried to thank her by saying *warigerig*, meaning literally "you are tiring yourself." One of their daughters, also bending at the waist, followed, carrying a charred teapot of boiling water. She put it next to the coffee and retired with a feline quiver to sit next to her mother. The second daughter brought a single coffee mug, an empty jar, and a hollowed coconut shell. Giggling, she placed these with the kettle. In English I told Piailug I recognized Nemoito from the film, but couldn't remember the names of his daughters.

"This one is Carlita," he replied in English, "and the other is— what's your name?" he teased. "Marcia," she said with a proud toss of her head. The boys scampered over to investigate the American and his bright new containers. One was Howie, the youngest child, the other Tom, one of Piailug's many grandchildren.

"Okay, Steve," Piailug ordered, "make coffee." He scratched the middle of his back with the blade of his machete while he watched.

Nemoito and Piailug had sixteen children, ten boys and six girls who ranged in age from thirty-three down to five. The three oldest boys, Antonio, Mesailuke, and Inaiman, had all married girls from other islands (since the brother-sister incest taboo extends to all one's cousins, it is often difficult for young men to find marriageable partners on their own islands). As custom dictates, each went to live with his wife's family but from time to time spent a season on Satawal. The fourth boy, Halig, worked on Saipan; the fifth, Battista, on Yap; the sixth, Uru, was a seaman on one of the government vessels. The seventh son, Jesus, attended the Jesuit high school on Truk. Only the three youngest boys, Bonefacio (age fourteen), Anton (age twelve), and Howie (age five), were still on Satawal. Anton, however, had been adopted by a childless family in the southern part of the island. All of the girls, Naimorman, Marigot, Emilia, Marcia, Carlita, and Sandra, remained on Satawal; it is very unusual for a woman to leave her ancestral home.

Piailug and Nemoito married after he became a navigator at age nineteen or so. She must have been a beautiful young woman, I commented, which Piailug confirmed enthusiastically. He was drawn to her not just for her beauty, he added, but also for her skill in the "work of the island": everything from routine chores like cultivating taro, weaving mats, and cooking to highly skilled crafts like folding the intricate, origamilike fresh-flower leis, and the complicated stripping, drying, dyeing, and weaving processes that transform banana and hibiscus bark into woven *turrh*. He told me that she was an extremely hardy woman as well. She became seriously ill once, when due to give birth to twins. Piailug was stranded on Lamotrek by calms (this was long before the government had installed a system of solar-powered high-seas radios on the islands). The respected navigator Ikimai sailed off to find Piailug, reaching Lamotrek after a difficult sail in light wind. He set off immediately, but was forced to West Fayu by contrary winds and then becalmed. By the time Piailug reached Satawal two weeks later,

Re Metau: The People of the Sea   45

Nemoito had suffered through the stillbirths and was recovering. "You know," he said with admiration, "Nemoito is *strong*."

As we drank coffee I reviewed my last-evening's notes and asked questions about the fighting stars. He answered patiently and completely, concerned that I understand well. When I finished, he lit another cigarette and exhaled.

"The ship returns this afternoon," he reminded me. "As I told you, I will take Nemoito and Bonefacio to Saipan and will come back on the next ship, in a month. You will live with Uurupa in Asugulap. When I return, you will come here to live with me." He glanced over his shoulder at the sun, at this point well into the morning sky. "Now we will go see the chiefs," he announced. "Then we will meet with Uurupa."

"Do you think you will come back in one month?" I asked nervously. "What if you don't?"

"I must see my son on Saipan," he repeated patiently. "If all goes well, I will return on the next ship. Then we will resume our lessons in navigation. But Uurupa, you know, Uurupa is my *brother*," he intoned soothingly; "he knows what I know. Don't worry, he will take care of you."

Piailug discussed something with his wife, then rose gingerly to his feet and, taking my hand, strolled with me down the path toward the settlement.

Galingatuk, the northernmost canoe house, was deserted. It held neither canoes nor gear. A few men sat in Woleatu, the next canoe house to the south, and they called out to Piailug. "*Inamo*" ("It's all right now"), he shouted back, waving to indicate he had no time. At Ropitiu, the canoe house of the Katamang clan, three young boys rigged their model sailing canoes. He fired off an order that sent them scrambling up to Asugulap. He greeted the men in the next canoe house, Ootenap, then paused behind one that stood in the center of all the rest.

It was named Lugarig, he explained, the chiefs' canoe house. Now we would pay our respects to Rewena, the eldest chief, also a *palu*. I followed him into the shaded interior, bending slightly at the waist, as he did. In the center of the great structure, he told me to sit and wait while he went to find the chief. I fidgeted with the wood shavings on the floor, trying to remember what I had read in the anthropological papers about etiquette in the presence of a chief. I recalled something about never being physically higher than one, so when the two men had reappeared and seated themselves, I scooted down the incline to place myself lower than they were.

"*Wenimum*, Rewena," I said, using the polite greeting as I extended my hand. He looked at it in puzzlement until Piailug said something to him in a low voice. Then he laughed and, with exaggerated movements, shook my hand.

"Thank you, thank you," I stammered in Satawalese, not knowing what else to say. "Thank you that I come to Satawal."

Piailug quietly cut me off: "Okay, Steve," he said in English. "Give the chief the cigarettes." I took them from the paper bag.

"Oh, sank you veddy much," the old man pronounced in English, then laughed and slapped Piailug on the shoulder. After that, evidently, Piailug explained his arrangements for my stay. He spoke softly but with force, ejecting his sentences in machinelike bursts, his even gaze leveled at the chief. Rewena listened solemnly and asked questions.

He seemed to be in his seventies, was wizened, almost fragile. Dolphin tattoos swam up the outside of both legs. On his shoulder was the triangular rising-sun logo of the Nanyo Boeiki Keisa Trading Company (NBK), with which many of the older men imprinted one another during the Japanese administration. A tattooed bracelet of overlapping triangles encircled his wrist. Dark lines radiated from it, tracing the tendons on the back of his hand. The lines terminated in dark "V"s at his knuckles, like the tails of the dolphins on his legs. From time to time, as Piailug talked, the chief leaned forward and backward, as if trying to get his cloudy eyes to bring me into focus.

When the third chief, Uliso (Thureng had stayed on Yap), passed by the canoe house, Rewena gestured to Piailug to call him. Uliso, one of the island's four master canoe builders, entered and sat down. Piailug nodded in the direction of the paper bag. Uliso acknowledged my gifts with a softly spoken "You tire yourself." He listened carefully (and without evident pleasure) to Rewena and Piailug. I wondered what the men were talking about and what would happen to me when Piailug left.

Soon the talking stopped. Uliso began to get up, but dropped back to the ground to take my extended hand. I shook Rewena's hand as well, thanking him obsequiously. He bowed with a smile, saying, "Sank you! Sank you!," then laughed wildly.

"Was everything good with the chiefs?" I asked Piailug when we were outside.

"No problem," he replied almost flippantly. "I told them you came to see Piailug, not the chiefs." He looked at me defiantly. "You came to see Piailug, not that other navigator."

I followed him through the dizzying assault of sunlight on the beach, up a small embankment, and into the main settlement. He took a wide path running north. The houses, cooking sheds, pigsties, and tobacco patches were heaped up on either side of the path, with no visible demarcation between one clan's compound and another's. Everywhere groups of women squatted around fires, roasting or pounding breadfruit. "Come and eat!" they greeted us. To most, Piailug simply held up his hand in a gesture of declination, but when one woman called he went over to chat and share his cigarettes. She offered me breadfruit, but with the sun blasting shimmering waves of heat from the coral path and courtyards, I felt faint and very thirsty. I asked for a drinking coconut instead. She bellowed at a young boy nearby, who scrambled up a thirty-foot tree to fetch several nuts. With a few deft strokes of her machete she stripped away the outer husk, as is done for children and visiting dignitaries, hacked off the top, and handed it to me. "Drink! Drink until you are full, full, full!" she exhorted with a laugh.

She was a cousin, Piailug explained. If I was ever hungry or thirsty I could go to her and she would feed me. I should think of her, too, and from time to time bring her cigarettes and coffee, and medicine when she was sick.

Back in Asugulap, we met with Uurupa in a small tin-roofed shack full of fishing gear. Piailug sat in a corner, smoking fiercely, turning from time to time to spit through an open doorway. At last he cleared his throat and spoke. Eguman, one of Uurupa's adopted sons and the island's Western-trained dental clinician, interpreted:

"We will speak of everything on our minds," Piailug said, somewhat formally. "You must tell us the whole story of why you came to Satawal and who you came to study with."

I did as I was told, with Eguman translating. When I finished, Piailug rattled off a burst of speech, gesturing in my direction. "It is good for you to explain this," Eguman translated, "for some people accuse Piailug of stealing you from the chiefs so he could take the gifts you brought."

Then Piailug turned to me directly: "Now you must finally choose," he said piercingly. "If you wish to talk with the other navigators, my brother and I will still help you in your work. We will be friends. You can give us whatever you feel compensates us for our efforts. You can even live here. But if you really wish to learn our navigation, we will take you as our brother. Then we can teach you all we know. Even if you have no money, we will teach you just the same. If you have things to give us, good—those things will help us on our island. Later, when you return home, if we need things we will write and you can send us what we need. But if you choose to be our brother, you cannot do whatever you wish—you cannot leave our village on your own, go around with people outside our clan, or talk with other navigators. For that, you will have to ask our permission. Do you understand, Steve?"

I nodded yes.

"Good. Then what is your choice?"

I knew that, traditionally, navigation was handed down in the family. Some of the most secret knowledge was taught only toward the end of a master's life, when the student himself was old and his hair had turned gray. To be adopted into Piailug's family was what I had most wanted, and I needed little deliberation to make my choice. But, again, I wondered why he should be so forthcoming. Maybe he felt it was his personal mission to teach navigation, now that the tradition was threatened. Again and again, I had gotten this impression in the hours of raw filmed interviews shot for *The Navigators*, and from my discussions with him on the *Microspirit*. It was clear, too, that he was offering a shrewd business bargain. Uurupa had already asked if I could get him a Polaroid camera and film so he could take pictures of his children and grandchildren, and I knew other requests would follow. Yet I sensed there was something more to these vows of brotherhood. I felt, although I could not then articulate, that my loyalty was being tested in a conflict with the chiefs that was politely masked but not resolved; that I was being asked to declare both personal and political allegiance to Piailug. I was uneasy about choosing sides so early, but I sensed that if I wanted Piailug as my teacher I had only this chance.

"I want to be like your brother," I affirmed.

"*Ina*," he said quietly.

Then he executed another long burst of speech, chopping the air with his hand.

"Piailug thanks you for the gifts," Eguman translated. "He says he will give two-thirds to the chiefs to distribute to the rest of the island, and he and Uurupa will keep the rest."

Uurupa had been listening with catlike attention, smoking tobacco rolled in newspaper. A long keychain was wrapped several times around the top of his head, and the keys dangled behind one ear. He was bigger than Piailug, and the angles of his face were less severe. He cleared his throat and spoke, startling me with his nearly perfect English.

"I am younger than Mau," he began, his rich, melodic voice rolling up from deep within his chest, "and he knows navigation better than I; but we had the same training. After our grandfather died, we learned from our father. When he died we learned from our uncle Angora, on Puluwat. If you are Mau's brother, then you are my brother. I will teach you all I can in the time you stay with me. What you have told us is good, for now we understand everything about you and the chiefs. We know you are a captain and that you came to see Mau." Then he asked how I would like my food prepared, and if I preferred to eat alone or with him. I said I would eat with him.

The meeting over, Piailug led me through the village and down a path through the undergrowth into a wide coconut grove.

"Our trees," he said, orbiting his machete above his head to shoot it downward, lopping off a shrub intruding onto the path. "If you need coconuts, tell one of the young boys to pick from any of these trees."

We came to a small pool surrounded by flowering hibiscus. "This is our place for bathing. We call it Fanagoon. You can come here to bathe." He speared a fallen coconut with the tip of his machete, hacked it open, cut the white meat into strips, and chewed several as he loosened his loincloth. He lowered himself into the pool, urging me to do likewise, then spit the white mass into his hand and rubbed it on his body.

"Just like soap," he said, "but better because it makes your skin strong beneath the sun." The oily meat left my skin feeling clean and pliant.

Finally he led me down another path back to Nemanong, crowded now with people helping with last-minute preparations for the *Micro-spirit's* return.

I helped Piailug carry his woven baskets of taro and breadfruit and bundles of coconuts to the beach. His clansmen loaded these into the skiff with his wife and son. As he boarded he turned to me: "I am going," was all he said.

The skiff pushed through the low surf to be hoisted aboard. Then the ship gunned her engines, spun, and steamed away. Three sea turtles, brought by the ship, lay upturned on the beach. Some young men hacked off their left hind flippers, pulled out their intestines, and cleaned them in the sea, trailing them through the waves like yellow ropes. Others piled dry coconut fronds atop the beasts and set them alight. When the fires died down they swept away the cinders and severed the junction between the turtles' breastplates and carapaces. Then they pried up the breastplates like manhole covers, revealing fantastic webs of muscles, veins, and organs, glistening like the workings of a wondrous machine.

Meanwhile the ship rode down the brilliant swath of the westering sun, crossed tracks with a supertanker, and disappeared. My quest to reach the islands had finally succeeded. I had found Piailug and been accepted as his student. Now, as I stood on the beach watching him sail away, I felt a bit sorry for myself. I went to Uurupa for sympathy but he took no notice, squatting in a large circle with the rest of the men, slicing the turtle into small pieces and separating them into piles of fat, organ, and flesh. Older boys distributed charred rings of roasted tripes. One boy gave me some of the fatty yellow stuff. Forcing back revulsion, I put it into my mouth and chewed. It was delicious, like bacon, and as I ate I became hungrier. Another boy gave me three chunks of roasted flesh and I gobbled those, too.

When all the meat had been cut, sorted, and counted, it was apportioned equally among the clans of Satawal.

6

The next day was Sunday, and no one worked. I awoke to a great crowd waiting patiently in my courtyard for me to make coffee. Children carrying glass jars arrived from distant parts of the settlement to have them filled with the prized liquid. Uurupa would explain that the child had been sent by so-and-so's cousin or brother or sister-in-law, and could I please give them some coffee, too. Some people asked for cigarettes, so I opened several packs to be distributed. Then a bell tolled to the south, and the crowd rose and wandered down the path to attend church services, performed by a layman. Uurupa took me to church, then attended a men's meeting in the chiefs' canoe house, to which I was not invited.

On Monday, the women cleaned up the grounds around my house and removed the junk from inside. Uurupa's wife, Insouluke, sat in the courtyard, weaving new palm-frond mats for the floor and doors, while her daughters swept the inside of the hut until it was clean and fresh. Uurupa and I built a bamboo desk and shelves for my gear. Then I unpacked my things and made my home with the Katamang clan of Satawal.

For the first week I was not allowed to wander around the settlement alone. When I tried to take photographs of a sailing canoe returning from a fishing trip, Uurupa sent one of his sons running down the beach to make certain I remained in front of our canoe house. He later explained that if I talked to anyone else or took photos outside our village, I might have to pay a fee.

I spent the days in Ropitiu canoe house, where Uurupa, like Piailug, a *sennap* or master canoe builder, supervised the renovation of the Katamang clan's canoe, *Suntory* (named for the Japanese whiskey). The *sennap* build their creations without blueprints or even measuring tape. The general proportions are controlled by a time-honored set of ratios: the height of the mast, for instance, equals the length of the hull; the length of the outrigger is half the hull length. To find the proper span of the crossbeams, the builder wraps a piece of string halfway around one of the forked ends, or "eyes," and stretches it to the hull's midpoint. The profile of the keel, the placement of the thwarts or seats, and the length of the booms are all dictated by similar ratios. But for the rest, the sharpness of the bows, the modeling of the underwater lines, the height of the hull, and the shape of the outrigger, the builder must rely on his master's teachings and his own experience and sense of aesthetics. Even then it is impossible to predict the true worth of the design, as many a frustrated America's Cup yacht designer knows. As the *sennap* say, "Only the sea knows if the canoe will be fast."

To construct a canoe the *sennap* will first fell a large, sound breadfruit tree, or a mahoganylike tree called *rugger*, and hollow it out for the keel, called the "heart." He fells more trees, splits them, and carefully carves them into planks. The whole vessel is lashed together with coconut-fiber rope. A sticky white compound of dehydrated breadfruit sap applied to strips of coconut husk between the planks makes the hull watertight. But over time the breadfruit caulking dries out and the lashings weaken. Every two years or so, the canoes must be rebuilt.

Suntory had been disassembled and her plank edges scraped. Uurupa had decided to try to make the canoe faster, and now the men of Ropitiu lightened the planks by thinning them with adzes. The younger boys steadied the planks for the older men, who were the only ones trusted to wield the heavy, razor-sharp tools. Men too old to work sat in the canoe house to chat and give advice while they rolled coconut fiber into rope on their thighs.

Old Olaman seldom hefted an adz. Like many of the old men, he was skinny and fragile-looking. His eyes were clouded over with cataracts and watered continually; he wiped the tears from his cheeks with the backs of his hands. Even though he did little of the heavy work, he was always in the canoe house while work was in progress. Each day he brought a fresh basket of dried coconut fiber to roll into neat blond coils of rope.

There was another old man, Rau (the name means "whale"). He stood about five feet ten and was still barrel-chested and muscular, but he evidently suffered from senile dementia, for he would spend days at a time lying on a bamboo pallet in a dark corner of the canoe house. Occasionally he would cry out and someone would bring him a cigarette. The boys told me that Rau had once gone crazy and tried to attack Piailug with a machete. Piailug, trained in the fighting aspects of *pwang*, a body of skills which also includes canoe repair and house construction, deflected his swing and brought him down with a blow to the stomach. But at other times the old man was completely alert, and when one of Piailug's or Uurupa's daughters brought him a plate of fish and breadfruit, he would converse amicably with her. Often, after staying up late to type my notes, I would take a stroll on the beach before going to sleep. I always watched for the glow of Rau's cigarette in the black interior of the canoe house. "Who is that?" he would call out. I would answer quickly, mindful of the story of the machete. Sometimes he would stroll out on the beach with me, to point out and name the stars. I eagerly attended his teachings at first, but became skeptical when I noticed that the stars changed names from night to night.

Next oldest was Neamirh, the elder of the Katamang clan. Neamirh was less than five feet tall, with sharp cheeks, nose, and chin and short, curly black hair. He was probably ten years older than Piailug, yet still in prime physical condition, with muscular arms and legs. He worked steadily, quietly, and efficiently, pausing from time to time to smoke.

Napota was Piailug and Uurupa's relative. He was big and fat, with an arrow tattooed on his chest. He always asked me to give him things. Uurupa told me to be "kind" to Napota for, as the eldest male in his wife's line, he wielded power in our village.

There was a handful of high-school boys: Steven, about sixteen, with a loud, unmodulated voice and a wild look in his eyes. Adam, Neamirh's son, who looked just like him, had been adopted by Uurupa. Two brothers, Amalug, fourteen, and Amalap, nineteen, could only be described as beautiful, with olive skin, deep-brown eyes, and high, feminine cheekbones. Each wore chains and flower leis around his neck and wrists and fresh hibiscus in his hair. Uurupa had adopted Amalug; Amalap lived with old, cloudy-eyed Olaman. I never found out who their real parents were.

Eguman, who translated for Piailug, was about thirty years old. He was married and had just had his first child. He had attended the elementary school on Satawal, where classes are taught in English with American textbooks, then went to high school on Ulithi. After attending technical school on Palau, he returned to Satawal to become the island's resident dental technician. He would work in the canoe house in the afternoon, after he had finished his morning duties at the small clinic located in Satawal's new cement dispensary. He was teaching the Head Start students how to brush their teeth and use dental floss, but, he lamented, the kids soon lost the toothbrushes and gave the floss to their fathers to tie fishing lures. Rau was Eguman's biological father.

The other two young men, Paul and Jesse, were Uurupa's nephews; as such they were considered his sons. Both of their fathers had died several years before, and Uurupa had taken full responsibility for their upbringing. Jesse, twenty-two, had attended the Jesuit high school on Truk. He spoke excellent English and each week translated portions of the Bible into Satawalese for the Sunday service. Paul, about sixteen, was very bright and polite. He had not yet graduated from high school. The previous summer Uurupa had taken Paul and the other high-school boys on a voyage to the eastern islands. On Puluwat they had become trapped by inclement weather, and the boys missed the ship to take them to Ulithi. Angered, the chiefs ruled they would have to wait out the school year on Satawal.

Uurupa and Piailug had built *Suntory* and now Uurupa was clearly in charge of rebuilding it, even though he was not the most senior man present. I spent my days in the canoe house working through my prepared list of questions. Paul seemed to take a special interest in me and became my translator, for, shy about his command of English, Uurupa would speak only his native language in the presence of his sons. I asked questions, Paul translated, and Uurupa discussed them with

Neamirh, Napota, and Olaman. Occasionally Rau would shout something from his cot. One of the men would then utter the definitive answer, which Paul would translate for me.

I started by making a sketch of the island, since Uurupa and the others kept referring to canoe houses, villages, and localities by name and I had no idea what or where they were. There were eight canoe houses, as Piailug had told me, one belonging to each clan. Lugarig, the chiefs' canoe house, stood in the middle of the others, dominating the terminus of the main channel. *Lugarig* meant "Middle, the Dividing," according to Uurupa, logical since returning canoes must enter through the channel to present their catch for division. North of Lugarig stood Ootenap, meaning "big canoe house," although no one knew if the name referred to the structure, which was no bigger than the others, or the number of men who belonged. Next was our canoe house, Ropitiu, so named because long ago the men would divide (*rop*) their entire catch into portions, and refuse to give the chiefs their share. Next was Woleatu, meaning "lair of lobsters" according to Olaman. Long ago the men of this house were fierce and well versed in the fighting aspects of *pwang*. Farther north was Galingatuk, whose name meant, roughly, "look up to it," for it was the last canoe house to the north.

Farthest south of Lugarig lay Sigafna, then Asuguo and Lepotig. No one knew the meaning of the first two, but Lepotig was the canoe house of the Masano clan. *Masano* means "the well of the eye." Legend holds that the Masano people sprang from the tear duct of a woman from Yap. *Potig* denotes the mucus flowing from the tear duct; thus the canoe house is the "place of the people from the well of the eye."

Next Paul helped me sketch the locations of the villages. All together there were nineteen, which collectively formed the *mesanafanu*, or "face of the island." Several villages, like Nemanong, were geographically separate and could readily be distinguished from the others. But the rest lay cheek by jowl in the settlement. Although the divisions between the villages, or *pwogos*, were clear to the people of Satawal, I never did learn which coconut, papaya, or banana trees marked the borders between them.

The names of some *pwogos* gave tantalizing clues to their history. Olaman recalled a story that the Pik clan once celebrated the completion of a dwelling house with a feast of dolphins; thus the name of their village, Nesattacu—"tempted to eat dolphins." Imwoligat, Eguman's wife's village, stands on the former site of the menstrual house, the "house of children." Some names are prosaic: Rapirugger simply means "at the base of the rugger tree," and Fainin "beneath the nin tree."

Satawal's culture is both matrilineal and matrilocal: one is born into the clan of one's mother and lives with the clan of one's wife. This makes a man responsible to two villages (and two canoe houses), his mother's, which he considers his own, and his wife's. For a woman, this means that from infancy to old age she may never dwell outside her own small village, or, indeed, her parents' house. The women of Asugulap were Uurupa's wife and her three sisters. The old woman who sat in her doorway glaring at me the first morning was his mother-in-law. The girls were their daughters and granddaughters. Piailug had also married into this clan, and until he had developed the abandoned Katamang village at Nemanong the previous year, he and his family had occupied the house in which I now stayed. Nemoito was a full-blooded Katamang, which Uurupa's wife and her sisters were not considered to be because their grandmother had been adopted into the clan.

When Paul had finished plotting the positions of the villages on my sketch, I asked if the rest of the island was divided and named. Uurupa said that Satawal's low-lying center, dominated by the taro swamp, is subdivided into numerous smaller plots owned by each of the clans. He waved his hands in irritation when I asked their names, saying they were too numerous to bother with and, besides, he didn't even know them—I would have to go ask the women, for the taro patch was their province.

All around the island, between the taro patch and the beach, a belt of higher ground held breadfruit and coconut trees, papayas, bananas, pineapples, and limes. This area, too, was greatly subdivided, with each woman owning plots of her clan's land. From these plots, the men, who technically own no land, must gather all the resources the sea will not provide: breadfruit trees yield food and lumber; breadfruit sap makes canoes watertight. Coconuts provide food and drink, copra brings in cash, and dried husks fuel the cooking fires, while woven coconut fronds become baskets and various mats for shielding canoes from the sun, roofing, sheathing, and carpeting dwelling houses, and dozens of other uses. Pineapples, bananas, papayas, and limes offer a welcome diversion from the monotonous diet of breadfruit and taro. A strange fruit called *afour*, which tastes like a cross between a potato and a mango, provides nourishment on a long voyage. Women dry and color fiber from hibiscus and banana trees, tie it into long strands, then string these on their backstrap looms to weave into beautiful *turrh*.

The land provides nearly everything needed to live: food and drink and shelter from the fierce winds of the winter stars. Land is a place to have children; a place to rest briefly before voyaging in the canoe of death. Land has always been the most precious of commodities. The old men recall legends of ancient warriors fighting bloody wars of conquest, and Satawal navigators roaming the sea in search of new islands. The clans of Satawal, for example, date their arrival on the island by the Slaughter of Saiow, when that fierce navigator and warrior from the Mortlocks took the island by surprise and killed every man, woman, and child but one, who escaped to tell the tale.

Yet, while the land gives taro and breadfruit, called simply "food," it cannot provide what is called "meat": fish, octopus, and sea turtle, which must be taken from the sea. Nor is the land itself always secure, for the vicious typhoons that sweep through the Carolines in summer can inundate whole islands, poisoning the taro swamp with salt water, smashing breadfruit and coconut trees, canoe and dwelling houses. On these occasions islanders have taken to their canoes to seek refuge on neighboring islands. In some cases whole fleets have been forced to venture out across the horizon, hoping to find a new home. On Yap, the outer islanders are called *re metau*, "people of the sea," for without their mastery of seafaring they would die.

There are eight clans of Satawal: Neyarh, Anatiu, Nosomar, Katamang, Pik, Souwen, Sousat, and Masano. The first three are the "Clans of the Chiefs," while the last five are the "Clans of the People."

Each of the chiefly clans produces one chief, the eldest son of the eldest woman in the clan. When a chief dies the title goes to his next-younger brother, not to his son. If he has no brother it goes to the son of his mother's next-youngest sister. If she has no son it goes to the son of the next-youngest sister, and so on. If none of them have sons, the title of chief goes to the grandson of the eldest of the sisters.

The chief's younger brother serves as his adviser and spokesman.

He is called the *maaneluke soamwoan*, the "bird outside the chief," according to Uurupa, but may mean "man (*muan*) beside the chief." In the public meetings in the canoe house, the *maaneluke* will often act as a foil to an unpopular resolution of the chiefs or will goad them into facing matters they wish to ignore.

Leading each of the Clans of the People is an elder, the *telap*. He, too, has a "bird outside" him who helps make decisions and disseminate the chief's rulings.

Any important island decision will be made after a meeting of all the chiefs, the *maaneluke*, and the *telap*, at which all sides of the problem are examined. But decisions are not made by the men alone. The Council of Elders, composed of old women, toothless and therefore considered wise, holds meetings and advises the chiefs of their opinions. When the women unite behind an issue, typically to reestablish the taboo on drinking tuba, they rarely fail to carry the day.

All three chiefly clans on Satawal are said to come from the Moenefar clan, which, in a coincidence of Satawal's legends with Western scientific findings, was the first clan to reach the Carolines from islands in the south. The power of the chiefly clans, therefore, apparently stems from their direct descent from the ancestral seafarers. On Satawal the chiefs are called the "captains" of the canoe of state.

The next Sunday I was summoned by Chief Rewena. At Uurupa's suggestion, I packed a gift of coffee, sugar, creamer, and cigarettes to please the old navigator. (He had been the most vocal advocate of the proposal to price my activities, I was discreetly told.) Uurupa avoided the main path through the settlement, taking me and Jesse, who came along to translate, on a circuitous route through the woods.

When we reached the chief's house, Uurupa motioned for us to remain behind. Bending at the waist, he entered the quiet courtyard and, in a respectful, almost timid voice, called the chief. Rewena emerged through the low door of his house, scowled at Uurupa, but smiled when he saw me. "Goot morning!" he enunciated pleasantly in English.

Still bending slightly, Uurupa followed him to the center of the courtyard. The chief sat on a mat and motioned for us to do likewise. Jesse came timidly, to sit like a little boy outside our circle. I made coffee for the old man and gave him cigarettes. "Sank you!" he said, turning to Jesse to ask if he was saying it properly. He and Uurupa exchanged pleasantries.

Then the chief gave Uurupa a command. Uurupa turned to me: "Now," he said softly, "our chief, Rewena, wants you to tell him the whole story of how and why you came here. Because he is the chief he is like your father—you should tell him everything, so he will understand."

Through Jesse I told him my story, beginning with how I had learned navigation on racing yachts. I told him I wanted originally to study with Piailug, but did not mention this in Madrich since I had not yet asked Piailug to be my teacher. On the *Microspirit* he had agreed, and I was content.

Then, as Uurupa had instructed me to do, I inventoried all the gifts I had brought and explained that I would give some to Uurupa and Piailug for their kindness, and the rest to the island.

Rewena thanked me for the gifts and for my talk. "We don't know as much as the ancient navigators," he said pensively. "We didn't have notebooks and pens and writing like the Americans and the Japanese. Some navigators were stingy with their knowledge. Others died before they could pass everything to their sons, and their knowledge was lost." Perhaps some of the other navigators could help Piailug and Uurupa teach me, he suggested. I wondered if this was a genuine offer or a veiled insult to the brothers.

Rewena sipped his coffee for a time, then dismissed us by announcing he understood everything. He thanked me again for my talk. When we left, Uurupa looked greatly relieved. "You spoke very well," he said; "our chief said he saw clearly that from the very beginning you came to Satawal to be with Piailug. Everything is now clear and straight."

Later that morning, in the chiefs' canoe house, I repeated my story to all the men of Satawal, having first given the chiefs a carton of cigarettes to distribute to the men. I sat in the wood chips on the ground speaking quietly to Jesse. He translated to Weneto, *maaneluke* to Rewena, who retold the story to the men clustering in, under, and atop the chiefs' canoe, named *Tiger*. When I finished my story, I passed around snapshots of my boat and of various islands and countries to which I had sailed. The men scrutinized the yacht carefully, asking questions about the rigging, sails, and keel. Then Uurupa and Napota divided the yards of clean white sailcloth, the fathoms of new fishing line, and the hundreds of gleaming fish hooks among the seven other canoe houses. Uurupa refused to take a share for Ropitiu, claiming they already had enough. Later I was told that Rewena beheld the gifts with delight: "This man truly knows what we need to live on this island. Everything will be free for him from now on—sailing, photography, all!"

PART II

The Talk of Our Fathers

7

When we heaved her along the freshly cut palm-frond skids, *Suntory* seemed to grow lighter, as if escaping the darkness of the canoe house called up some urge from her wooden planks. In the half-light we fitted the lee platform and stepped the mast. Then we pushed again, and the keel squeaked down the long row of skids to the sea. A dying moon hung in the western sky, and the beach and village still nodded in the fine mists of sleep. Even the tradewinds were light now, just before daybreak, and the sea deceived us with her quiescence, her eyes half closed.

We stripped off our loincloths and stood naked in the warm water to hold the canoe as she tossed her head to the low swells humping over the mid-tide reef. Uurupa had no need to give orders. The scene had been enacted hundreds of times before by these men, their fathers, grandfathers, and great-grandfathers. It had probably been done this way for thousands of years. Paul and Jesse carried the heavy booms and new sail down from the canoe house and loaded them aboard. Then we maneuvered the canoe around the coral heads in the *lealulu*, the shallow, narrow pool just inside the breakers, to the main channel. Already the other canoes, *Aloha*, *Rugger*, and *Tiger*, had slipped through the channel and were making sail at the face of the reef.

Satawal slid away as we gathered speed, a dark ellipse, embraceable in the wave of an arm. Behind her the sky began to heave in the labor of daybreak. The wind increased. Far ahead we could see the other three canoes reducing sail by pulling the gaff and boom that spread the triangle of canvas. Uurupa looked up at our straining sail, then ahead, as if to gauge the distance to the others. He turned to Jesse, sitting aft at the steering paddle, and sliced his arm through the air above him. We would press on, to catch up with the others. It was a clear, exhilarating morning, and skipjack tuna were running on the deep-sea reef. Every seaworthy canoe on Satawal was racing out to fish for the day.

The previous week, we had finished rebuilding *Suntory*. The planks had been lightened, recaulked with breadfruit sap, and tightly relashed with coconut-fiber rope. The lashing holes had been stopped with a cementlike mixture of lime and water, which had dried for five days. Then she had been repainted, her hull glistening black and topsides bright yellow. Uurupa had then asked me to help build a new sail, since I was the only one who understood the vagaries of adjusting and operating the Chinese hand-crank sewing machine Piailug had purchased on Yap.

As we'd laid the dacron sailcloth on the beach, I'd suggested we cut the sail flatter than the traditional design and add both a downhaul and an outhaul to help control the shape in different wind conditions. Also, I wanted to omit the heavy rope customarily lashed around the perimeter.

"No, no, no, no," Uurupa had said, shaking his head, laughing gently at my naïveté, "this is not how we make sails here on Satawal. Never, not even many, many years ago, did navigators ever make sails like that."

"But we always make sails like this," I insisted and gave a long-winded lecture on the aerodynamics of sail design and the structural properties of dacron sailcloth. Uurupa remained unconvinced, and I finally resorted to teasing:

"Do you want your canoe to be slower than the others, or do you want to fly past them as if they were anchored to the reef?"

"Do you really make sails this way in America?" he asked, softening; finally he caved in: "You must be right," he reasoned dejectedly, "because this sailcloth is from America and you are an American navigator. So you must know about these things."

"You will see," I consoled him teasingly. "When we sail right past the other canoes, then what will you do?"

"Oh! I don't know!" he exclaimed, clowning before Paul, Jesse, Eguman, and the rest of the young men who had come to help. "I'll just jump in the water and—*pssssst*—go find a shark!"

As we sewed the sail together under the palm trees, Olaman came by, muttered, and walked away, shaking his head. Soon other old men followed. Uurupa grew worried: "The old men say that no one has ever made a sail this way before."

"It will be a fast sail," I assured him, hoping I was right, for I had never sailed aboard a Micronesian outrigger. I labored furiously through Saturday and Sunday to finish the sail for Monday's fishing expedition. "Are you sure the Christian God will not break our sail because we worked on the Sabbath?" Uurupa had asked nervously.

Now I was eyeing the sail. The clew, the corner attached to the end of the boom, was pulling away from its lashing. I told Uurupa we had to drop the sail to fix it, but he just waved me away and concentrated on the other canoes. Soon it tore completely and the sail flogged in the wind. He ordered the sail dropped, shooting suspicious glances at me. Fortunately, I was able to effect a quick repair, and we proceeded.

Today *Suntory* had a complement of eleven: Uurupa; his sons Paul, Jesse, Adam, and Eguman; Amalap and Napota; Terei (another of Piailug's sons-in-law); skinny old Assaf, who had married Uurupa's youngest sister-in-law; tubby, irreverent Iti, who had also married into the Katamang clan; and me. Paul now traded places with Jesse on the steering paddle astern. Amalap sat near them. Assaf, Uurupa, and Terei sat on the central bench, and the rest of the young men stood by to handle the sail. I was placed on the lee platform with Iti and Napota, where with my cameras, notebooks, and inexperience I wouldn't interfere with the serious business of catching fish.

Uurupa watched the boats ahead and Satawal astern. Later he told me that he maintained his course to the reef, called Wuligee, by lining up the southern tip of the island, Apenaiaaow, with the eastern tip, Wenimung.

Now we were well offshore, and big swells rolled majestically out of the northeast. As they lifted us skyward and the clear wind pressed the sail, we would shoot ahead, lunging down the face of the wave like some swift fish. Assaf frantically trimmed the sheet as we gathered speed. The rest of us shouted with exhilaration. Then, as the swell outran us, we slowed, wallowed down the backside, and lolled in the trough. The wind lightened in the shallow valley; the other canoes disappeared. Then, as the next wave lifted us, the sail would fill again, *Suntory* would spring forward, and the cycle would begin anew.

Soon we had driven past the three other canoes to gain the lead. To stay with the fleet, Uurupa ordered us to reduce sail by hauling in the brailing line between the *ira muan*, the "man's timber" or gaff, and the *ira rauput*, the "woman's timber" or boom, so named because it is weaker. (It is not the only part of the canoe named after the female anatomy. At the very top of the mast, or *ayu*, the boatbuilder carves a small nub in the wood. "This is called the *tololayu*," Uurupa had told me with an air of anticipation. When I asked what that meant, he burst out mirthfully: "The clitoris of the mast!")

By seven, Uurupa judged we were on the reef, given the slight greenish tinge to the normally blue water. He ordered Assaf to release the sheet, letting sail stream like a flag. *Suntory* slowed and came to rest with her outrigger upwind. Soon the other canoes caught up, let fly their sails, and hove to close by. Satawal lay barely visible on the horizon.

The largest canoe of the fleet was *Aloha*, which belonged to Ootenap canoe house. Today she was guided by the young navigator Matto, a former student of Piailug's. Matto, nicknamed "Mitch" after a Navy officer who frequently visited Satawal in the fifties (the officer had no eyebrows and, when he was a boy, neither did Matto), was as fat as a sumo wrestler, yet warmhearted and gentle. The old navigator and canoe builder Ikerip, now in his seventies, sailed the chief's canoe, *Tiger*, while *Rugger* was navigated by Regaliang, younger brother of Muanirik.

After shouting back and forth between the canoes, the men settled down to chat, smoke, and check their trolling lines and poles. The poles were about ten feet long, of either bamboo or Fiberglas, the latter being salvaged from a wrecked Japanese fishing boat on West Fayu. They were not fitted with reels; instead, six feet of heavy trolling line was permanently secured to the ends, and from the line dangled small silver tuna lures. The lures' hooks were barbless, and the fisherman had to maintain constant, even pressure on the line or the fish would wriggle free. But the advantage of this type of hook was that a fish would quickly disengage itself once landed, and the fisherman could get the lure back in the water.

When I asked why we were waiting, Uurupa told me it was customary to fish Wuligee only between 8:00 A.M. and noon. At other times, he claimed, the tuna would not bite. He recalled expeditions in the past when they had caught over a thousand tuna per boat: "Our canoes were so full we had only this much between the water and the top of the hull," he exclaimed, chopping one hand across his other forearm as a form of measurement. Tuna was smoked and dried; canoes sailed down to Lamotrek and Elato to give it away. They even fed tuna to the pigs and dogs. In the last few years, though, the catch had not been so good. Uurupa felt this was due to the disregard of the fishing taboos: now the young men wore flowers and aftershave lotion while fishing; they brought with them lemons and limes and ate fish, discarding the bones in the sea. Most important, some failed to abstain from intercourse and masturbation during the fishing season, thereby bringing pollution aboard the canoes. Uurupa warned me never to lend my lines and lures, lest my gear become tainted. Once imparted, the contamination was permanent, and the gear would never attract fish. But increasingly Taiwanese, Japanese, and American tuna seiners had been buying licenses from the FSM to operate in Carolinian waters, and Uurupa admitted that they might account for decreased catch rates.

The canoes waited, calmly riding the swells like sea birds. Men intently scanned the water for signs of tuna. Visible on the fishing grounds were several *pway*, flocks of wheeling birds diving on herring chased to the surface by the tuna. This was the most obvious sign of fish, one even I could detect. But when the sea was smoother, the incredibly sharp-eyed crew could sight the tuna without birds, in *wee*, schools rushing and shooting just beneath the surface.

At cight o'clock, Regaliang gave a signal and we hauled in our sails and raced off toward the nearest *pway*. Men unreeled their trolling lines and held their poles ready. I borrowed one of the extra bamboo poles, rigged the tuna lure, and waited excitedly as we approached the edge of the first school. When the first fish hit one of the trolling lines everyone cheered. Fish hit a second line, then a third, and were quickly reeled in. I looked around at the men with poles and, following their example, trailed my lure through the water. Uurupa shouted to Paul to come up on the wind. Suddenly we were in the thick of the school. Tuna bit everything in the water. Eguman, in the stern, jerked his pole upward with a hoot, craning a big skipjack into the canoe. Uurupa methodically dipped his pole, pulled out a fish, dipped his pole, pulled out another one. Fish exploded all around the canoe. Everyone was hauling them in, shouting at the fish and one another, yelling the men's favorite bawdy expression: *Yanna tingie annie!* ("The cunt flies to you!").

I waited, kneeling on the lee platform, my lure dithering in the water. Presently, a fish hit. I jerked my pole, pulling the flailing creature from the water and up to the very edge of the lee platform. Then the boat lurched; I fell on Napota, knocking him over; he yelled and the fish wriggled off the hook and into the sea. "What kind of fisherman is this American?" clucked Uurupa. The rest roared with laughter. I reassembled my dignity and returned my lure to the water. Another fish hit. I started to pull up but was afraid of losing it, so I reeled in both pole and line hand over hand and triumphantly secured the fish. Iti and Napota howled with glee. "That's a pole, Steve," Iti advised, making an obscene jerking gesture. "You use it like this!"

By then we had sailed right through the school and out the other side. "Let's tack," someone shouted. "No, wait!" someone else yelled. A chorus of voices: "Over there! Let's tack!" Suddenly we were tacking. Bodies flew around the canoe. Some reeled in their trolling lines; others took positions on the bow and stern. Then the whole rig, gaff, boom, and sail, was lifted up, using the mast as a crane, and shifted to what had just been the stern. The steering paddle was passed back and rigged, and a minute after initiating the tack we were shooting off in the other direction.

I had been demoted from pole to trolling line, but as we reached the outer edges of the school, mine was the first to be struck. I reeled it in speedily, everyone yelling advice and encouragement as I landed the fish. We came into the thick of the school and pandemonium broke loose as the fish hit the poles and burst from the water. Around us the other boats were having similar luck, their crews hooting and yelling.

At one in the afternoon the canoes hove to, to compare catches. We had taken forty-five, *Rugger* fifty-two, *Aloha* forty, and *Tiger* thirty-nine. Not great but not bad either, Uurupa commented.

The captains decided to call it a day. The wind had slackened now, and the long swells of the early morning had softened into more manageable lumps. As we thrashed upwind toward Satawal, spray hissing at *Suntory's* bow and outrigger, it was time for what the high-school boys called "free chow." Amalap stoked up a coconut-husk fire in the salvaged oil pan we used for a stove and, when the coals were glowing red, blackened both sides of a whole tuna and hacked it into shares.

The charred outside had a smoky flavor, and the raw inside was sweet and cool.

After the meal, the beat home turned into a race. Crews adjusted rigging and sails and discussed the relative merits of the contestants. We had been the faster canoe sailing downwind primarily because we had not reefed our sail as early as the others. Now, sailing to windward in lighter air, we had a fair contest. I went forward to tighten the down-haul, which I called, in English, the "speed," since it was easier to say than "downhaul" or "Cunningham," its proper yachting name. Uurupa eyed the other canoes, then took the sheet himself to squeeze as much speed as possible from *Suntory*. I waited anxiously to see how my new sail would perform.

To my relief, we pulled into the lead. By the time we had reached the reef pass, late in the afternoon, we were more than a mile ahead of the second canoe. Later, on the beach, Olaman rushed over to pump my hand and thank me for the sail. I accepted the credit, but the old sail was so worn that any new one would have shown what the canoe could do; Piailug and Uurupa had fashioned a fast and nimble sailor. Still, I was proud of my contribution, and glad to prove I, too, was versed in the ways of the sea.

Once the canoe had been guided through the channel, we carried the glittering cargo to Lugarig canoe house for distribution. Then we guided *Suntory* back up the *lealulu*, to beach her before Ropitiu. When I asked why we didn't save ourselves work by beaching the canoe near the main channel, Uurupa explained that if we did, anyone could take it.

A large crowd of men had gathered. Saumek, the master of tattoo, led a rhythmic chant to which everyone moved, heaving the canoe up the steep foreshore along the row of skids to the canoe house. There the remaining water was bailed from the hull and the canoe covered with coconut-frond mats. Lastly, Uurupa hooded the *mas*, the "eyes," or forked decorations, on either end with mats and tied them securely. When I asked why, he said that the "eyes" keep a constant lookout for the island. If they are not covered when the canoe is at rest, they will keep watching and become tired. I must have looked dubious, for he shrugged and exclaimed, "Oh, just—what do you call it—superstition!"

As is customary, the women had prepared a post-voyage meal, which some boys now brought down from Asugulap. Today it consisted of taro, rice, and a delicious dish called *kkun*, made of pounded breadfruit covered with coconut milk. I squatted in the circle near Uurupa, scooping up the sweet, warm, creamy breadfruit and licking it from my fingers. One by one the crew finished eating, fetched their wooden boxes of fishing gear and smoking tobacco, and wandered home to sleep. Early the next morning—and every morning for the next two weeks, until the tuna became sporadic—we would fish the reef.

8

In the evenings, Uurupa and I would bathe at Fanagoon or the men's pool at Neunemeuyang. Then we would return to our canoe house to watch the day end. He was beginning to teach me the *kapesani lang*, or "talk of the skies," the art of forecasting the weather by analyzing the shape, color, and arrangement of the clouds at sunrise and sunset.

Over these weeks I came to know him. When Satawal had converted to Catholicism after the war, he was given the Christian name of Tobias; if I was taking notes he would carefully refer to himself by both his names: Tobias Uurupa. He thought he was forty-five, although he was not sure. When the Americans came to Satawal after the war, they assigned ages to the children by judging their size. But Carolinian children grow slower than American ones, so their new ages were often less than their actual years. He was still an infant when his father died, and a teen-ager when his aunt and uncle sent him to Puluwat to study with Angora. Although he had received much the same education as his older brother, he had not been initiated in *pwo*, for by the time he was of age the ceremony was regarded as pagan and no longer performed. Then he returned to Satawal and married, but his wife never conceived. They adopted ten children instead, most of whom were now married with children of their own. He learned English in high school, first on Yap and later on Ulithi, when the Outer Island High School was built there in 1964. He attended with his oldest sons and nephews, Eguman, Mesailuke, Inaiman, and Antonio.

After high school, he accepted training and a job as a medical technician at Yap Memorial Hospital. "I took it because I thought I would make something of myself," he said. "I thought I would go on to college in Hawaii or Guam—I didn't know where, but I thought I would leave these islands." He worked on Yap for a year; then a member of the chiefly clans, jealous that Uurupa, from a low clan, should have such a position, arranged for his dismissal. He returned to Satawal and devoted himself to navigation. He proudly told me of his voyages throughout the central Carolines, including one to Saipan with Piailug. He planned more voyages that year, when the sailing season began.

Uurupa clearly admired his older brother: "Other navigators know more of the talk," he said of Piailug, "but none is braver." Often, when I would pose a navigational question, he would begin with this disclaimer: "We will check with Mau when he returns, but our master, Angora, taught . . ." Because he was not *pwo* he was not accorded the same respect as Piailug. Yet he admitted he hadn't wanted to become *pwo*, for it would have placed him under the severe, nearly ascetic strictures, the taboos of the *palu*, in which the navigator was proscribed from eating food prepared by menstruating women, from having sexual relations, and even from meeting with women and children for specific intervals before, during, and after a sailing or fishing trip. Yet Uurupa was not content to have his reputation wholly eclipsed by his brother and thus sailed as incessantly as Piailug—when not to more distant islands like Truk, Puluwat, and Woleai, to closer ones like Lamotrek, West Fayu, and Pikelot. One evening I asked if there was a rivalry between them.

"Rivalry? What is that?" he asked. When I explained the meaning of the word he laughed: "Only about a hundred miles of rivalry! The distance from here to Puluwat!"

But there was another factor besides the friendly competition with his brother that motivated him to voyage. He had congenital *retinitis pigmentosa*, as far as I could determine from my *Merck Manual*, and was steadily losing his vision. As a boy he had learned the names of all the stars, but now he could no longer see them. He was beginning to lose his day vision as well and wondered how he could navigate if he became blind. He asked for medicine to cure him. I read him the prognosis, which seemed grimly ironic, from the *Merck Manual*: "No therapy is effective . . . career counseling [is] all that can be offered."

After our evening cloud-watching lessons, when it grew dark and the stars shone like the tips of cold steel arrows, Uurupa would take my hand in his strong, callused paw and as meekly as a child would follow me up the path by the canoe house to our home at Asugulap. There we would be served dinner in the courtyard by his wife and daughters. Then I would light my Coleman lantern and take out my notebook, and we would discuss navigation until late at night.

I thought of blue-water navigation as a system that integrated chart and instruments. The chart gives the Western navigator the means to find his course to an objective, the hand-bearing compass lets him check the speed and direction of the current when departing land, the steering compass lets him keep his course at sea, and the sextant enables him to fix his position using the sun, moon, stars, and planets. He will model on the chart all the events of his passage. By projecting the boat's distance run across the course sailed and factoring in the set of the current, he can produce a dead-reckoning (DR) position. Then he can plot the lines-of-position from sextant observations, correcting his DR position and updating his measurement of the current's strength and direction. He uses this updated information to produce the next DR position, which he again checks with sextant observations. If Western navigation is compared to a chess game, and the various procedures to the rules of chess, the chart is the board on which the game is played. Winning, of course, means getting to one's destination.

Micronesian navigation, I realized, is also an integrated system; instead of being based on charts and instruments, it relies on a vast body of lore and the navigator's own senses. The *palu* knows from *wofanu* the course to his destination, the star under which the island lies. At night he maintains his course by following that star, one of the principal stars of *paafu*. If it has not yet risen or is too high to steer by, he selects one of a number of substitute stars that travel the same arc or path through the heavens. These stars are often unnamed, Piailug later told me; the student learns them from his master over years of apprenticeship.

By day and on overcast nights, the *palu* must rely on the swells. This technique, called *pukulaw*, or "wave tying," requires him to analyze the various component swells that make up the confusion of waves on the sea's surface. In the tropical Pacific, where the steady tradewinds blow from easterly quadrants for most of the year, the wind pushes up long, low groundswells that march across the sea in steady lines. The vector of the swells' march remains steady, enabling the skilled *palu* to maintain his direction by keeping a constant angle between the swells and his canoe. Where two or three swell systems interact, the navigator will steer by what are called "knots," the peaks the swells make as they come together, like the converging wakes of two motorboats. At dawn and dusk, he must check the swells' vector against the stars. At night, if the sky is overcast and there is no moon to light the swells on the ocean, he must steer by the pitch and roll of his canoe in the seaway. This technique is simply called *meaify*, Piailug told me, "to feel." It is the ultimate test of a navigator's skill.

Navigators are taught to recognize eight "waves"—one from each octant of the compass. The most dominant are the swells from the north, northeast, and east that are created by the strong winter tradewinds. As the winter winds diminish and the voyaging season begins, swells come from the southeast and south. In late summer, during the season of the west wind, swells come from the southwest, west, and northwest. *Pukulaw* has now, almost universally, been supplanted by the magnetic compass.

To measure the current when departing land, the navigator performs *fatonomuir*, "facing astern," to find the star under which the island has moved. The navigator will then know from the *kapesani serak*, "talk of sailing," the precise series of course corrections he must make to reach his destination. When out of sight of land, the *palu* can check the current by reading it directly, either in the shape of the swells or by using the ripple technique Piailug had tried to teach me on the *Microspirit*.

Thus far, Micronesian navigation, like Western navigation, satisfies the three requirements for any successful navigational system: to determine the course to an objective, to maintain that course at sea, and to measure and compensate for the displacement from the correct course by current or other factors such as leeway and storm drift. What I didn't fully understand was the precise way in which the *palu* tied together and modeled the events of a passage—the Micronesian equivalent of the chart. From my preliminary research I knew this was done in a mental plotting system called *Etak*. In my first weeks with Uurupa, we investigated the *Etak* modeling technique in detail.

The nautical chart is like a road map. Islands, reefs, and continents are laid out in their correct relation to one another according to Mercator's projection, which distorts the earth's features such that by sailing a straight course the navigator can still reach his destination on the curved earth. A compass rose is printed on the chart so the navigator can easily use his parallel rulers to find the compass bearings between points, bearings that, after compensating for magnetic variation, he will actually follow to his target. North, of course, is always at the top of the chart. The chart is superimposed with lines of latitude and longitude graded in degrees and minutes. Sixty minutes constitute one degree; one minute of latitude equals one nautical mile.

Imagine a voyage from one island to another, lying directly north, or 360° (we ignore the problem of magnetic variation here). If there is no current to displace his vessel, all the navigator has to do is follow his compass to his destination. To plot his voyage on the chart, he simply marks off the distance run, which he knows from his taffrail log, on the line of his course—just as a driver would position himself along a motorway by noting his odometer reading.

In a slight variation of this example, the navigator takes leave of land steering north, as before, but then, as the island drops beneath the horizon, he backsights with his hand-bearing compass. If there is no current, the island should bear south, 180°. But it bears 190° instead, meaning a westerly current has carried the boat east. By plotting this bearing on the chart and noting he has traveled ten miles in two hours, the navigator can measure the spread between his nominal course and his actual course and thus determine that the westerly current is running at one nautical mile per hour. To compensate for this current, the navigator steers 10° to the west, or 350°.

Micronesian navigators have a radically different, though elegant and ingenious, method of tracking their relationship to the islands around them. In *Etak*, the canoe's progress through the water is mentally gauged by picturing an island off to one side of the course moving under the star points on the horizon behind it. This island is called the *lu pongank*, which simply means "in the middle and athwart." It is not actually seen during the voyage, yet, as a known location in the locus of converging star paths, it is essential to the *Etak* modeling process.

When sailing from Satawal to West Fayu, the navigator constructs his *Etak* sequence like this: He knows from *wofanu* that West Fayu lies under the setting position of the Little Dipper, Lamotrek lies under setting Gamma Aquila, and, from West Fayu, Lamotrek lies under setting Shaula. Between setting Gamma Aquila and setting Shaula lie five star points: setting Altair, setting Beta Aquila, setting Orion's Belt, setting Corvus, and setting Antares. If we imagine these lines to be focused through Lamotrek and radiated across the course between Satawal and West Fayu, they will divide it into six segments, also called *etak*.* As the navigator sails, he will mentally track his position along the course by visualizing Lamotrek moving under the stars spread across the sky behind it.

"The course between two islands is called the *yalap*, the great path," Uurupa explained one night as we sat side by side on a mat in the courtyard, the lantern dangling from the frond of a young coconut tree. He had just sketched the three islands Satawal, West Fayu, and Lamotrek in my notebook, which he was using as a blackboard.

"You imagine that you are standing on Satawal," he said. "Then you must think of the star over Lamotrek—you do *wofanu*." He drew a line between Satawal and Lamotrek on the sketch. "This path runs from the rising of Paiiur to the setting of Paiifung." He looked up to make sure I was following. "Then you must think where Lamotrek is if you stand on West Fayu," he continued, drawing that line. "This path runs from the rising of Egulig to the setting of Mesaru. Okay?"

I nodded. He continued.

"And you already know the great path to West Fayu runs from setting Mailapellifung to Machemeias." He drew the course from Satawal to West Fayu.

"Now you count—you do *paafu*—from setting Paiiur, the direction of Lamotrek from Satawal, to setting Mesaru, the direction of

---

*Lower case indicates *etak* as a unit of distance; upper case denotes *Etak*, the system.

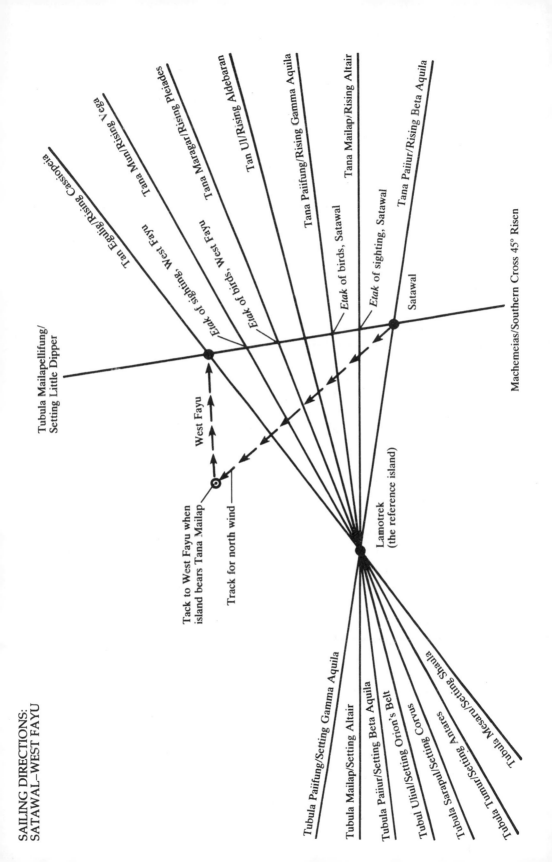

SAILING DIRECTIONS:
SATAWAL–WEST FAYU

Tubula Mailapellifung/
Setting Little Dipper

Tan Eguliig/Rising Cassiopeia

Tana Mun/Rising Vega

Tana Maragar/Rising Pleiades

Tan Ul/Rising Aldebaran

Tana Paiifung/Rising Gamma Aquila

Tana Mailap/Rising Altair

Tana Paiiur/Rising Beta Aquila

Setting of sighting, West Fayu

West Fayu

Etak of sighting, West Fayu

Etak of birds, West Fayu

Etak of birds, Satawal

Etak of sighting, Satawal

Satawal

West Fayu

Tack to West Fayu when
island bears Tana Mailap

Track for north wind

Lamotrek
(the reference island)

Machemeias/Southern Cross 45° Risen

Tubula Paiifung/Setting Gamma Aquila

Tubula Mailap/Setting Altair

Tubula Paiiur/Setting Beta Aquila

Tubul Uliul/Setting Orion's Belt

Tubula Sarapul/Setting Corvus

Tubula Tumur/Setting Antares

Tubula Mesaru/Setting Shaula

Lamotrek from West Fayu: so then you have [counting on his fingers]: setting Mailap, setting Paiiur, setting Uliul, setting Sarapul, setting Tumur, setting Mesaru. You see? Six *etak*."

This is how Uurupa mentally set up his *Etak* configuration as he prepared to sail, before he had even left the beach. At sea, he would keep it firmly in mind at all times: "I keep the star paths in my head wherever I go," he said. "Even now the paths run through the place we sit, but I don't think about them very hard because I am on the land and am safe. But at sea I have to think very hard. I keep the paths in mind even when we fish Wuligee reef. I don't have to think too hard, of course, because we can see the island, but I must always be prepared in case we get caught in a storm."

The *etak* closest to an island is called *etakidigina*, the *etak* of sighting. It spans the distance from the island to the point at sea at which the island slips beneath the horizon. On all voyages there are two *etak* of sighting: one for the island of departure and one for the target island. In the case of the Satawal-West Fayu voyage, these *etak* would be referred to as Etakidigina Satawal and Etakidigina West Fayu.*

The second (and second-to-the-last) *etak* in any voyage is called *etakidimaan*, the *etak* of birds. It is delineated by the farthest range of certain seabirds, predominantly noddies and terns, which at dawn fly eighteen to twenty miles from their islands to fish for the day and at dusk return to their roosts. These species always fly a direct course to and from their island, enabling the *palu* to use them to expand the size of the target. If, during his final approach, a navigator is unsure where the island lies, he will heave to within the *etak* of birds, wait for dawn or dusk, and carefully observe the flight paths of the birds.

The other *etak*, named by the star paths that demarcate them, are of variable length, depending on the distance between islands and the number of star paths intersecting the course.

There are two important features about the *Etak* process. First, since the navigator has no instrument to measure his speed and is out of sight of land, he can only imagine the movement of the *lu pongank* across the picket of star points behind it. He judges his speed by watching the water flow past the hull, or by some other simple method.

---

*The *etak* of sighting is further subdivided. See Appendix 2.

PAAFU: THE STAR COMPASS

Paafu: "Numbering the Stars" of the Star Compass

Paafu, the young boy's first lesson in navigation, teaches him the primary navigational stars. A circle of thirty-two lumps of coral is often used as a teaching aid. Banana fibers between the principal axes demonstrate reciprocal relationships. A small canoe of coconut fronds helps the student visualize himself in the locus of "star paths." Eight coconut fronds show the eight swells used in *pukulaw*, or "wave tying," a method of steering by the ocean waves.

Note that while the actual azimuths, or compass bearings, of the rising and setting stars are not evenly spaced around the horizon as depicted in the *paafu* array, Micronesian navigators believe they are, with the exception of Gamma and Beta Aquila, which rise close to Altair to form the northern and southern wings of Mailap, the "Big Bird." Since the *paafu* array is a conceptual aid, this fact does not affect the navigator's use of star courses at sea.

Now the magnetic compass has almost universally replaced steering by the stars. The compass was introduced during the German administration, according to Satawal's elders. Navigators assumed that its thirty-two points corresponded to the stars of *paafu*. With the points appropriately renamed, the *palu* used the compass to maintain direction at sea. It therefore had no structural impact on the rest of the indigenous system.

Magnetic variation in the vicinity of Satawal is four degrees east, meaning that north on the magnetic compass will be four degrees east of true north. Navigators sail a slightly different course and use different sailing directions when steering by a compass instead of the stars.

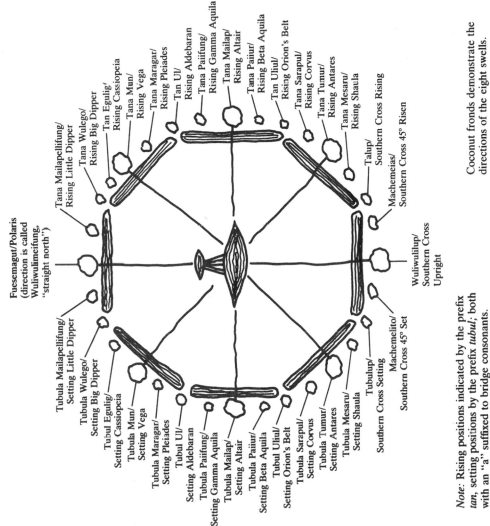

Fuesemagut/Polaris (direction is called Wuliwulimeifung, "straight north")

Tana Mailapelliifung/ Rising Little Dipper

Tana Wulego/ Rising Big Dipper

Tan Egulig/ Rising Cassiopeia

Tana Mun/ Rising Vega

Tana Maragar/ Rising Pleiades

Tan Ul/ Rising Aldebaran

Tana Paiifung/ Rising Gamma Aquila

Tana Mailap/ Rising Altair

Tana Paiiur/ Rising Beta Aquila

Tan Uliul/ Rising Orion's Belt

Tana Sarapul/ Rising Corvus

Tana Tumur/ Rising Antares

Tana Mesaru/ Rising Shaula

Talup/ Southern Cross Rising

Machemeias/ Southern Cross 45° Risen

Wuliwulilup/ Southern Cross Upright

Tubula Mailapelliifung/ Setting Little Dipper

Tubula Wulego/ Setting Big Dipper

Tubul Egulig/ Setting Cassiopeia

Tubula Mun/ Setting Vega

Tubula Maragar/ Setting Pleiades

Tubul Ul/ Setting Aldebaran

Tubula Paiifung/ Setting Gamma Aquila

Tubula Mailap/ Setting Altair

Tubula Paiiur/ Setting Beta Aquila

Tubul Uliul/ Setting Orion's Belt

Tubula Sarapul/ Setting Corvus

Tubula Tumur/ Setting Antares

Tubula Mesaru/ Setting Shaula

Tubulup/ Southern Cross Setting

Machemelito/ Southern Cross 45° Set

Coconut fronds demonstrate the directions of the eight swells.

Note: Rising positions indicated by the prefix *tan*, setting positions by the prefix *tubul*; both with an "a" suffixed to bridge consonants.

Piailug said he would sometimes focus on the splash of bilgewater as it is bailed from the canoe. *Etak*, therefore, is purely a mental construct the navigator imposes on the real world, a conceptual framework that integrates the other lessons of navigation, *paafu*, *aroom*, *amas*, and *wofanu*.

Second, *Etak* is a dynamic model. Unlike the Western construct, in which the navigator represents his vessel moving among stationary islands, *Etak* posits the canoe as stationary, and the islands moving on the sea around it. It evolves from the sea-level perspective one has when standing on the deck of a vessel observing the relative motion of islands and land features. *Etak* is perfectly adapted for its use by navigators who have no instruments, charts, or even a dry place in which to spread a chart if they had one. The Western navigator, in fact, constantly shifts between the bird's-eye view he has while scrutinizing his chart, and the fish-eye view he has on deck. *Etak* allows the Micronesian navigator to process all his information—course, speed, current drift, and so on—through a single, sea-level perspective.

Uurupa's example depicted the simplest kind of voyage in which, because of fair winds and no current, the navigator could sail directly to West Fayu. If the navigator were faced with a strong current and adverse winds and forced to tack upwind to West Fayu, his course, and thus his *Etak* plot, would be more complex.

There was one feature of the system that greatly puzzled me. If the *etak* of sighting and the *etak* of birds are of fixed length, I asked Uurupa, delineated by the height of the island and the fishing habits of birds, how can these segments *always* correspond to the intersection of star paths with the great path? When one is sailing from Satawal to Lamotrek, for instance, five stars radiate through the *lu pongank*, West Fayu, to divide the course into four *etak*. Therefore the *etak* of sighting and *etak* of birds must be longer on this passage than on the passage to West Fayu.

The Satawal-West Fayu *Etak* configuration is the paradigmatic case, Uurupa explained. On this voyage, the independently measured segments, the *etak* of sighting and *etak* of birds, happen to correspond exactly to the passage of Lamotrek under the appropriate stars. In other words, at the *etak* of sighting, when Satawal sinks beneath the horizon, Lamotrek has moved beneath the setting position of Altair; at the farthest range of seabirds, Lamotrek has moved beneath the setting position of Beta Aquila; at the midpoint of the voyage, called *yaw luke* (the "middle path"), Lamotrek is squarely under the setting of Orion's Belt. This is the only voyage in which such a coincidence occurs.

Uurupa stressed that the ability to track the movements of the islands beneath the stars in any sea condition, even when tired, cold, and hungry, was the most critical skill in navigation. "You see," he confided, "some old men know much more navigation than I do, they know all the *pookof* and all the talk. But they cannot navigate because they cannot keep the movement of the *lu pongank* clear in their minds."

On subsequent nights Uurupa recorded the *wofanu* and the *pookof* for the Caroline Islands, describing each creature. He then went on to a piece of lore called *itimetau*, which uniquely names the seaways (*metau*) between all islands. The sea between Satawal and West Fayu, for instance, is called *Metau Pongank*, the "sea that crosses," so named because it runs north-south, athwart the east-west alignment of most other sea routes and perpendicular to the cardinal direction, east, under Mailap, the "Big Bird." From Satawal to Pik runs the "sea that stands"; from Satawal to Lamotrek, Oairek; from Satawal to Puluwat, Apinallay. In the past, the names of the seaways were kept secret, because evil sorcerers who knew the *metau* on which a canoe was sailing could destroy it with a chant. Uurupa knew all the seaways from Truk in the east to the Philippines in the west.

He then had me record a similar system called *pwipwimetau*, or "brother seaways," which pairs all similarly aligned sea routes. If a *palu* forgets the star under which one island lies, he can derive the course from its brother seaway. He was very pleased I was recording his knowledge and wanted me to send him a transcript to give to his sons, in case he was lost at sea. He had taken copious notes while studying with Angora but had left his notebooks with his stepmother, Neamoun; not comprehending what they were, she used them to kindle a fire.

The respect I had for the commitment it took to become a *palu* was growing. There was no powerful mathematical model one could apply, as in Western navigation, nor were there primers and instruction books in case one forgot something. The *palu* had only his senses and his memory. So critical was memory to navigation that it defined his

ETAK CONFIGURATION FOR
SATAWAL-LAMOTREK VOYAGE

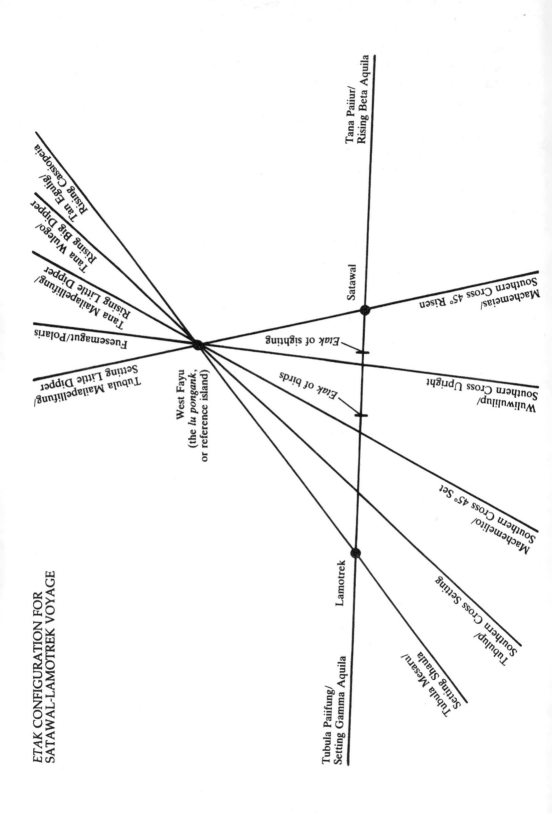

Tan Egulig/
Rising Cassiopeia

Tana Wulego/
Rising Big Dipper

Tana Mailapellilung/
Rising Little Dipper

Fuesemagut/Polaris

Tubula Mailapellilung/
Setting Little Dipper

West Fayu
(the *lu pongank*,
or reference island)

Tana Paiiur/
Rising Beta Aquila

Satawal

Machemeias/
Southern Cross 45° Risen

Etak of sighting

Etak of birds

Wuliwuliup/
Southern Cross Upright

Machemelito/
Southern Cross 45° Set

Lamotrek

Tubuliup/
Southern Cross Setting

Tubula Mesaru/
Setting Shaula

Tubula Paiifung/
Setting Gamma Aquila

notion of courage. In the interviews for *The Navigators* film, Piailug had said: "To navigate you must be brave and to be brave you must remember. If I am brave, it is because I remember the words of my fathers. . . . When I voyage, I forget everything else and think only of what my grandfather, father, and master taught me. Then I am not afraid."

Uurupa laughed his rich, throaty laugh. "Oh, I don't know where navigation came from," he replied to my question, a few nights later. "I just heard a story, a story about the spirit Anumwerici."

Sagur, a spirit and chief, lived on the island of Pulap with his daughter, Inosagur. As she bathed in the lagoon before the canoe house one morning, she beheld a rainbow. It became a spirit, Anumwerici, which came to her. The spirit had eaten all the inhabitants of Truk and Naminuoito; now he intended to eat the people of Pulap, too.

But Sagur told his daughter to fetch a little piece of taro and a small drinking coconut. Although Anumwerici complained this would not be enough, each time he tipped the cup containing the taro to his mouth it was refilled. The same thing happened with the drinking coconut. Anumwerici ate and drank his fill. Never, he said, had he been so satisfied.

In gratitude he taught Inosagur navigation. He placed her in a small coconut tree and by magic made it grow above the clouds. Inosagur could see all the islands, all the creatures of *pookof*, and all the reefs, banks, and shoals. When she had memorized the stars under which everything lay, Anumwerici again made magic to shrink the tree, depositing her gently on the beach.

He told Inosagur she would soon bear a son, whom she would name Fanur. She would teach him navigation and make him *pwo*. Later she would have a second son, whom she would name Wareyang and whom Fanur would teach and initiate in *pwo*. All of this came to pass, and navigation spread throughout the islands.*

---

*Later I heard another version of this story, in which a large *kuling* bird, instead of Anumwerici, ate all the people of Truk Lagoon before finally reaching Pulap. Inosagur fed the bird from the inexhaustible coconut shell, and in gratitude the *kuling* bent over and parted the feathers of his head. What first appeared to be lice turned out to be a map of all the islands, reefs, and sea creatures of *pookof*. When she had learned the locations of everything, Inosagur gave the bird many baskets of food, which he tied to his back and belly. Flying home to Uman, he fell into the sea and drowned.

The name Fanur means one who receives *pwo* from a woman, whereas Wareyang means one who receives *pwo* from a man. Thus, said Uurupa, Wareyang was the more powerful navigator. Now there are two schools of navigation, Fanur and Wareyang, and even today, Uurupa concluded, Wareyang navigators are considered more formidable than the Fanur. (Uurupa and Piailug are Wareyang, whereas the navigators of the chiefly clans are Fanur.)

"That's a good story!" I exclaimed.

"Oh, that's what I heard," Uurupa laughed in disclaimer, "but I don't believe this story, I really don't believe it!"

"So where did the *pookof* come from, then?" I asked.

"Individually they are called *epar*,"* he corrected, "and they came from Fanur and Wareyang." One day the brothers were checking their fish traps. Wareyang paddled the canoe from the bow while Fanur, in the stern, hauled up the traps. Fanur wanted to play a trick that would give him an advantage over his younger brother, so he told him to keep paddling and claimed the traps were empty. But secretly he took each fish from the trap, spoke to it, and placed it back in the sea: "Now you will stay here, under rising Mailap from Satawal, so I will know you," and "You, you stay here under setting Paiifung from Puluwat." All the creatures remained in their places in the sea, and now Fanur navigators still know more *epar* than the Wareyang.

"You see!" laughed Uurupa. "That's what they said, but I don't believe this. How can birds come from a fish trap? And whales? How can you put a whale in a fish trap?" He waved his arm and concluded: "That's why I say *epar* is important. But much more important is *wofanu*. You will not see the *epar* every time, but you *must* see the island."

"So are these creatures really there," I asked, "or is this just superstition? Have you actually seen *epar*?"

He searched his memory while counting on his fingers: "*Ut, rue, un, fan, niim.* Hmmm. Yes, five times," he announced at last. "I have seen *epar* five times. I once saw the pod of whales between here and Lamotrek, called Yoliwa, bearing setting Mwargar from Satawal. Many navigators have seen this *epar*. Twice between here and Lamotrek I saw

---

*When I later asked Piailug what the word *pookof* meant, he said "to tie." Then he picked up a palm frond, tied knots in it, and bent it into a ring. The system is seen to tie a ring of knots—the sea creatures—around each island. *Epar* means "to fix" or "to aim." When the *palu* sights a sea creature from *pookof*, he can fix his position with respect to the islands.

Lugoisum, a fat white tropic bird with red feet and beak. Near West Fayu I saw Apiaoumuun lusessen, a pod of dolphins with small snouts. Near Truk I saw a turtle—we call it Nauwinimaan; it has a red back.[*] I saw it on a voyage to Truk when we had to tack upwind the whole way. On the fourth day I saw Nauwimimaan and I knew that Truk lay under the rising Uliul. I changed course and the next day we reached the island."

"So is this turtle always in the same place?" I asked. "I mean, if you left Truk to sail back to the turtle would you see it again?"

"No, no, no," he chuckled. "It is not our custom to sail off looking for *epar*. When we sail we go to the island."

"But suppose you wanted to see it; would it still be there?"

"We don't sail for *epar*," he repeated. "We sail to reach the island. This is what our master taught us."

"But suppose you sailed to Truk five times," I persisted, "and the wind was the same each time and you sailed along the same track. Then wouldn't you see the *epar* each time?"

"No, no." He shook his head tolerantly. "You might reach the spot at night and thus would not see the turtle; or if you reached it in the daytime, the turtle might be a little to one side or the other of your course, and you still wouldn't see it."

"Okay. Look!" I said, determined to make my logic clear. I drew a sketch of Truk, Satawal, and the turtle. "Now, you leave Truk to sail to Satawal, and you reach a point just south of the turtle. . . ." He watched as I made a diagram, as if to learn why I was so insistent. "Then the wind dies. But there is a current from the south which pushes your canoe north, right into the turtle. Then would you see it?"

"Oh yes, of course!" said Uurupa. "This happens many times. The wind dies and you are just drifting. That is when you see the *epar*."

"So if you took a buoy . . ."

"What is that word: 'buoy'?"

"A float. You take a float and find the turtle and anchor the float to the bottom. Then you sail away and return to find your float—will the turtle still be there?"

---

[*]Note that in Piailug's version of *pookof* (Appendix 6) the pod of dolphins is named Epwinegerik. *Pookof Truk* is not listed. *Pookof* may vary from navigator to navigator and from the Wareyang to the Fanur school.

Uurupa looked upset. "Yes. Yes, that must be true."

"So!" I concluded, snapping shut the steep trap. "The *epar* is there all the time!"

Uurupa squirmed on his mat.

"Always there?" he asked himself tentatively. "Yes, I really believe that." Then, more definitely: "Yes, I really, really believe the *epar* always remain in the same place. But remember what I told you?" I said our master taught us to voyage for islands and not to see *epar*. You can't just go sailing to find *epar*! No!

"Here in Micronesia," he explained patiently, "all we have to sail on are our small canoes. They are made of wood, and they are not strong like your canoes of steel. In these islands, we don't have charts and sextants like navigators of America. And, because of that, we have the *epar* instead. If we get lost, that is when we look for the *epar*. You see, the spirit of voyaging gave us the *epar* to use *only when we are lost*."

One night I tried to get him to record the story of Anumwerici. He demurred, saying his English was not good enough, and asked me to tell it to him so he could study how I told it. I repeated the story as I remembered it, calling Anumwerici a spirit. He asked me what exactly "spirit" meant in English, and I told him it meant "ghost."

"Then what about the Holy Spirit they talk about in church?" he asked. "Is that a ghost, too?" I said it was.

Then he faced me directly and asked if I was afraid of ghosts. I was about to laugh his question off as silly, but something in his tone of voice made me answer truthfully: I supposed I was a little afraid of ghosts.

"How can that be?" he questioned, narrowing his eyes. "I thought Americans were never afraid of ghosts."

I shrugged and said I thought everyone was a little afraid, but we were taught not to believe in them.

"I am really afraid of the ghosts," he said in a low whisper. "Really, really afraid."

Somewhat alarmed, I asked him why.

"Because there are spirits of the land and spirits of the sea," he whispered, explaining he must speak in English. "Here in the woods is a very bad spirit, named Lealiwan ["She of the Woods"]. Pregnant women should never be in the woods alone after sunset or before sunrise, or even on a cloudy day. The spirit might say, 'I wonder why this woman always comes into the woods? Maybe I will eat her.' From ten in the morning to four in the afternoon is the proper time for a woman to be in the woods."

He went on to explain that the sea spirits are universally malevolent and will cause severe illness. Piailug was "eaten" by a sea spirit once while night-fishing. He fell ill and could not move.

A good spirit named Narun appeared to her medium Illellpuumaan, mother of the navigator Ikimai. In a deep trance and speaking in tongues, the old woman could hear the spirit's remedy, a mixture of *teek* grass and parts of the *alet* plant to be burned in an earth oven, an *oom*. Piailug lay in a litter over the oven for four days, then recovered.

When he was a young boy, Weneto, Rewena's brother, became sick after eating a spirit-inhabited fish he had caught on the reef at low tide. His stomach had swollen to the bursting point when Narun appeared to Illellpuumaan to give her the cure. The good spirit came again when Felix, son of Regaliang, nearly died. Even Uurupa himself had become sick from sea spirits.

Certain behavior attracts sea spirits, he cautioned me: "In the summer, when we fish the reef in our paddling canoes, you must never, never fish later than the others. If you have been fishing during the day, you must not stay out after sunset. Otherwise the sea spirits will notice you, and after several months will make you sick." Then he added in a barely audible whisper: "Be very careful on Wenimung reef because of Punorrun, an evil spirit who lives there. Never call other fishermen by their names, or the spirit might follow them home. And never spit. Instead just pick up a mouthful of seawater and rinse your mouth. If you spit, the spirit can jump into your body."

Fascinated, I wrote everything down in my notebook, but by about nine-thirty I wanted to stop because I could hardly keep my eyes open. When I mentioned how sleepy I was, he grew very concerned and demanded an explanation.

I said I had arisen about three that morning, gone to urinate on the beach, then watched the stars for a time.

"Do you always walk around at night alone?" he demanded.

I said no, just down to the beach. He told me to go on. I had returned to my hut, but when I tried to go back to sleep I kept having to get up to shoo away a rat gnawing at my food box. By then it was dawn.

He watched me closely, as if to determine whether I had been eaten by a spirit in my wanderings, then cautioned me again never to walk about at night alone.

On Sundays, Uurupa and I would sit in my hut drinking coffee until the gong signaled the beginning of church service. He always went to church, more, it seemed, to cover all metaphysical contingencies than because he was a true believer. The first week we went, he asked me for a nickel to contribute to the coffer. He suggested I contribute, too. When I asked why, he shrugged and said, "I don't know. Perhaps the God of the Christians will get mad at us if we don't." After that I always gave him donation money.

After church we would usually talk about navigation. More than Piailug, Uurupa seemed to understand the Western institution of logical inquiry. He knew how I thought because he had gone to high school and trained as a medical technician—it was partly how he thought as well. He was more patient than Piailug, and much less harsh. I was relaxed with him. Because our ages were closer, we were more like friends, or brothers.

He was very curious about Western navigation. After church one Sunday he had me explain to him and Paul and Jesse how to find courses and distances on the chart, and how to use the hand-bearing compass to measure the current. His sons comprehended the processes readily, asked many questions, and explained the concepts to him in Satawalese. They were eager to learn more the next Sunday. They especially wanted to learn how to use my sextant.

When they left to play basketball with the rest of the boys— Satawal was selecting a team for an all-island tournament—Uurupa took me through the taro swamp and into the woods to look for a suitable tree for a new boom for *Suntory*. He located one but would not cut it, as "the God might get mad if we work on Sunday." Then he led me along another path, which emerged on Satawal's deserted northern beach, called Pegifung, which means "north side." He pointed out the waves breaking on a portion of the reef called Teiifung. Before leaving on a passage, he said, navigators sometimes come here to check the current. If it is setting from east to west, the water will be smooth here and rough at a similar reef elbow, called Neafass, to the south. If the current is flowing from west to east, the water will be rough here and smooth at Neafass.

Then he explained that the way in which the white crest of a whitecap folded over would indicate the direction of the current. Whitecaps, of course, are caused by the local wind, and therefore will always topple in the direction of that wind. They seemed a useless sign to me; they would merely indicate the direction the wind was blowing. But he said that if the caps tumbled over gently and seethed into a long streak, the current was running with the wind. But if they seemed to peak abruptly, then fall and be drawn back to windward, the current was flowing against the wind. If one combined this sign with the ripple technique Piailug had tried to teach me, one could read the current directly from the surface of the ocean. I tried to observe these signs while he sat quietly.

A supertanker hove over the southern horizon, steaming through the wide channel between Satawal and Lamotrek. Soon another appeared to the north. The current was coming from the west, I concluded, watching the waves breaking on the reef and the whitecaps farther out. The tankers slid past.

"I think Rewena must be right," Uurupa said suddenly. "Do you remember what our chief told us? He said the navigators of the old days must have known the sea better than we do. But they didn't have writing and notebooks, and some navigators hoarded their knowledge and didn't teach it before they died. Now we only know part of what they once knew." He paused and went on:

"It used to be that when we cut our tuba we would make just two bottles. We would take the first to the canoe house to share. We would drink a little, talk about navigation, and tell stories. When the first bottle was gone we would take the second to our master—we call him our *raap*; it means the 'trunk,' or 'base,' of a tree. We would ask and ask and ask about navigation. This is how we came to know.

"But now, when we sit in the canoe house to drink, the young men just want to sing and make jokes. Now, you see, there are many young men and just a few old ones. We drink for a time and the old men say,

'Now we will talk of navigation.' And the young men say, 'Oh, why are we going to tell those stories? Now we want to sing and laugh. For now we are drunk!' And the old men just nod. After this happens two or three times, they never bring it up again."

I said I was afraid for navigation on Satawal. It had died out throughout the Pacific as islands adopted Western customs. Even on Satawal, I thought it had only a few years to live.

For a time, he was silent. Finally he turned to me and said, his voice cracking: "This year my sons are on Satawal, but next year they will return to high school. Why is it they want to learn your way of navigation but they *never, never* come to ask me about mine? Why is this? I really want to know."

It was now the month of Ceuta, our April. Na, the storm star forming the dorsal fin of Cu, the Dolphin, had finished storming as the new moon appeared in the evening sky. The end of the fighting of Na heralded the beginning of *leraak,* "the year." The strong winds of winter were diminishing and the voyaging season would soon begin. Skipjack tuna were still running on Wuligee, and two canoes went to West Fayu, returning with turtles, fish, and a multitude of sooty terns. One morning Auhror, the old man I had met in the men's house in Madrich, came up to me clutching two of the frail birds. He presented me with one, then summarily dashed his against a coconut tree and began to pluck it. "Good to roast," he mumbled, and wandered back to his house to cook it. I named mine Wareyang and placed it on a perch in the small coconut tree in my courtyard, but in a week it grew sick and died. With the tuna from Wuligee and turtles from West Fayu, the edge of winter's hunger was dulled. Breadfruit grew plump on their branches, and, nourished by the light rain, flowers bloomed in fragrant clusters under the palm trees near the canoe house.

Things seemed to be going very well for me. Whatever conflict there had been with the chiefs had apparently been resolved, and, given Uurupa's command of English, I was quickly learning navigation. I looked forward to voyages to West Fayu, Pikelot, and Puluwat. I received word that Piailug was delayed leaving Yap and would be gone another month, but I didn't really care, so pleasant was it to be with Uurupa.

Early one morning he was summoned to the radio. His uncle Eguwan was sick on Lamotrek and, believing he was dying, wanted his relatives to come and spend his last days with him. Uurupa and several other navigators made plans to sail the next morning. I would go along.

At dawn we slid *Suntory*, *Aloha*, and *Rugger* into the water and anchored them before the chiefs' canoe house. We loaded sails and booms, water, coconuts, and extra rope and stout branches to use in case of breakage. Then the passengers came aboard: old women with coconut-frond baskets of taro, breadfruit, and salt turtle for their relatives; men with their plywood boxes of fishing gear, tobacco, and Zippo lighters; younger women with their babies; children and teenage girls. The women took their traditional place on the lee platform, separated from the rest of the crew. The men and teenage boys sat on the outrigger platform and main hull. There were twelve people on *Suntory*, fifteen on *Aloha*, and nine on the smaller *Rugger*.

Throughout the preparations the people of Satawal gathered on the beach. The men smoked and talked in the canoe houses; the women and infants waited in the shade of the palm trees. It was a solemn leave-taking; only the children playing in the water waved as we raised our sails and filed away on a course of setting Mailap.

Eguwan, however, started to recover after several days. Then Uurupa received another message. The *Microspirit* would reach Satawal in a week. He was to take it to Yap to resume his job at the hospital (evidently, the chief surgeon had had him reinstated). We waited for fair weather, then, with a crew of five, sailed *Suntory* back to Satawal, leaving his passengers to be picked up by the ship.

Uurupa wanted me to come to Yap with him so we could continue our studies in his free time. But I wanted to wait for Piailug, and, having worked so hard to reach Satawal, I was loath to leave it now. Also, I feared our relationship would be different on Yap. In Madrich there would be no place to talk in private, and even if I rented a hotel room, Uurupa would constantly be seen with me, a white man, on the island of his traditional masters. Besides, Muanirik was there, and I didn't want to stir up sleeping jealousies. "Never mind that!" Uurupa said defiantly. "I don't care what the chiefs or the Yapese say." But it seemed clear he did.

When the ship was about to leave, Uurupa and I faced each other in the surf. He stared at the water between us as we shook hands, his face streaming with tears. "I am really going to miss you now," he said without shame. Then he brightened, wiped his cheeks with the heel of his hand, and laughed: "Now I think I will jump off the ship and go find that shark!"

I got a case of cold beer from the ship, along with my mail, and spirited it back to my hut. When it grew dark I shut my doors, lit my lantern, and very slowly drank the beer, read the letters from my wife, and cried.

A mood of lassitude settled like a mist over the island. The winter winds returned, lashing us with cold rainsqualls as we sailed out to fish Wuligee. The tuna became sporadic, then disappeared completely. Hunger came again; dogs were killed and roasted in earth ovens.

On *Suntory*, the cementlike stopping compound used to seal the lashing holes had been mixed improperly and was now leaking. We pulled the canoe into the canoe house, removed the bad plugs, and allowed the canoe to dry out. Then work stopped. With no navigator to form the nucleus of a crew, the young men spent their afternoons languishing in the shade or playing cards. Some went trolling in small sailing canoes near shore; others wandered off to join the crews of other canoes. My investigations came to a standstill. I worked on my language skills instead, spending dull mornings reading the Woleian grammar book and afternoons being tutored by Paul or Jesse. Other times I would wander through the quiet canoe houses to perplex the old men, patiently rolling coconut fibers into rope on their thighs, with my tortured Satawalese.

The stars rose and set; weeks passed; more squally weather set in, pinning all the canoes ashore. From time to time the horrid squeal of dying pigs pierced the overcast morning as their throats were slashed and their blood drained. No word came from Piailug. The wind died and it became hot and sticky.

Boredom set in, and loneliness. One day, as I walked around the island to take photographs, a huge container ship hove over the horizon and passed by several miles offshore. I wanted desperately to be aboard that ship, sailing back to my wife and home, back to my own culture and away from this strangeness.

Then I lost my patience. One afternoon a rooster kept dashing at my plate of food, stealing it even as I ate. I killed it with a stick. The next night I hit a barking puppy with a stone; it ran into the woods, whimpering. I hunted it down, trapping it in the brilliant beam of my flashlight. I'd lofted a coconut above my head, and was about to smash the scrawny pile of bones and fur quaking at my feet, when I caught myself, and reeled back to my hut.

9

Piailug had introduced me to his uncle Maanusuuk, my first day on Satawal. Dolphin tattoos surged up the outside of his legs like salmon swimming upstream to spawn; a birdlike filigree adorned his chest and a rising-sun logo darkened his shoulder. He had more tattoos on his wrists. The old man was reclining atop a paddling canoe in the shade of the canoe house, his head pillowed on a coconut, apparently asleep. But when Piailug called softly, he rose, fully alert. I found his gaze disconcerting: it had a penetrating, luminous quality, as if with no effort or intrusion he could see my heart and read my motives.

Piailug told me Maanusuuk was his "father," for in Satawal's language there is no distinction between "uncle" and "father" (or between "aunt" and "mother" or "cousin" and "sister" or "brother"). But, Piailug said, Maanusuuk was his father in a very real sense, for he had cared for him and Uurupa when their biological father died and saw to their education as navigators. He was now my father, too, Piailug stressed. I was to think of him often and bring him cigarettes and coffee.

After Piailug left, I didn't avoid Maanusuuk, but neither did I seek him out. The times I saw him in the village or canoe house, he seemed to be watching me. With a slight pang of conscience, I made it a point to take him cigarettes once or twice a week. When I handed him the small gifts, his whole face would brighten and he would bow his head deeply in thanks. He had an air of expectancy about him, as if he had been waiting for me.

One evening after Uurupa had left, I waded into the shallows before the chiefs' canoe house to photograph the returning canoes. The fleet appeared on the horizon, a half-hour away. Maanusuuk slowly walked across the beach and lowered himself into the warm, clear water to bathe. I was fairly conversant in Satawalese by then, so we began to chat.

I said I was anxious to get on with my research, sidetracked since Uurupa had left, and hoped Piailug would return soon. The old man asked what I had learned so far and why I wanted to learn their navigation anyway, since I was already an "American *palu*." I told him I thought their navigation was both useful and beautiful, and soon the *palu* would die and the lore would be gone. But I wanted to learn about more than just navigation, I went on. I hoped to learn about *itang*.

"How do you know about *itang*?" he asked, never taking his eyes off me. I had read about it in books, I replied, adding that I wanted to learn about it because it seemed very beautiful. But while the anthropological literature made teasing references to *itang*, not much of the actual language had been recorded, and Westerners seemed to know little about it.*

I had come tantalizingly close to *itang* earlier on Satawal. The day before he left for Yap, Uurupa had taken me to a place in the woods near Fanagoon to drink with Onalap, a highly respected navigator visiting from Pulap. Paul came along to serve the drink and listen. Uurupa

---

*The authors of one paper described *itang* as "a remarkably involuted, circumlocutory, elliptical and metaphorical mode of speech and form of oral literature." They went on to identify different classes, or "bowls," of esoteric knowledge: for war, magic, meetings, navigation, and calling breadfruit. (Saul Riesenberg and Samuel Elbert, "The Poi of the Meeting," *The Journal of the Polynesian Society*, 80[2]: 1971 [June], p. 219 [quoted in Ochs, cited below].) Another writer reports that *itang* denotes a class of diviners and magicians whose "power . . . knowledge and an esoteric form of speech known only within their ranks, set them apart from other men." (Thomas Gladwin, *East Is a Big Bird* [Cambridge, Mass.: Harvard University Press, 1970], p. 125.) Another researcher comments that it "is an esoteric knowledge containing the wisdom of politics, diplomacy and human relations employed primarily to overcome troubles on the island or between islands and secondarily as a demonstration of a specialist's wisdom." (Peter Ochs, "Learning Sea Lore on Pulawat Atoll," unpublished research notes, 1970, p. 134.)

explained that in the old days they used to catch flying fish by setting lines rigged to coconut-shell floats: "When we have set our coconut shells on the sea, we do a little song to make the flying fish bite our lure." Suddenly both men hopped to their feet to sing the "flying-fish song." They waved their arms and laughed wildly as they tried to coax the fish to their imaginary lures. It was such a delightful song I ran back to fetch my tape recorder and notepad, but by the time I returned, Onalap had decided the song was silly and I should learn something much more important instead. He recorded a short chant. I asked Uurupa what it meant.

"Oh, I am very sorry!" he laughed. "How can I translate when I don't even know what it is! Maybe later Onalap will explain it to us." Then he lowered his voice and concluded very seriously: "It is *itang*. Onalap advises the chiefs of Pulap. They must listen carefully, because he knows."

I asked what *itang* was. He answered elliptically: "*Itang* lets you take care of everything, this leaf [pointing], this tree, this boy—*everything* on our islands."

Then he left for Yap, Onalap sailed back to Pulap, and the meaning of the *itang* remained mysterious.

Maanusuuk studied me calmly and intently as he splashed himself with seawater. "Do you want to learn *itang*?" he asked.

"Yes," I said unhesitatingly, "I would like to learn."

"All right, then, I will teach you. Come to my house this evening." I was stunned. I understood that *itang* was rare and secret; it was hard to believe that I could have free access to it so easily.

Paul led me to Maanusuuk's house in the early evening. Although it was hot, the old man instructed us to close all the doors, after first checking outside to make certain no one was listening. I handed him the tape recorder, explaining where to speak into it. He chanted with his eyes closed, weaving gently like sea grass. His wife sat in a corner, also chanting.

He finished and handed the recorder back to me. "That is the talk of wisdom," was all he said. Then he wanted to stop, for he was afraid someone would overhear. He said he would come to my hut in two nights.

I prepared my tape recorder and typewriter, got out some cigarettes and coffee, and waited; but he did not come. I feared he had had second thoughts. The palm fronds chattered in the evening wind, and sea birds streaked overhead, returning to roost. The darkness seemed composed of small particles swirling like snow around the sea and island. As the trees at the far end of the courtyard faded, Maanusuuk appeared, led by his young grandson. His gaunt image was grainy, like an old photograph. He smiled, bade me the polite *wenimum*, and swiftly ducked through the low doors.

When the village children found out he'd come, they swarmed into my hut. The women came too, and sat down, two in each of the five timber doorsills, smoking and chatting. Maanusuuk sent his grandson to find Paul to translate. I made coffee for the adults, passed around cigarettes, and gave ship's biscuits to the children. When Paul arrived, the ladies withdrew with the wriggling children to chat in the courtyard by the cooking shed. Maanusuuk then had us close the mat doors, I lit my Coleman lantern, and he began his lesson.

First he re-recorded the whole series of chants, then had me play it back so he could make sure it had gotten into the machine correctly. When he was satisfied, we began the long process of translation and transcription. By late that night we had finished the first chant. Paul checked every word with him until he was satisfied we had apprehended the various levels of meaning.

> *Floating leaf swept out,*
> *Floating leaf swept back,*
> *The leaf of the* tong *tree*
> *(The leaf of our love),*
> *Which stands before the canoe house.*
> *His ears are full of talk,*
> *His ears are full of talk.*
>
> *But where is she?*
> *She, Neanuaas?*
> *Why does she not pull*
> *The feather of the egret?*
>
> *So it can decorate*
> *That canoe of dark stomach.*
> *So it can sweep the opinions of*
> *The earth of our island.*

She, Neanueet,
She, Neanuaal,
We will meet together;
We will stitch together;
We will resolve;
My talk, the meeting, the agreement.

This *itang* impels the chiefs to resolve conflict, he explained. The *tong* tree grows on the beach in front of the canoe houses. Its leaf, representing the care of the chiefs, has been swept away from shore by conflict. Now it is carried back by the *itang*. The chief must pick it up, thereby signifying that his care and attention will be focused on the current conflict. The stanza's last two lines praise the chief for his wisdom, which he has learned from his parents and elders. Because of this, and because of his perspicacity, he will already know about the conflict, which is never mentioned. Maanusuuk cautioned that if one negates the last lines by saying "His ears are *not* full of talk," it is highly insulting.

The second stanza begs Neanuaas, the spirit of wisdom, to restore order and beauty to the island, the canoe of state. The seat of wisdom and the emotions is held to be the stomach (the solar plexus), not the head. To say the island has a dark stomach is to criticize its condition and leadership. The *itang* bids the spirit to brighten both the island and the chief's dark thoughts with white egret feathers.

The final stanza appeals to two more spirits, She of the Meeting, who gathers a clan or an island together after a dispute, and She of the Resolution, who forges unity of thinking. This stanza declares that all individuals in a clan, clans on an island, or islands in an archipelago compose a single people who must be brought together by the care of the chiefs under the ruling principles of *itang*.

I asked him if he had ever had to use this *itang*. He didn't answer, but Paul said that once, before American times, the chiefs of an island conspired to kill an entire clan. Word of the plot leaked out and one old man, alone and armed only with the talk of wisdom, confronted the chiefs. By this, he saved the clan.

Maanusuuk came to my hut often over the next weeks, always after dark, helped along the path by his grandson, whom he wanted to teach.

The next *itang*, he told me, is used to control someone who steals and fights or consistently disregards the rules of the island.

Who is he, anyway?
Man with unbent knees.
There is whispering outside
Yet he acts like a chief,
A crooked timber.

Why don't you cut
The skids of his canoe?
So he will stand up straight
Amid this problem?

Say it and say it,
Tell me and tell.

Typically, the offender—the "crooked timber"—is a young, rebellious man. An elder would go to the youth's uncle or father, who, ashamed he had been spoken to in *itang*, would compel the young man to mend his ways.

A canoe is pushed from the canoe house to the water on palmfrond skids. Without the skids, the canoe cannot move. Thus the *itang* asks the father to destroy the skids on which his son's lawlessness is launched and help him mend his character for all to see.

Maanusuuk told me of a man who had to use this *itang*. There had been a rumor that this man plotted to kill someone from the chiefly clans. He stopped the rumor by confronting the chiefs and the purported victim in the canoe house. Maanusuuk explained that the man placed a rusty adz and knife in front of the chiefs. "Look," he said, "these blades cannot cut; therefore I am not 'the crooked timber.' If I know the talk of wisdom I can kill no one." The chiefs rose without comment and thereafter the gossip stopped.

There is a spirit called "Dark Stomach," Maanusuuk said, a spirit of "unbent knees." She took the form of a human being but her insides were hollow and empty of knowledge. She came to the Island of the Middle Heavens from the Western Sky refusing to *aparog*, to bend with respect to men and chiefs. The other spirits then cut her knees, back, and arms to make her bend.

There are two more spirits who "play" in the *itang*, Maanusuuk said. She of Hiding enters people's stomachs to conceal their evil intentions from others. She of Why reveals that which She of Hiding has concealed.

The next *itang* is used when the threat of violence swirls around an individual. The victim, or an elder representing him, recites it to the chiefs, reminding them that he is like a fish struggling in the current of vicious talk at the corner of the reef. The speaker offers the chiefs the refreshment of the "coconuts of brightness," which is the *itang*; he may actually present a type of small yellow drinking coconut as part of the ritual.

> *I, I am struggling*
> *On my island;*
> *Corner of reef where the current runs strong.*
> *I will bring in*
> *For the chiefs to drink*
> *The coconuts of brightness.*
>
> *Stone-meets-inside*
> *Stone-meets-chiefs.*

The last two lines compliment the chief. In Satawalese, "meets inside" is composed of the words *chu* ("meet") and *long* ("inside"), which when spoken together sound like *aoulong*. The *aoulong* is the portion of the reef on which the waves break. The chiefs are considered the "reef," for they absorb and protect the island from the waves of the outside world. They must never break or falter, despite the fact that waves beat on them incessantly.

"Stone-meets-chiefs" refers to power. Everyone has some type of "stone," or inner force—even children. But the chiefs' is one of power.

Another *itang* is used by the *palu* who comes to a strange island after many months lost at sea. He speaks it quietly to the *saisaulig*, the man who greets incoming canoes to learn of their intentions and origins. If the *saisaulig* is wise—that is, if he understands *itang*—he will merely twirl his paddle in the air and return directly to the island. Then the chiefs will order each village to prepare food for the starving sailors and care for them until they are ready to sail home.

> *I come from the sea suffering,*
> *I arrived at your channel,*
> *I struck upon your reef.*
> *I push away from that sea of hunger;*
> *My stomach touches my backbone.*

If the navigator is too weak to talk, he can merely take a coconut-shell cup and hold it upside down, meaning "empty."

Then Maanusuuk fell ill and we did not meet for more than a week. I brought him aspirin for his fever, cigarettes, and coffee. I met his wife, who complained that her eyes hurt under the brilliant sunlight, forcing her to seek out the shady paths or remain in her house until late in the afternoon. She asked me to cure her, but the *Merck Manual* indicated she might have glaucoma and I had no medicine for it. Instead I gave her a visor and some sunglasses.

When he recovered, Maanusuuk returned, and, as before, the women and children crowded into and around my hut. He told one of the many fables of Palulap, the great navigator, a very long story called "The Island of Wuung," about a spirit who took the form of the canoe house's ridgepole:

Palulap's two sons, Rongelap and Rongerig (who some claim are Fanur and Wareyang), felled a tree for a new canoe. But when they returned to the log the next day, it stood upright. They felled it again; the following morning it stood upright. After four days of this, Rongerig made magic to Seulang, the patron spirit of the canoe builder. His workers then built the canoe in just two days. Rongelap became jealous, for he thought Rongerig had been taught special knowledge; he killed him and threw his body into the sea. But Palulap saw everything and brought Rongerig back to life. Thereafter, Rongelap hated both his father and his brother.

Palulap told both sons to voyage. Rongelap sailed first, and at sea ignored the advice of Palulap's sister, whom he found floating in a large wooden bowl. When he made landfall at Wuung's island, he ignored the greeters, who took the form of floating sticks and coconuts. At night, when Rongelap and all his crew slept in the canoe house, Wuung lowered himself down and devoured them all.

When eight days passed, Rongerig knew his brother was dead. He set off in his canoe. He greeted Palulap's sister respectfully, and fed her the navigator's special food. He recognized the flotsam as greeters and fed them small bits of coconut. He knew Wuung's nefarious tricks, and in the end burned him and his canoe house to the ground.

The children, munching ship's biscuits, watched the tape recorder and the brilliantly glowing Coleman lantern, with eyes wide open. The women listened carefully, smoking, asking questions at critical junctures. The moral of the story, I took it, was that one should respect one's elders and learn from them traditional skills and right behavior. Maanusuuk talked with the women for a time before he had his grandson lead him down the path to his village. The women sat a while longer, then took their children, now snoozing in the corners of the hut, home to sleep.

"What exactly is *itang*?" I asked when Maanusuuk returned several nights later. I had gone through all my notes and prepared a list of questions.

"It is the talk of wisdom," he answered, "the talk of light. *Itang* is deep talk. If one is wise, he will understand it; if he is not wise, he will not understand. It is a shield for the man who possesses it, for it protects him on any island. Because it has the power to restore order, it is the most important kind of knowledge."

When I asked how it did this, he said that when spoken to a chief it would shame him into righting injustices. I found it hard to imagine how mere words and not weapons could protect anyone in my society, so I asked if a chief couldn't simply disregard the *itang*.

"Then the chief would be irrational, unfit to be a chief," Maanusuuk responded quietly.

He seemed not to grasp my point, so I asked, "But couldn't a chief say, 'I am not irrational; I know exactly what I am doing, and I am powerful enough to kill you despite the *itang*'?"

He thought about this for a time: "The purpose of *itang* is not power," he said. "It seems to open our stomachs [again, the seat of knowledge and the emotions] to the chiefs to enable them to see our true feelings. Then they will understand and will be ashamed that they didn't see the problem before, that we had to point to it in *itang*."

"But why *must* a chief obey it?" I persisted.

"*Itang* is the talk of light," he explained again. "A chief will be ignorant of it only if he is irrational. If so, he is unfit to be a chief. Therefore, if he is a chief he must respect even a single word of *itang*.

"But if he deliberately goes against the *itang*, something bad will happen to him. We call this *reah* [retribution]. It is sent by the Alulap [literally "great spirit"], who hears the people talk of their dark chief. Only those who are wise can learn *itang*, those who are good."

Next I asked how a master decided if his student was worthy to learn *itang*. Paul discussed this with him, then explained that the old man had watched me from the beginning, and decided on the basis of my behavior. He stressed that if I had come alone asking about *itang*, he never would have taught me. But because I was a brother to his sons, Piailug and Uurupa, he considered me his son as well. Besides, I was a captain myself and ought to know these things.

Itang was the most important knowledge, he reminded me; I should never discuss it with others, nor should I use it unless absolutely necessary. To do so could only be for self-aggrandizement and would thus be a violation of the precepts of wisdom.

I asked if there was any more to learn.

"There might be more," Paul said, translating the old man's answer, "but he has told us all he knows."

Then Paul explained that Maanusuuk had referred to me as "his son, the chief," meaning that he took me as his son and at the same time accorded me the respect due a chief. Maanusuuk watched me with moist eyes, as if ashamed he had no more to teach. Suddenly the full force of my tactlessness and ignorance struck me. Wavering between tears and awe, I cast my eyes down and asked Paul please to tell Maanusuuk, our father, I was deeply honored to be considered worthy of knowledge and hoped for the wisdom to use it well. After this he came no more.

Because of the perfect memory of the tape recorder and written notes, I had recorded in several weeks what would normally have required months or even years to learn. Maanusuuk had already taken Paul aside to teach him, and if the young man were to continue his traditional education, Maanusuuk would do so again and again as Paul progressed through the lessons of navigation to take command, finally, of a canoe. In facing the dangers and responsibilities of command—storms, calms, hunger, fatigue, loss of discipline or the confidence of the crew, hostility from strangers on distant islands—Paul would learn for himself how moral judgments are made, guided by *itang*. As he learned the *itang*, he would be learning the way of the *palu*; the language would become mapped onto the flow of human interaction, in which he as a navigator would be a locus. The role of the *palu* would thus be a complete way of life.

Over time, I came to understand that Maanusuuk had given me his greatest possessions, the secret of his personal power. It struck me also that I could have only a shallow insight into the nature of his gift. I was not of Satawal and would remain there only long enough to discover why I had come. The language of light unfolded over time and experience. It was like some reactive chemical that helped to form wisdom when added to the clear liquid of reflection.

It was now the end of April. Long, dark squalls crept out of the northeast to soak the island with rain. When a young woman named Maurenoor went into labor, the women from all the villages gathered by her house. Food and fish were prepared and served, and a midwife stood by. For two days the women waited; then Maurenoor gave birth to a girl.

We began the four days of *roe*, when all the men fish for the family of the newborn. Because the wind prevented the canoes from being launched, the chiefs temporarily suspended the taboo on spearfishing, which is instituted when stocks of reef fish decline. We scoured the reef for small fish, taking our meager catch to the chiefs' canoe house, where it was strung on coconut fronds and then presented to the celebrating family. They, in turn, divided the fish among the women in attendance, who brought their shares back to their own villages for their husbands and children.

But after the second day of fishing, the baby became sick. A light rain fell late in the afternoon, and the women sitting in the family's compound covered their heads with their sitting mats as they sang dirgelike songs. The next day we began another four days of *roe* to mark the death of the infant. Maurenoor and the rest of her clan shaved their heads as a sign of mourning.

The star Na struggled free of the sea and rose to name the moon beneath it. May, the month of Na, was supposed to be the month of plenty. For a time, canoes made daily trips to Wuligee, until the tuna again disappeared. I was asked to try to locate a rich, deep-sea reef called Orrairepar, with Western navigational methods. The reef's position is mismarked on the charts, however, and I found only seawater. After this, the wind fell still and the canoes were pulled into their canoe houses. I had nothing to do. I tried to work on my language skills but was too restless to concentrate. I had had enough foreignness. I was tired of the dogs, the flies, the shit on the beach; tired of squatting in the dirt to eat boiled taro and burned breadfruit. Finally I received word from Piailug telling me to join him on Saipan. I tried to wait patiently for the ship.

As the ascension of Cu marked the beginning of June, the school year came to a close. On Ulithi, the children boarded the *Microspirit* to return to their home islands. Satawal, meantime, graduated its eighth-graders with a feast. The girls rubbed themselves with orange turmeric, applied lipstick to their mouths and cheeks, and performed traditional dances wearing coconut-frond skirts. When they finished, the older women followed, claiming that although the girls were young and energetic, they could not dance as well as more mature women. Then the men, not to be upstaged, danced with even greater power and abandon. All the clans sat in clusters in the green grass, eating smoked fish and roasted turtle.

As the *Microspirit* discharged its teeming cargo of jubilant students, I prepared to go aboard. Maanusuuk was sick, and in my rush to leave, I didn't take the time to say goodbye. I asked Paul to tell him I would return soon with Piailug, but I knew I was probably on my way home. Several days before, when I had gone to tell him I was leaving, he reminded me that I was his son now, and he was my father. I knew I was not behaving as a son ought to, but I was desperate to leave. I told myself I would make it up to him when I returned by bringing him fine presents.

From the ship's deck I watched the people of Satawal gather before the chiefs' canoe house. A great collective shout went up as they sprayed holy water from plastic bottles to drive the spirits of illness back on board. But the roar of the ship's engines defeated their cries, and as the vessel spun and gathered way, the people of the sea faded into the shadows.

10

The ship made a swift three-day passage to Yap. There I boarded the next flight to Guam. Upon arrival, I telephoned Saipan to learn that Piailug had gone to Hawaii for a reunion of the crew of the 1980 *Hokule'a* voyage and would return to Guam in several days. I was to meet him there and accompany him to Saipan. From there, we would return to Satawal on a private yacht.

I had never noticed how small Piailug was. At first, scanning the passengers filing through U.S. Immigration, I didn't see him. Suddenly he and his wife and son stood before me. The freshly waxed floor of the arrivals lounge gleamed like the still waters of the *lealulu* on a quiet summer evening. He was half a foot shorter than I and dressed in ill-fitting trousers, a gaudy flower-print shirt, and sandals. He looked like a poor old man, maybe a sampan fisherman in Hawaii or a gardener. Had I not known him, I would have passed him by as someone of no consequence. He stepped gingerly on his left leg—he'd mentioned that he suffered from gout but I'd never seen it bother him.

"It's good to see you. It's great to see you!" I effused, shaking his hand.

"Yes, me too," was all he said. He looked around warily. The glowing signs of the rental-car booths cast swaths of green and yellow and red across the polished floor. Nemoito tugged uncomfortably at her polyester skirt as she waited patiently amid a small mound of baggage. Bonefacio wore shorts and a T-shirt and carried his belongings in a small knapsack. He had grown since I saw him on Satawal and, although he stood near his mother, was eagerly taking in the sights and sounds of the airport.

"Well!" I boomed. "Did you drink lots of tuba on the airplane?"

"No, no, no," Piailug answered quietly. "I was afraid to drink. I was afraid about the papers. The man would ask about the papers and maybe if I forgot something he would get mad at me and say, 'You, go away!'" He jerkily waved his hand.

The differences between us suddenly flew up around my awareness like fluttering moths. I was white, by appearances prosperous, with credit cards and an American passport; I could go anywhere in the world. Piailug was dark-skinned and poor; he had papers to allow him—after proper questioning and scrutiny—into Guam and Saipan, the islands of his traditional masters. His sons, who spoke English and were familiar with the ways of the West, were far better adapted to this world. He was an anachronism, a throwback to a way of life that had begun to disappear here 150 years ago.

I led them to the gate, where we caught a short commuter flight to Saipan. As we waited there for our ride, I tried to begin a conversation.

"What did you do in Hawaii?" I asked.

"Nothing," he answered.

"Did you party?"

"Some."

"Did you go fishing?" He brightened and told of trying to catch sea turtles from his host's motorboat until his companions told him it was against the law. After I had explained that green turtles are an endangered species, he nodded and would say little else. I wondered if he was still committed to teaching me.

"Now I want to work and work and work," I told him in Satawalese. He nodded and said maybe we could talk tomorrow.

Soon his son Halig arrived in a new Mazda pickup, casually greeted his family, and loaded the baggage into the back. We would be guests of a prominent Carolinian politician, he explained, a distant relative of Piailug's. We climbed aboard and motored through the lush countryside to our host's house.

Saipan is a much bigger island than Satawal, about thirteen miles long and seven wide. A ridge of volcanic hills runs down the middle like the backbone of a skinny dog. To the south, past the modern airport, the fertile mountains tilt gently into the sea, rising on the other side of a channel to form the island of Tinian. To the north, the mountains end in a series of lofty palisades known as Suicide Cliffs because hundreds of families, deceived by Japanese propaganda about the barbarism of the invading Americans, leapt from them to their deaths.

Saipan is part of the Commonwealth of the Northern Marianas, with a political relationship to the United States like Puerto Rico's. It is an island with plenty of water, sun, and beautiful scenery. Modern hotels have been built on the white sands along the calm eastern shore, and Japanese come here to escape the damp chill of Tokyo winters. Two hours from Japan by air, forty-five minutes from Guam, an hour and a half from Taiwan, it seems poised for development with the rest of the Pacific, far removed from Satawal and the people of the sea.

From the Satawalese point of view, Saipan is their own. Legend holds it was first discovered by Agoroup, a famous navigator and chief. The name Saipan comes from the Satawalese *saii pwen*, meaning "empty earth," for when Agoroup first found the island it was devoid of people (they had in fact been killed by the Spanish). Agoroup purchased the island from the governor of Guam, the legend concludes, and it was thereafter settled by outer islanders.

The legend conforms somewhat to the facts. In 1821 the explorer Otto von Kotzebue reported that Carolinians had been voyaging to the Marianas since before the arrival of the Europeans, to barter for turmeric and shell belts. They broke off contact upon hearing of the cruelty of the white man. In 1787, and again 1788, the navigator Luito led a small fleet of canoes from Lamotrek to the Marianas to trade for iron and metal tools. On the return voyage he was lost at sea. Suspecting Luito had been captured by the Spanish, Carolinians again broke contact with the Marianas. In 1804 the vice governor of Guam, Don Luis Torres, made a good-will tour through the Carolines, after which the trading voyages resumed. Thereafter, each April, at the beginning of *leraak*, canoes would rendezvous in the wide, protected lagoon at Lamotrek and with cargoes of seashells, turtle shell, rope, and woven mats would sail northeast, under the setting Ursa Major, to Guam. Most returned in May or June, before typhoon season and the strong winds of *lefung* pinned them in the Marianas for another year. But some captains stayed, and soon Carolinian canoes were carrying trade and official Spanish communications throughout the Marianas.

In 1816 a fleet of 120 canoes bearing more than nine hundred settlers left Lamotrek and the surrounding islands (presumably including Satawal) after a series of typhoons rendered the islands unable to support full populations. Most of this fleet was lost in a gale. Upon hearing of the disaster, Torres invited the Carolinians to settle on Saipan. By 1840 many had accepted his offer. The Carolinians lived much as they had on their own atolls, clothed in loincloths and *turrh*, living on fish, turtle, and taro, and trading between the islands of the Marianas archipelago.

Marianas-Caroline voyages were again abandoned when the German and later the Japanese administration forbade them. But in the early 1970s the trade route was reopened by the Puluwat navigator Hippour, who, using a Western sailing vessel, demonstrated his way of navigating to researcher David Lewis. Not to be outdone, Satawal navigators soon made voyages in their own outriggers. Piailug first made the voyage in 1974, sailing his canoe alongside that of Chief Rewena. He again made the voyage in 1979 to deliver an eighteen-foot canoe to a relative as a gift.

On Saipan, the descendants of the original Micronesian settlers refer to themselves as Carolinians and speak a similar dialect. Many elder women maintain their clans' links to the outer islands, although few have ever visited their ancestral homes. This gives the Satawalese a *pied-à-terre* on Saipan, a portal to the West with familiar people, customs, and language, and, unlike Yap, a place where they are not stuck on the lowest rung of a caste system. Piailug has visited often and in 1978 taught Carolinian culture in the public schools. But the younger men are especially attracted; some come seeking jobs, others just to get a taste of the outside world. Piailug's son Uru attended high school here, then returned to Yap to work on the government field ship; Mesailuke came to satisfy his curiosity, working odd jobs for several months before returning to Satawal to marry and start a family. Halig came and settled, working for a local contractor. He had a good job, he told me, and planned to stay. Over the next weeks he often dropped by our host's house to do his laundry or watch television. Occasionally he sat with us as Piailug explained some point of navigation, but never asked questions or sought instruction on his own. Piailug did not make an issue of this and seemed to accept that his son was now of a different world.

Piailug began teaching me immediately, with the same intensity as before. I spent the mornings working on my notes while he carved a beautifully detailed model sailing canoe for our host. In the afternoons we held our lessons, and in the evenings and early mornings we sat on the beach to watch the clouds and discuss the talk of the skies. Sometimes we stayed up late or rose very early to watch the rising stars break the horizon from Suicide Cliffs.

I spent the next weeks immersed in the technical details of the talk of the sea, filling my notebooks with diagrams of sailing directions, lists of *wofanu*, sketches of creatures from *pookof*, and drawings of the reef channels around the islands. Piailug worked quickly, as if to transmit and record his knowledge as efficiently as possible. He was conscientious about our lessons but otherwise ignored me, preferring the company of his relatives. Unlike on Satawal, here I was excluded from Carolinian society and regarded with suspicion.

By this time I had a fairly good, if still academic, understanding of Micronesian navigation. I understood that *wofanu* was the *palu's* chart case, that *Etak* was his mental plotting sheet, and that *fatonomuir*, "facing astern," was the key to determining the direction of the current. Now I was particularly anxious to learn the sailing directions, called the *kape-sani serak* or "talk of sailing," which set forth the sequence of mid-course corrections the navigator must make to compensate for the current he measured in *fatonomuir*.

During our voyage to Lamotrek, I had asked Uurupa what course corrections the sailing directions dictated for the slight southerly current we'd observed.

"When sailing to Lamotrek we sometimes keep a course of setting Mailap the whole way," he abbreviated, hoping to put a quick stop to my prodding. "Sometimes we change to setting Paiifung, Ul, or Mun." When I askcd what he meant by this, he would say only that the sailing directions contained everything. Then, since the weather was rough and he had twelve people aboard, he turned his attention back to his job.

Now, on Saipan, Piailug explained the "talk of sailing" in detail.

We worked at a picnic table in a small pavilion before our host's beach house. He sat on one side, I sat on the other, with the notebook between us.

He began with the Satawal-Lamotrek voyage, directing me to construct the *Etak* sequence as Uurupa had earlier done. He reminded me that West Fayu was the *lu pongank*, that there were four *etak*, and that the intersections of the star paths with the great path did not correspond with the actual *etak* of sighting or the *etak* of birds.

Even though the star course from Satawal to Lamotrek is setting Gamma Aquila, Piailug explained, the sailing directions dictate an initial course of setting Altair. At "One Tooth,"* the navigator backsights. The star under which Satawal has then moved determines the series of course changes. For every whole star point Satawal moves at "One Tooth," Piailug alters his course one-half star point. (For all discussions we assumed wind from the northeast.)

If Satawal remains under rising Altair—i.e., if there is no current— the navigator alters to a course of setting Gamma Aquila at the midway point. If Satawal moves north, under rising Gamma Aquila (indicating a current from the north), he steers midway between the setting positions of Altair and Beta Aquila at the midway point; if Satawal moves under rising Aldebaran, he aims toward Beta Aquila. Similarly, if Satawal moves south to rising Beta Aquila, indicating a current from the south, he sails setting Altair the whole way. If Satawal moves to rising Orion's Belt, indicating a stronger current, he steers halfway between the setting positions of Altair and Beta Aquila. Lamotrek will come into view on the starboard side, to windward; this is desirable, since it is easier to reach up than run downwind in a Micronesian canoe.

But the *palu* cannot expect to make landfall by mechanically following the sailing directions, he cautioned. He must be attuned to the wind and water for signs of change. I had witnessed this earlier, on our voyage to Lamotrek. When Uurupa backsighted, Satawal had moved between rising Mailap and rising Paiiur. According to the sailing directions, therefore, we altered course to a quarter-point north of setting Mailap. Later, when the wind picked up and the waves grew larger, he wanted to steer setting Paiifung, since we would now make greater leeway, with the waves and the wind pushing us south (moving Lamotrek

---

*See Appendix 2.

to the north). He delayed this correction because I, used to Western keel yachts, which make little leeway, thought we were on course. Consequently, Lamotrek broke the horizon between setting Gamma Aquila and setting Aldebaran instead of just off the starboard bow, where it should have appeared.

The sailing directions for each voyage are uniquely configured. In contrast to the Satawal-Lamotrek directions, which call for variable course changes made at the midpoint of the voyage, the directions for the Satawal-West Fayu voyage instruct the navigator to change to the same course but at different *etak*.

The navigator sails an initial course of setting Little Dipper. If, at One Tooth, Satawal remains under Crux (Southern Cross) at 45° risen, he alters course to setting Big Dipper at Satawal's *etak* of sighting. If Satawal moves between Crux rising and Crux at 45° risen, he alters to setting Big Dipper at Satawal's *etak* of birds. If the current is stronger and Satawal moves under Crux rising, he alters to setting Big Dipper at the midway point. If, on the other hand, the current has set the canoe to the east and Satawal moves under Crux upright, he immediately alters to setting Big Dipper. If the current is stronger and Satawal moves under Crux at 45° setting, he immediately alters to setting Cassiopeia.

The sailing directions for the upwind passage from Satawal to Pikelot take yet a different approach. After leaving the main channel before the chiefs' canoe house, the navigator sails around to Wenimung reef. Satawal now bears setting Altair. He tacks north and at One Tooth tacks east again to skirt the *etak* of sighting until Satawal finally disappears. When he judges he has reached the path of setting Big Dipper as it radiates through the reference island, West Fayu, he tacks north again. For the rest of the passage he keeps tacking to cross the great path at the *Etak* points.

Piailug envisions himself tacking within the outspread arms of a Y-shaped fish trap, called an *amei*. The southern arm is formed by the line from Satawal to rising Vega; the northern arm by a line from Satawal to rising Little Dipper. Pikelot lies in the center of the fish trap, under rising Big Dipper.

Piailug told me that although it is often wet, slow, and uncomfortable to beat into the wind, as the most casual sailor knows, it is navigationally easier than guiding downwind passages. Downwind, even a small error can result in missing the island. Upwind, one tacks back and forth in front of the target many times. Similarly, long passages are often easier than short ones. Steering errors, current shifts and the effects of wind shifts tend to cancel one another out on a long seaway; but on a short one, a single unnoticed shift in current may take the canoe far off course. The short passages therefore are called *metau rhiperhip*, "seas of kicking."

Over the next weeks, Piailug detailed the talk of sailing for voyages to Lamotrek, West Fayu, Pikelot, and Puluwat. These directions, prescribing the sequence of course compensations for all the permutations of wind and current one could anticipate on these seaways, contained a formidable amount of data. When I asked if he knew more, he said this was everything he had learned from Angora before he died. It is important to learn the talk of sailing, he said, but far more important to develop the ability to construct one's own sailing directions by projecting the star courses of *wofanu* across the sea and envisioning the reference island moving according to the current and one's course. With this skill—and with the correct star courses—one can sail anywhere in the world. He had done precisely this on his voyage from Hawaii to Tahiti, he said. Using the Marshall Islands as his *lu pongank*, he constructed an *Etak* sequence from star courses he had learned from his grandfather.

Before the advent of the compass, he told me, voyages could be initiated during the day by ranging from two known points onshore. For passages to West Fayu, for example, the navigator could align Faieruni, a large rock south of Sigafna canoe house, with the middle of three breadfruit trees in the forest behind. This gave him the desired course of setting Mailapellifung. He could then gauge the current by watching the trees on either side. If the rock and the northernmost tree lined up, he knew his true heading was setting Wulego—i.e., the current carried him west; if the rock and the southernmost tree lined up, his true heading was Fuesemagut—i.e., the current carried him east. There were similar ranges, called *yaopiyop*, for voyages to Pikelot, Lamotrek, and Wuligee reef. Now, however, this system has fallen into disuse, victim of the power and convenience of the magnetic compass.

As the days and nights passed, Piailug and I continued working. I recorded *pookof* for Satawal and the surrounding islands, constantly astounded at the specificity of the descriptions of the *epar* and at the sheer volume of information he had committed to memory. Bearing north of

Satawal, for instance, at the *etak* of birds dwells Eguwan, a tan shark making lazy movements in the water (his uncle on Lamotrek is named after this creature). Bearing setting Orion's Belt is Lugoisum, a red tropic bird (these are usually white), now very old. Under setting Pleiades, just before Lamotrek's *etak* of birds, is Yoliwa, the pod of killer whales Uurupa had sighted. Piailug said that in 1950 or so, these whales attacked a flotilla of canoes. Under rising Big Dipper at Satawal's *etak* of sighting dwells a *tagalar*, a swordfish of the species *Xiphias gladius*. I told him that we had seen a swordfish in this general vicinity. He became intensely interested and asked detailed questions about our course and range from Satawal. Finally he decided we must have sighted this *epar*.

Since Pikelot is well screened by reefs, most of its *epar* have to do with features on the reefs. Bearing setting Altair from Pikelot is a portion of Moen reef called Pelifaimo. It is covered with gravel (*faimo*), by which sign a navigator can recognize it. Under setting Cassiopeia lies a reef called Orraitigilimaan. Its distinguishing feature is a bird (*maan*) hovering over it that calls "tig-i-tig-i-tig."

When we had finished the sailing directions and *pookof*, we reviewed *wofanu* for all the islands of the Carolines. Then Piailug taught me *fu taur*, literally "star channel," a system by which the navigator lines up a known feature on an island with a star point behind, to locate the reef channel at night. When making a dark landfall, the navigator who knows *fu taur* can find his way through the channel to the protection of the beach or lagoon. Without this knowledge, he must lay offshore, waiting for morning light.*

With *fu taur* I came to the end of the formal lessons of navigation. Again, because I was writing the material in notebooks and recording it on tape instead of committing it to memory, I had compressed into a matter of months a course of instruction that normally took years. What I had to do next, Piailug said, was to apply his instruction to actual voyages. For that we needed to be on Satawal.

Late one night Piailug began to tell me of his childhood. The palm fronds fluttered in the light tradewinds, and from where we sat in the beach pavilion we could see the pale streak of moonlight shimmering in Saipan's wide eastern lagoon. It might have been Satawal if not for the noise of the cars on the coastal road behind the house.

---

*Sketches of the star channels can be found in Appendix 10.

His grandfather Raangipi first took him aside to teach him navigation, he said. Raangipi, whose name comes from the word for "turmeric," the symbol of light, was small but tough and sinewy. Both his legs bore dolphin tattoos (with which, traditionally, both men and women decorated themselves—the women inside their thighs—for they were considered highly erotic), and his arms bore the short bars and stripes that were the style before the Japanese colonial administration. Each morning at sunrise, his grandfather would wake him and they would eat breakfast. Then, instead of playing with his friends on the beach, Piailug would accompany the old man on his daily rounds. If a canoe was under construction they would work with Piailug's father, Orranipul. Otherwise they would tend Raangipi's coconut trees or go fishing. Piailug would wait in the canoe while his grandfather peered into the water, his spear poised and ready. When he saw a fish, he would dive in to spear it. Piailug would then string the fish on a coconut frond. These were the days before steel spears and diving masks were imported by Japanese traders. Raangipi fashioned his own spears from strong wood and rolled his fishing line from the dried bark of *yarama* tree and hibiscus plant. He crafted his trolling lures and hooks for bottom-fishing from the shell of the hawksbill turtle, called *mau*, for which Piailug was later nicknamed.

Throughout the day, when he stopped to smoke or relax, Raangipi would teach navigation. "Sometimes he got mad at me when I didn't listen," Piailug recalled with a chuckle, "but I was only five or six, and my head was not strong. I could only follow him a little."

At night Piailug sat with the men in the canoe house while they drank and told stories. "Those old navigators talked about navigation every day," he recalled. "It was a custom. I listened, listened to their stories of sailing to West Fayu and Lamotrek, Pikelot and Puluwat. Then, when it was time to sleep, I would lie down beside my grandfather. He would always tell me that if I learned navigation I would have a name and people would respect me. I would eat the navigator's food and when I voyaged I would be higher than a chief. I listened and I thought, 'Maybe to be a *palu* is good. Maybe I will learn navigation.'"

On voyages to the neighboring islands Raangipi taught him about the stars, swells, and birds. "I was bigger then," Piailug recalled, "and I could think a little better. I tried to make my head strong to remember what my grandfather taught me." When Piailug was eleven or twelve, Raangipi died.

Piailug then studied with his father. They continued with *wofanu* and the sailing directions, then went on to boatbuilding and fishing. When Piailug was thirteen, Orranipul died, too, leaving him without a teacher or father. This is when his aunt Neamoun and uncle Maanusuuk adopted him and Uurupa, still a toddler, and arranged for their education with the highly respected navigator Angora.

When Piailug was fifteen or sixteen, Angora came to Satawal to perform the most important ceremony in Piailug's life, *pwo*. This symbolized his coming of age and initiated him into the secret teachings, responsibilities, and special status of the full-fledged *palu*. The uninitiated were not *palu*, Piailug stressed, but merely *arreuw*. Only a *palu* could lead a flotilla of canoes or sit in the navigator's place in the canoe house; only a *palu* carried the distinction of the name; one who was *arreuw* had always to follow.

Pwo was simple in ritual but rich in significance. On the day of the ceremony, Piailug bathed himself and dressed in a new loincloth woven especially for the occasion, and was dusted with turmeric. Then he drank a special potion made from various plants steeped in a drinking coconut. "They called it the medicine of brightness," he explained. "You drank it before they put *pwo* on your body so that your master's words would come into your head and into your stomach."

His family gathered in Sigafna canoe house, since Lepotig, the Masano clan's canoe house, was filled with canoes. The women brought in a large bowl of breadfruit upon which they piled hundreds of *turrh*, gifts to Angora, the master of *pwo*. Gifts were exchanged among the friends and relatives who participated as well. Then Piailug rested his arms on the pile so that Angora could tie young coconut shoots around them. The arm tying is critical, Piailug explained, for it invokes the care and the guidance of Anumwerici to "heat the *palu*'s words," to make his magic strong.

Then Angora peeled off the *turrh* to bare the great bowl of breadfruit. With a sharp clamshell he divided the food, offering small portions to Fara, Sapu, Fanur, and Wareyang, the spirits of the four schools of navigation.[*] Then everybody ate and drank. The men sang and danced to bawdy songs to celebrate the coming of age of a new navigator.

But not everybody came to celebrate, he remembered: "My *pwo*

---

[*]Only the latter two "masts," or schools, are extant. No one I interviewed remembered details of the Sapu and Fara schools.

was held when Christianity first came to Satawal. Many people were afraid to come—afraid of the Christian God." *Pwo* was never again celebrated on the island.

For the next month he was sequestered in the canoe house. He drank only coconut juice and ate certain species of fish and specially prepared food. Angora and two other navigators taught him day and night, in relays. When the month was over, he made his first voyage to West Fayu as a full-fledged *palu*. "It was the first time, and there was fear inside me!" he admitted. "I didn't want to eat! But when I got back to Satawal my fear was finished, and in two days I wanted to sail again."

Shortly thereafter he sailed to Puluwat for further study with Angora: "I went to ask him about more *pookof* and *wofanu*. I wanted to learn *pwe* and magic, too, but I was afraid to ask. That was the time when the Christians came."

Piailug and his crew made voyages in the Puluwat area, to Pulusuk, Tamatam, and Pulap, before running downwind to Satawal with the returning easterlies at the beginning of *lefung*.

For the next two years, with the westerly winds in late *leraak*, he returned to see his master. "I stayed with him so we could discuss navigation. Day and night we talked. He didn't like it when my head was blank. Sometimes I went with the other young men to drink and 'scratch around' for women: he got mad. He would speak quietly but strongly: 'What is this, man? Why do you play around? It is bad. You must come to me to ask and ask and ask.'"

I asked if he remembered anything more. "No," he replied slowly, still lost in his recollections, "I can't think of anything else. It has been long; long."

Angora died in the late 1970s, and Piailug has never returned to Puluwat.

The summer had reached its zenith and began to wane. Piailug left to stay with his relatives in the southern part of the island. I remained in the house on the beach, loath to give up the comforts of Western living. Each morning, after swimming in the lagoon and reviewing my notes on the terrace, I would drive to the southern village to continue my studies. Often I would ask Piailug to go with me in my rented car to talk, for I was uncomfortable discussing navigation in front of the others.

On Satawal he was a power to be reckoned with. He had had the force of will and the political acumen to place me in his clan and protect me, in spite of the chiefs' contrary designs. But on Saipan he himself was a visitor, and seemed to be wary of his own position in the Carolinian community. Since the island was more Western than not, he left me (justifiably) to fend for myself. The Carolinians there knew nothing about me, not who I was, or why I had come, or the nature of my connection to Piailug and his clan. From the beginning I was eyed with suspicion, which my lack of patience and my poorly concealed contempt for the behavior of many, who accepted food stamps and public assistance and yet on the weekend drank their entire week's earnings in all-night parties, only served to exacerbate. The courtesy I received stemmed from the fact that I was with Piailug, who was regarded with respect, even awe. His voyages to Saipan and Tahiti had left a deep impression.

One Saturday I accompanied him to a fiesta. Men butchered a fat hog and roasted it over a spit. Big pots of beans, breadfruit, taro, and other savory dishes cooked slowly over a glowing pit of coals. All afternoon the partygoers ate and drank. Late into the evening, the drinking continued apace. People danced to Hawaiian music blasting from a stereo.

I wandered aimlessly, carrying my cameras since I had been asked to take pictures. Four young men loomed out of the dark: "Hey, brudda!" one leered. "You are only one and we are four. Why don't you give us that bag of cameras?" I backed off, alarmed.

I found Piailug sitting at a picnic table. Soon two men sat next to me. One asked what I was learning from Piailug. A little navigation, I answered, warily. The other demanded to know how much I was paying him. I remained silent. "You are stealing his knowledge!" the first one hissed. "Tell us your arrangements with him!" the other sneered. "What will he do when you have stolen all his knowledge and left him with nothing?"

I looked to Piailug for intercession, but he just sat there, cupping his beer in both hands, his head bent low to the table.

"You Americans are all the same . . ." the first one was saying. "You are shit!"

I went like a pariah into the night.

A few days later one of the men apologized, mumbling that he had been crazy with drink. I accepted, but remained wary. Piailug shrugged off the incident as hostility born of drunkenness, but seemed very uneasy to be the cause of conflict.

Then he stopped teaching me. For three days I went to ask him questions and each day he avoided me. When I brought him cigarettes and other gifts he resumed his lessons, but I knew I could not continue much longer. I was tired and emotionally spent. I needed to go home, to be with my wife, simply to sit and try to absorb my experiences thus far. My patience, by nature scanty, was used up. A small voice within warned me to leave now, before I became more antagonistic.

A wealthy American who made his home on Saipan was to have taken us back to Satawal on his yacht. But his business plans changed and he canceled the trip. In the face of that, I scheduled a flight home, and Piailug began to think about returning to Yap to wait for the *Microspirit*.

On one of my last days on Saipan, I took him shopping for knives, fishing line, hooks, and other gear. Then we sat in my car on the beach and I asked about sailing magic. He seemed tired of all my questions.

He repeated that he had never learned the magic: "I wanted to, but by that time the Christians had come and they told us to forget all of it."

"Is that good or bad?"

"I don't really know," he pondered, more interested in the discussion now. "I myself think it's bad. We threw away our magic and then we threw away our customs."

"That's why I want to write it down," I put in quickly, as if to justify my persistent questions.

"Yeah," he said acidly, "it's good that you are writing it all down. But when you return to Boston, keep what you write—don't send it to those people on Satawal." I asked why.

"Because those young men never come to ask me about navigation," he snapped.

"Are they lazy?"

"Lazy? No. They just don't want to learn."

The wind had died away completely and the reclining sun beat fiercely on the water. Wavelets nibbled at the beach. He smoked in silence, then exhaled with a sigh.

"Remember what I told you?" he asked. "When I was small and I went with my grandfather to the beach, the younger men would always come to sit in the circle. An elder would ask someone to talk about his skill. If he was a *palu* he would talk about navigation; if he was a *sennap*, about building canoes; if he knew *katoepaipai* or *katoaragnap* or *katogoose* [magic rituals to summon floating logs, tuna, and octopus to the island], he would tell us about that. When he finished, the elder would have the young men repeat what they'd heard. When I was young, I wanted to hear what they talked about. But now the young men on Satawal don't seem to care. When I talk about navigation, they just say, 'We don't want to listen to that, we want to get drunk!' 'Okay,' I say to them, 'you can laugh and get drunk, and when I die everything will be gone!' Now there is only Ikimai, Ikerip, Muanirik, Regaliang, Rewena, Uurupa, me. That's all."

He took a fierce pull on his cigarette and stared out to sea. I asked if the navigators had tried to teach. He smoked for a moment, then went on, his words tumbling out with anger and sadness:

"Several years ago the chiefs said we would have classes in navigation so the kids resuming from high school could learn. We came together in the canoe house and we taught. Me, Ikimai, Rewena, Regaliang. In only three or four weeks all the students ran off. Now there are only a few of us navigators. We stay and wait to die. Nobody asks us.

"When I started sailing between the islands," he went on bitterly, "there were only a few young men on Satawal: me [counting on his fingers], Tugrai, Raisor, Asoman, Rasaalp, Raparig-maybe twenty. But now look, there are probably a hundred, and only one or two are learning anything at all. But when it's time to drink, eh hey! They are all quick! Quick to drink and quick to fight. Yes, it's crazy."

"So what will the people of Satawal do?" I asked.

"Nothing," he said abruptly, then paused to light a fresh cigarette. "In several years, if you are still alive, you will come back to Satawal, but you won't see any navigators. We will all be dead." He stopped talking and stared out to sea.

"Do you see yourself as the last one?" I asked.

"Perhaps," he answered thoughtfully, "perhaps. Now I depend on my son Bonefacio. He is a good size to learn. I have started to teach him, but it depends on my body. If I am still alive, I can teach for a long time. But maybe in a year or two I will die . . . and then I can't teach." His voice trailed off, long and sad.

"Why?" I asked, alarmed. "Why one or two years?"

"I don't know," he said, chuckling at the sound of panic in my voice. "I am not a god."

When I said goodbye he was up in a coconut tree, preparing it to produce tuba. He wore a loincloth, having given up Western dress when not in public. I stood below, dressed in slacks and a clean polo shirt, the engine of my rental car idling. The vast differences between our cultures seemed to be compressed into the vertical distance between me on the ground and him in the tree.

"I am going now," I shouted up as he showered me with wood shavings. "I will try to get back to Satawal in six months."

He paused, knife in hand, to look down at me. "Six months?" he asked, counting on his fingers. "What, under Tumur?"

"Yes," I shouted, "January."

"Okay, Steve," he said matter-of-factly, "you are going. I will wait for you on Satawal." Then he turned back to his work.

11

The succeeding flights blended together like a cross-country bus ride: Ponape to Honolulu, Los Angeles, Houston, and finally Boston. It was wonderful to be going home. I drank gin-and tonics from plastic glasses and stared out the window at the sea or the darkness. I had been to Satawal and back, I reflected. I had accomplished at least part of what I wanted to do. Piailug had adopted me as his brother (although with him in his mid-fifties and me just thirty he was more like a father) and entrusted me to Uurupa and Maanusuuk. They had taught me with care and patience. Piailug had taught me a great deal, too, but I felt disappointed; I had somehow expected a closer relationship with him.

Uurupa, with both a traditional and a Western education, treaded a path between the West and old Oceania. His command of English had considerably eased my introduction to Satawal's culture and navigational methodology. Perhaps with Uurupa as my initial guide I had learned much more, much more quickly than if Piailug had remained on Satawal.

Maanusuuk, in contrast, was wholly of the old world. His world view was probably as non-Western as was possible in a living islander. He had opened a door onto the seascape of old Oceania by giving me his greatest gift, although I still didn't know why he had chosen me to receive it. I could make no claims to understand either Uurupa or Maanusuuk, but I thought I would in time; there was nothing enigmatic about them.

But Piailug seemed all smooth curves and jagged angles to me, a turbulent mixture of conflicts. In the first moments we met I had witnessed both hemispheres of his character: he gazed fiercely, probing me as if to detect hidden flaws, only to laugh teasingly and accept me as his student. On the *Microspirit* he had answered my questions with the utmost patience and attention. He struck me then as a man of measured discipline, one who had welded together the physical and intellectual elements of navigation, the ideal Oceanic navigator. His spectacular drunk shattered that naïve fiction. He was self-destructive, filled with bitterness and rage. Yet I was drawn to him as I was to my own father. I wanted his love and respect. I admired his resourcefulness, his skill and boldness, his courage.

He had traveled more extensively than any of the other navigators, making canoe voyages throughout the eastern Caroline Islands, and had been to Guam, Saipan, Hawaii, and Tahiti. He clearly knew the attraction the West held for the younger men; he himself was attracted. He often voiced his fear that, since navigation was woven into the social fabric of his island, it would disappear as the adoption of Western customs frayed that fabric. "First we threw away our magic and our taboos," he had stated again and again; "now we will throw away our navigation." And yet, just as my own father had let his children grow up like wild plants, I had seen Piailug spend little time with his own sons.

If Piailug knew and feared the West, he was also very curious about it. He was a restless experimenter: unlike others on Satawal, even Uurupa, he was willing to adapt new ideas and methods if useful. He listened carefully when I pointed out a flaw in the traditional canoe design that caused the planks of all the canoes to crack at the stemhead. I told him of a special polysulfide caulking compound that would be far superior to breadfruit sap between the planks, and he wanted me to get some to test. I suggested we put reefing points in the sail we had built, to enable the canoe to keep sailing in strong winds. He thought that a novel solution to a constant problem. He wanted me to help him design a bracket so he could mount an outboard motor on *Suntory* for propulsion in calms. He was the only boatbuilder on Satawal to use a chain saw, wielding the fuming machine one moment and trading it the next for an adz, using that tool as his ancestors had done for thousands of years. He had reopened Nemanong village, abandoned to the ghosts of the Katamang people who perished in the smallpox epidemics during the Japanese administration. He intended to build a new canoe house there and equip it with his own canoes, so he would no longer have to contend with Katamang men who resisted his will. In all of this, he seemed quite Western: he believed his own actions could influence his destiny.

On Satawal, where a man lives on his wife's land and cares for his mother's, where canoes are owned in common, each canoe-house member claiming a share according to his contribution of timber and labor, where harvests of fishes and turtles and even gifts of cigarettes are divided equally by the *souwienet*, the "master of dividing," a man could not gain social position by amassing material goods. Rather, he achieved it by mastery of the arts: navigation, canoe building, house building, fishing, divination, and medicine. Of these, a *palu* carried the highest distinction. A chief was a chief because of his heredity; but a *palu* was a *palu* because he had the right stuff. The respect accorded him provided the greatest incentive for a young man to learn the skills required for the island to survive. This was, of course, why Piailug himself had become a navigator.

He told me he had been chosen to guide the *Hokule'a* by chance. He had accompanied Mike McCoy, a Peace Corps volunteer, to Hawaii when the initial planning for the voyage was taking place. McCoy had proposed him as a candidate, and he was selected over a navigator from Puluwat because he spoke some English.

Publicly, Piailug said he made the voyage to show the Hawaiians and Tahitians what their ancestors knew and the young men of Micronesia what they would lose if they didn't seek the knowledge of their fathers. Privately, he added that the Hawaii-Tahiti voyage was a great challenge; if he succeeded, his prominence would be ensured everywhere, including Micronesia. Nowhere, I was beginning to realize, was his reputation more important to him than on his own island. That a film producer and his crew had come on a chartered yacht, complete with lights, cameras, sound recorders, and generators, to film Piailug for American television was a tremendous coup. An American *palu* arriving on the *Microspirit* proved that his fame had reached all the way to far-off Boston, that Americans would come to see him and not his archrival, the navigator of the chiefly clan.

He was probably little different from his ancestors, who struck north from the New Hebrides on voyages of discovery and colonization—to prove themselves at sea, to escape overcrowded islands, and to exercise their will to rule. Instead of voyaging to establish himself on new islands, he voyaged to establish himself in new cultures and to achieve pre-eminence in his own.

In his aggressiveness, his restlessness, and his independent mind, he was almost a caricature of the rugged individual. It was ironic to me that in a culture in which the desires of one are subjugated to the needs of many, it was this man who longed to preserve the traditional society that could not accommodate nonconformists such as himself.

Even his notion of courage seemed Western. On Saipan, I had asked about the magical rituals previously used to bring strength to the navigator at sea.

"In the old days the navigators used magic to make themselves strong," he answered, "but now, nothing; they just pray. Before they leave and at sea, they pray. But I, I make myself strong by *thinking*—just by thinking! I make myself strong because I despise cowardice. Too many men are afraid of the sea. But I am a *navigator*; I don't want to stay long on land. Sometimes, when I am caught in strong winds and big waves, I am afraid—oh yes, I am afraid. But when the wind dies and the waves are lower, I make myself strong again to search for the island, and to keep going."

Piailug was a master of the lore and practice of navigation. He was also a master of the *umau*, a cycle of songs and dances traditionally performed during the periods when picking coconuts was taboo to allow the trees to regenerate. Each evening the islanders gathered in a canoe house. The children tended a large fire while the men danced and sang. Late at night, as the children nodded off to sleep, the women would slip away, only to rush back in, their identities masked. They would select partners—not necessarily their husbands—and spirit them into the darkness to enjoy this time of ritual license.

The Carolinians on Saipan wanted to learn these traditional dances, so, each evening after work, the men would meet at the beach, where Piailug would patiently teach the dance steps and the accompanying words. When it grew dark, the men turned on their car headlights and he would continue with the dances, eyes closed, hands tracing strange patterns in the eerie light, singing of spirits sailing between the islands on ethereal canoes. Clearly, he felt a deep connection to his own tradition.

Yet, early in my stay on Saipan, I had asked him if he knew *itang*, the talk of wisdom. Modestly, he answered that he hadn't wanted to learn it: it was confused talk and thus could be of no use. I pressed him for an explanation, but that was all he would say.

Maanusuuk had stressed that *itang* was the *most* important kind of knowledge. Once I had even asked the chiefs if they knew it. All quickly denied, then in hushed voices asked how I had even heard it existed. Yet Piailug, a master of lore, dismissed it as confusion. *Itang* was what navigators used to protect their crews, what fathers used to protect their children; how could he make himself a master of land and sea lore but ignore the most vital knowledge? If he had learned it, would it have dissolved his bitterness and rage? Did I know something he didn't?

Over the next months, as I translated my tape recordings and compiled my notes, I struggled to understand just who Piailug was. Although I had been to his island, made admirable progress in learning his language, and managed to record a great deal of his navigational lore, I could not say I knew him at all. I saw him driven by two impulses: an incredible will to prevail, to save his name, his way of navigation and way of life; and rage and anger. In the end, all I really had was a scattering of images: In Nemanong, Piailug gently stroking a puppy, whimpering because it had two broken legs; on Saipan, Piailug drinking all night with his relatives and at three in the morning going with me for our star lesson. "It is my job to drink," he laughed, toting a six-pack. He was fully cogent for the lesson. Another time on Saipan, a retarded boy with snot dripping down his chin and covering his chest and hands grabbed hold of Mau. He peered intently at the boy for a short time, then gently, reassuringly, sadly, grasped his shoulders with his weathered hands, as if to fill him with strength.

Finally I was left with a single remark. Once, after talking many hours about technical navigation, I asked if the talk of navigation was beautiful. He said it was useful, because it gave one the means to sail from island to island. No, not like that, I explained, I mean beautiful, like a woman. "Yes, like that, too!" he laughed, then became pensive.

"I don't know what the others would say," he said, forcing the words out in a kind of pain, "but in my mind I say the talk of navigation is beautiful. In my body it's the same: I feel the talk of navigation is beautiful."

Because of Piailug's generosity and commitment, I learned about Micronesian seafaring very quickly. Had that been my only goal, I would not have thought of returning to Satawal. But I had asked questions I needed to answer, begun relationships I needed to explore. In the process of compiling my notes and journals I had (unwittingly) tried to articulate my motives for returning. I had written:

> *Traditionally the navigator is the mediator of the physical and the metaphysical elements of the sea. The knowledge of both is essential. The secular is not sliced away from the spiritual, the physical from the metaphysical. The* palu *is bound to serve his people. He is bound to provide food for them, to heal them, to build canoes for them, to resolve conflict for them. He is a husband to his people, a father to his children, a social creature who is nothing without the society he serves. He is hero as rabbi or priest; a much different kind of hero from the Western existential loner.*

In my patchy ideal of manhood, one harnessed one's skills, strength, and vision in service to one's people, one's family.

In the Caribbean, while on my voyage from England to San Francisco, I had met a woman who accepted my invitation to sail to Panama. She continued on to the Galápagos, then returned to the United States. Upon completing my voyage, I visited her in Boston; later we were married. Now we wanted children. What kind of father would I be? I wondered. What kind of man? What kind of husband? How could I put all my aspirations together into an integrated package? After college I had become a yacht captain; now I wanted to be a writer. Yet my own father had abandoned writing when he had had children. Would I have to do the same?

When I once showed my father a portrait I had written of a Marquesan hunter I met on my voyage, he had savagely attacked it. Later, when I described ideas for a book on the Oceanic navigators, he only half-listened, then shrugged and suggested I might be able to patch together a magazine article. It seemed he didn't want me to succeed, or even to try—as if his support for my adventuring ended at seafaring and was fundamentally conflicted, if not withdrawn altogether, when he realized my goal was to become a writer. Before my first trip to Satawal, I had resolved never to seek his advice and to ignore both his criticism and his praise. Now, as he was mired in a marriage neither party had the strength to end, I was even more determined to succeed.

But I didn't dismantle the fiction of my father, I just transferred it to Piailug. *He* must be the father and hero I thought my own was not; he must embody the ideal of integrated manhood my own did not—my father the "Western existential loner." And yet of all the navigators on Satawal, Piailug most resembled my father. Like him, Piailug possessed great strength which he seemed to dissipate by raging against the world. Like him, Piailug had high expectations for his children, yet stubbornly refused to tend to them, to bring them up with the qualities necessary to succeed.

If I confused Piailug with my father, I identified myself with both. As I probed their characters, I had to ask myself to what extent I was not just like them. Could I succeed where they failed? Could I surpass my own father? What would *that* mean?

But there was another reason I wanted to go back. As a navigator who could record and preserve the lore that lived only in memory, I had come to have a connection to Piailug and his people I had not anticipated. One winter evening, as I worked on my notes, I spontaneously typed a paragraph about an old man lying on a litter over an earth oven. The medicinal smoke curled around his body as he waited calmly for death. Three weeks later, I received word that Maanusuuk had died. Why had he taught me the *itang*? Had he a premonition of death? What was I to do with this knowledge now?

It had been ten months since I had last seen or heard from Piailug. When it was clear I could not make it back in January I had sent him a letter to tell him I was delayed. But I'd heard nothing from him, and even as I boarded my flight to Hawaii I did not know where he was. I had heard he was on Woleai felling logs for a new canoe. Then someone told me he was on Yap, waiting to return to Saipan. I received another report that he had remained on Saipan. I wondered if he would still teach me or if he thought he had fulfilled his commitment. There was nothing for me to do but to find him and stick with him and see my quest through to the end.

When I got to Yap I found that Piailug had indeed spent several months on Woleai to fell and hollow a large tree for the keel of a new canoe. He had shipped it back to Satawal aboard the *Microspirit* and was now working on it there. Uurupa was with him, having left his job at the hospital when Maanusuuk became ill. When I talked with Piailug on the government radio, I asked if there was anything he needed. He asked me to bring some paint for the new canoe. I offered to bring more, but all he needed was the paint.

The high-school year had just ended, and on the *Microspirit* a carnival atmosphere prevailed. Day and night the students roamed the ship, conversing excitedly, playing disco music on portable stereos and singing songs to a strummed guitar. We steamed through the islands, each appearing as a small, dark nub on the horizon, growing larger until it spread before us in a dazzling panorama of green palm trees and white beaches. As the ship lowered her boats, a celebration would begin for the arriving students. Then, as the ship hoisted her boats and steamed away, one could sense the festivities dying as the island was left alone at sea. Rainy weather set in and the students huddled under a large tarpaulin suspended over the cargo hatch.

When the *Microspirit* anchored at Lamotrek, I went ashore to pay my respects to Eguwan, Piailug and Uurupa's uncle. I found him on the main path, coming down to greet the skiff. When I asked if he remembered me, he peered through his cataracts as if searching the misty image for some clue. Finally he took my hand and held it. Curious children swarmed all over us.

In the evening, everyone from the ship and the island gathered in the grassy clearing near the beach. "The Slaves," a rock band formed by some University of Guam students, twanged out songs on battered electric guitars powered by the town generator. A Lamotrek man wearing lipstick and a ratted wig hung with beads, combs, and bits of cloth danced suggestively, eliciting squeals of laughter from the girls on the far side of the clearing. As it grew dark, the band retired and the boys built a bonfire in the clearing. Then the women danced in a long, undulating line. The blaze and the rhythmic swaying of their arms and bodies created a scene like those rendered by one of Captain Cook's artists, John Webber, two hundred years earlier. At that moment, it seemed as if little had changed—or, indeed, could change. When the dancing was over, I turned to Eguwan to tell him I was leaving. The old man again took my hand and said: "Tell Piailug and Uurupa you came to see me here. I make you my son, like them. I am your father. Please tell them." It was as if I really could recapture that lost world glimpsed by Captain Cook, as if I could reach back to a world of stars and wind and spirits.

At dawn the ship hove under the lee of Satawal. When I went ashore, men came to welcome me back. I found Piailug lying on a mat in his newly built canoe house in Nemanong, crippled by gout. He greeted me as matter-of-factly as he'd said goodbye a year before, but laughed as he tried to deflect my slaps to his shoulder, enjoying my enthusiasm.

"You said you would come back in Tumur," he reminded me, "so I met the ship that came in January, but you weren't on it. I thought perhaps you weren't coming. The next ship brought your letter, so I waited for you."

It was several weeks before I realized the implications of this statement. He had been invited back to Hawaii the next winter to accompany the *Hokule'a* on a two-year good-will voyage throughout Oceania. He wanted to complete the new canoe and help me finish my research before he left. This might be my last chance to be with him. I felt very fortunate, as if a small door had opened in the flow of time and human lives, and one family had invited me to enter.

PART III

The Canoe
of Palulap

12

Before dawn two days later, I woke to rain hammering on the tin roof of my hut in Nemanong village. Wind rifled the glistening manes of the palm trees. I was about to fall back to sleep, assuming the turtling expedition to West Fayu would be postponed, when Piailug came in, struck a match, and lit the stove.

"Make coffee, Steve," he ordered in the tentative voice in which he spoke English. Sleepily I asked if we were still going. He claimed the rain would soon stop and seemed unconcerned even as the squall renewed its attack.

I crawled from beneath my mosquito netting, groped for a flashlight, and began to make coffee. He scratched his back against one of the rough-hewn house posts. I asked how he knew the rain would stop.

"It has been five days since the new moon appeared in the west," he explained. "The star Ul has finished storming. Since it rained all night, I think it will clear today. If it had been clear last night and started raining this morning, I would think Ul was not quite finished fighting and we would have two more days of rain. But now it will be good weather. Maybe a little rain today, but not too much."

The squall ended as it grew light. Piailug slurped his coffee and smoked a cigarette. "Pack everything you need," he ordered, "your cameras, notes, some coffee and sugar, cigarettes for the crew. We will try to leave with the other canoes." Then he tossed the dregs through the open doorway and limped off into the gray dawn.

By eight-thirty we had skidded the canoe down the beach into the shallow *lealulu*, loaded up the mast, sail, food, and supplies, pushed out through the main channel, and were under way. Our initial course was setting Big Dipper. By ten-thirty we were at *rongirup*: Satawal showed as several green mounds on the horizon. The wind held steady from the northeast. Motch, Piailug's cousin, a gentle, good-humored man in his late sixties who looked no older than Piailug, was at the sheet. Rovigno, Piailug's son-in-law, sat aft at the steering paddle, rigged for sea in his red "Truk Island" T-shirt, turquoise wool gloves, and a green hardhat salvaged from a Japanese fishing boat. Skinny old Assaf, married to Uurupa's youngest sister-in-law, squatted in the hull to bail. Bonefacio, feeling seasick, slept on one of the two benches traversing the middle of the canoe. Maria, Assaf's eight-year-old daughter, hummed quietly to herself in the shade of the mainsail. I sat on the outrigger platform with most of the baggage. Piailug perched on the rail near Rovigno, steadying himself with the backstay, glancing back to Satawal, just visible in the distance.

Two canoes, *Aloha* and *White Horse*, with a half-hour's head start, were about two miles distant, sailing beneath a gray bank of cloud. There was a metallic sheen to the sea and sky, unsettling to me, for I didn't know if it was the tail end of the inclement weather or the forerunner of more. A few squalls crossed our track far ahead, beetling downwind on fuzzy legs of rain. No one seemed concerned. Motch and Assaf joked back and forth. Motch watched the compass and occasionally called out "*Mwan-oh!*"—meaning "man" or "right" (one's right arm is called the "man's arm," for it is stronger than the left, or "woman's arm"; the suffix makes the expression more melodious). Rovigno took his foot from the steering paddle, letting it ride to the surface; the canoe responded immediately, swinging upwind. When Motch wanted Rovigno to steer the other way he yelled "*Rauput-ah!*"— "woman" or "left." Sometimes he simply called "foot," meaning Rovigno should press down on the paddle, making the canoe fall off wind,

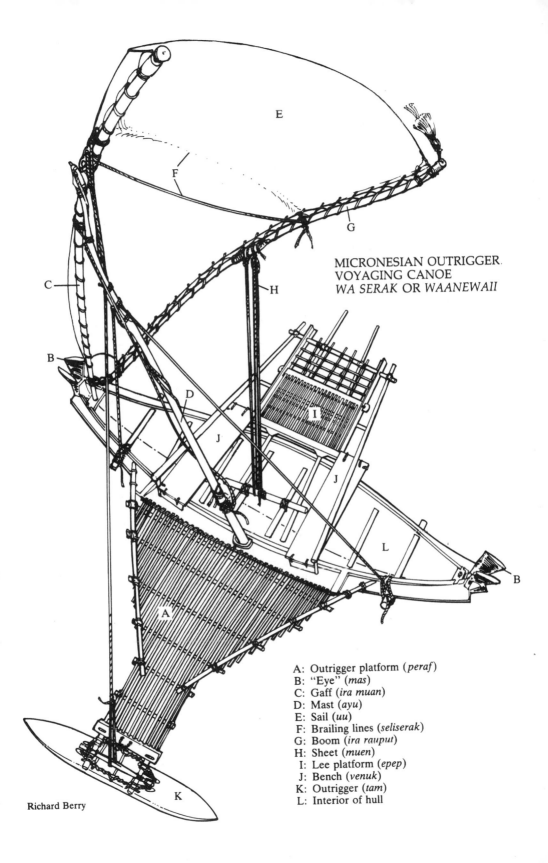

MICRONESIAN OUTRIGGER
VOYAGING CANOE
WA SERAK OR *WAANEWAII*

A: Outrigger platform (*peraf*)
B: "Eye" (*mas*)
C: Gaff (*ira muan*)
D: Mast (*ayu*)
E: Sail (*uu*)
F: Brailing lines (*seliserak*)
G: Boom (*ira rauput*)
H: Sheet (*muen*)
I: Lee platform (*epep*)
J: Bench (*venuk*)
K: Outrigger (*tam*)
L: Interior of hull

Richard Berry

in this case to the left. Satawal disappeared astern, a green planet setting into the sea.

Piailug had contributed little to the banter. Now he seemed completely absorbed in the world of sea sounds and wave patterns. He
glanced from the compass to the island and scanned the sea. Everyone
quieted as we did our *fatonomuir*. Satawal had not moved, Piailug announced at last; it still lay squarely under the position of Crux half-
risen; there was no current. As Satawal disappeared at the *etak* of
sighting, he quietly ordered a course change to setting Little Dipper.
Unless conditions changed, we would hold this course for the entire
passage.

Aloha was being guided by the bawdy Iti, who had teased me while
fishing Wuligee reef the previous year. Matto navigated *White Horse*.
The two canoes were still ahead but far to windward, and Rovigno
speculated they had not accurately gauged the current. Soon they fell
off and steered parallel to us. Steadily we closed the distance, and by
early in the afternoon had sailed right between them to pull into the
lead.

By my estimation we were at the midpoint of the voyage, with
Lamotrek bearing halfway between setting Orion's Belt and setting
Corvus. Piailug said we would reach the midpoint soon, then fell silent,
scrutinizing the waves and sky. Rovigno lit cigarettes for everyone.
Maria and Bonefacio slept undisturbed in the shade of the sail. The
miles and time slipped away as the cutwater hissed at the waves and
the sail creaked against its coir lashings. A supertanker appeared on
the horizon, steaming south; soon a second appeared, headed north.
There was no cause for alarm, though: they would track far to the west
of us.

After passing *yaw luke*, Assaf served lunch. With a machete, he
sliced one of the fat packages of breadfruit wrapped in banana leaves
into portions and passed them around. Then he gave each of us a drinking coconut. Piailug refused to eat, because there was no fish. When
the meal was over, conversation resumed and Piailug ordered a round
of tuba. Earlier, as we had prepared to leave, all the men had poured
their morning's harvest into a large plastic jerry can for us to take.
Assaf skinned a coconut to make a cup from the inner nut, then started
passing it around. The prospect of sailing with a crew of drunks made
me nervous, but I told myself it was no different from drinking beer on
a Sunday race around the buoys.

Assaf began drinking heavily. Motch teased him about one of his girlfriends long ago—when he had finally asked her to marry, someone else had already made her pregnant. Everyone laughed, and Assaf, pouring more tuba, laughed loudest.

By two-thirty the wind had increased and veered to the north. Piailug ordered us to steer halfway between setting positions of the Big and Little Dippers. By my estimation we were nearly at West Fayu's *etak* of birds and should reach the island by five-thirty. Piailug affirmed this, reminding me that Lamotrek bore setting Antares. Bonefacio and Maria woke and sat quietly. Assaf lapsed into drunken silence. Piailug chanted a song about a legendary navigator named Weito:

Who is the man
Who made the talk,
Called the tail of bluefin tuna,[*]
There, in the channel of Moguchis?
He will recite, a little,
The creatures in the sea,
So they will know how they are aligned
On Arrouw.[†]
He will haul up that fish trap
With the tail of ayufan,
That it can lead him to Puluwat,
That it can.

No one talked. The water skipped past. The sail lashings creaked with the motion of the boat; the bottom of the outrigger slapped the waves. The tankers slipped beneath the horizon, leaving us alone in our own world.

By three-fifteen we were clearly within West Fayu's *etak* of birds. Many sooty terns swam and dove in the waters around us. Assaf slurred his words badly, and whenever he spoke Piailug called him a penis and As-

---

[*]Refers to *perhyan ayufan*, "the tail of bluefin tuna," a navigational system similar to *wofanu* but laid out in the shape of a fish's tail, which lists star courses from Moguchis, the northern channel of Truk Lagoon, to various islands.
[†]Arrouw is the seaway between Truk and Puluwat.

saf laughed drunkenly. Rovigno harshly told him to stop drinking, but he refused.

By three-thirty, Piailug told Bonefacio to stand up and look for the island. We were, in fact, heading straight for the channel through the reef. "Now, Steve, do you believe in me?" he asked, responding to my unspoken anxiety. I simply shook his hand. Sighting the island broke the mood of introspection. Assaf asked Rovigno for more tuba. He refused, but Assaf insisted, "Go on, penis, drink!" Piailug yelled angrily. Then, in English, he ridiculed the old man, saying he had a penis one fathom long. He laughed so hard he almost fell off the canoe. Assaf, who spoke no English, laughed drunkenly with him.

I asked and was allowed to take the steering paddle, sitting way back aft with my foot in the water, the whole canoe spread out before me like a seabird, outrigger plunging through the waves on one side, sail boomed out to the other. In the distance, West Fayu nipped at the horizon. Rovigno and Motch coached me, and soon the canoe settled into a groove, picked up speed, and skimmed toward the island. Piailug proudly handed me a cup of tuba. I was suddenly very happy, steering a canoe, sailing with my teacher, my foot in the warm water. Rovigno said I was the first American to steer a Satawal canoe; as doubtful as the claim was, I was very satisfied to show that I could handle myself at sea.

I steered through the reef pass into the lagoon, through a narrow channel up to the beach. At the last minute, with great flair, Piailug ordered the sail dropped. The canoe spun beam to the wind and stopped ten yards from the beach. *Aloha* and *White Horse* arrived, and the crews squatted around big pots of turtle stew prepared for us by the crew of *Tiger*, who had been on the island for a week.

By then it was growing dark. Stars welled up in the sky, clear now after a vivid red sunset. Clouds of sooty terns, called *krugas* after the sound of their cries, circled noisily before perching in the trees. The dank, tangy odor of guano seeped out of the woods to cover the beach and the small grassy clearing where Piailug had built a thatch-roofed sleeping hut for his crew. I leaned against the plastic cooler I used as a sea chest, scribbling notes, while the rest of the men changed their loincloths, laid out their sleeping mats, and took their few treasured belongings—lures, cigarette lighters, plastic jars filled with homegrown smoking tobacco—from their wooden boxes. Piailug put out coconut-frond mats for himself and Bonefacio and instructed me to lay mine next to his. He moved with difficulty, I noticed, wincing as he stepped on his gouty foot.

Soft laughter filtered up from the fire, where Joseph, a young man from Woleatu canoe house who had been attending college in a small town in Virginia, talked with the old man Nefaifai, whom some called "Two by Four" because that was the only English he knew. The waxing moon sailed high in the sky. Delicately feathered cirrus clouds wisped across its face like swift, translucent birds. As the wind lightened and the waters of the lagoon became calm, the two men by the fire rose to search for turtles coming up on the beach to lay their eggs. Behind me Piailug snored. Assaf moaned, unconscious on his mat. His daughter Maria lay beside him, her hands clasped over her stomach like some small and delicate primate.

I crawled in next to my teacher and tried to sleep. As the moon set, the wind died and a moist heat rose from the earth. Centipedes wriggled up through the coarse weave of the mats to slither across our naked legs and bellies. Their armored shell excretes a powerful acid that raises sinuous blisters on one's skin the following day. Motch woke, scratched, cursed the insects, and lay back to sleep. Piailug, deep in sleep, flung his arm across me and then his leg. "What? I'm not your wife!" I joked, but he only snorted and rolled over. I went down to sleep on the beach, but soon a platoon of small sand crabs marched up to investigate and skittered across my legs and torso. I gave up, went back to the hut, wrapped myself in a plastic tarp against the centipedes, and fell asleep.

West Fayu—called Pigale by the Carolinians—is a tiny island. The narrow grassy path from one side to the other stretches barely the length of three football fields. It is forested in palm trees and a variety of branching tree in which the terns roost, but is not large enough to support a fresh-water lens. Two sinkholes offer a bath, but drinking water must be collected from the tin roof of the chapel. Without water, permanent habitation here is impossible.

A long reef stretches out from the island like crooked arms to enclose the lagoon. Here tuna can be caught and sea turtles come to mate in the protected waters and lay their eggs in the island's warm sand. The jagged coral heads shield a profusion of fishes: red squirrelfish, very good eating; blue, buck-toothed parrot fish; red-and-black butterfly fish; various species of brilliantly colored wrasses; Moorish idols; bloated, spiny puffers, which rely on their ugliness for protection; thick-skinned triggerfish, which grunt when hooked or speared; and man-ray flatfish and scorpion fish, which, rendered nearly invisible by their camouflage, are ready to sting the unwary diver with their poisonous spines.

The crew of a single canoe, fishing this reef for half a day, can catch more than twice as much as all the men of Satawal on its impoverished reef. The men of Satawal rely on West Fayu to feed their people. Teen-agers, anxious to secure canoe passage here so they can get enough to eat, refer to it by their English moniker, the "Island of Free Chow."

West Fayu belongs to Lamotrek and her subordinate islands, Satawal and Elato. In the past, navigators from both islands sailed here to fish and hunt turtles. But the Lamotrekans gradually turned to outboard motorboats to get around their protected lagoon, and now they have no oceangoing canoes capable of making the voyage. The people of Satawal have West Fayu to themselves.

I woke Piailug at five so we could look for sea turtles. Groggily he told me to go on by myself, then rolled over and went back to sleep. By the time I returned, he was squatting over a small fire to boil water for coffee. Motch and Rovigno fished up bits of turtle liver from the bottom of the stewpot. Assaf sat alone, smoking forlornly and coughing.

The other crews returned from their early-morning foraging, with strings of sergeant fish netted in the shallows and bundles of dead terns. These they plucked, skewered, and roasted over a roaring fire, then dumped the charred little bodies—beaks open and eyes singed closed— onto a mat of palm fronds for division. Each man gobbled them, heads and all. I was given a share, which I ate. "Yummy," I commented in my journal, "just like eating your parakeet."

The sun stood just off the eastern horizon, bathing the sea and our small patch of sand with a fleeting sense of morning before it leapt up to heat the blue furnace of the sky. After breakfast the men assembled their Tupperware tobacco containers, lures, lines, and spears, loaded the canoes, and filed out into the waters of the lagoon. We cruised slowly, the men watching for mating turtles as their fathers, grandfathers, and great-grandfathers had done before them in this very lagoon. The looming hulks of a freighter and a fishing boat aground on the reef were the only evidence that West Fayu was in the twentieth century.

The freighter had hit the reef at a full eighteen knots, stranding itself high and dry. When the crew was finally rescued by the U.S. Coast Guard, the Satawalese looted to their hearts' content. First they found the officers' lounge with liquor cabinets intact. They drank their fill, then stumbled into the cargo bay, where they beheld row upon row of shiny new Toyotas, keys in the ignition, enough gas in the tanks to drive them on and off the ship. "Do you know how to drive these things?" the older men asked the younger. "Oh yes!" they answered. "We saw someone do it once on Yap." The cargo bay became an instant bumper-car course. The men careened about in scant control of their charges until they ran into something or something ran into them. When one car was smashed they would merely start up another and go charging off again. Eventually the cars were dismantled and the bits brought back to Satawal. Even now, tires serve as fenders for the canoes; upturned steering wheels, the shafts sharpened to a point, are used to husk coconuts.

The Japanese fishing boat had a much more useful, if less entertaining, cargo; hundreds of fathoms of tarred nylon fishing line, heavier mooring line, and various floats and buoys. In the bosun's locker were gallons of yellow and black paint. (This is when the canoes of Satawal changed their color from the traditional red and black to yellow and black.) In the living quarters they found stacks of Japanese sex and martial-arts comic books, which found their way back to the canoe houses on Satawal. Some of the older, Japanese-speaking men read them, while the young men and boys simply leafed through, looking at the drawings. But since the pictures were merely of breasts, an everyday sight on Satawal, instead of thighs, considered highly erotic, the magazines were tossed back into a corner of the canoe house, the pages used to roll cigarettes.

As we sailed back and forth over the far end of the reef, Piailug examined the bottom with great concentration. Finally he ordered the sail dropped and the canoe anchored to coral heads. All three crews took to the water with their spears. The older boys and men worked quickly and rhythmically, spearing fish, biting them behind the eyes to kill them, and skipping them across the water like flat stones to be collected and strung on coconut fronds by the younger boys. Everyone hooted and shouted, exuberant at the quantity of easy prey.

Piailug fished by himself, spearing a few, but mostly seeming to look around. He ignored me as I swam with him. Abruptly he stood up on the shallow reef.

"You see that shark?" he asked casually. I didn't. He pointed to a four-foot-long whitetip in the distance.

"Does it bite?" I asked, somewhat alarmed.

He reassured me that it attacked only if provoked. But suddenly he tensed into full alert as a large, sinister-looking blacktip stalked along the bottom. "That one is unpredictable and vicious!" he said, then commanded the crews to move back to the canoes. Immediately he submerged again, cocking his long handmade speargun, holding it poised and ready.

The shark was joined by a second, and the two cruised nearer and nearer. Piailug waved me back toward the rest of the group, who had already suspended fishing to form a circle, their spears pointing outward. Slowly we worked our way back to the canoes. Piailug swam out in front of us, all senses keyed to the sharks. When the larger one angled toward us, he rushed at it, thrusting his speargun into firing position. The shark veered away and withdrew to a safe distance, watching.

At the canoes Piailug stood guard while we loaded the strings of fish and jumped aboard. Then he untied the anchor lines and heaved himself onto the outrigger platform. We sailed off to work another portion of the reef.

Again the spears twanged on the coral heads and fish flew through the air. But sharks came again and Piailug called it a day. The canoes crossed tacks as we raced back up the lagoon.

The next morning we returned to the reef. This time, however, Piailug decided to drive the fish into a seine net instead of spearfishing, since he felt the clang of the spears drew the sharks. But the sharks came anyway, and we soon had to move to another part of the lagoon.

Piailug, standing on a shallow patch of reef, his mask atop his forehead, glowered as he directed us to anchor the net to the bottom. Then, in a wide semicircle, we herded a school of fish toward the net while he barked commands. To those who didn't snap to he yelled, "Penis! What are you doing?"

But the school was kept under control, even through some complicated maneuvers around the anchored canoes, and driven squarely into the net. It was a big catch and everyone cheered—everyone but Piailug, who growled at us to load the fish quickly aboard the canoes, perhaps mindful of the danger of sharks.

We tacked back up the lagoon in silence. He sat by himself on the outrigger platform, shooting reproachful glances at the water, the set of the sail, and the distant island. He seemed lost to us, isolated by his anger. I reflected that Uurupa, after a successful day's fishing, would have laughed and joked with his crew—I had seen him do so in such moments of leisure while sailing back from Lamotrek. There was no doubt Piailug was in command and no doubt he deserved to be; his crews caught more fish, handled the canoe better, made passages faster and with more accuracy than others. No one could dispute his skill and bravery. But at moments like this he seemed so stern and lonely and unapproachable. I couldn't help wondering if he wouldn't be different if he had learned *itang*, the talk of light.

In the afternoon the cry went across the camp: "Turtles!" Everyone dropped what he was doing, grabbed a diving mask, and ran to the northeast corner of the island, where, in the surf on the distant reef edge, a pair of turtles were swimming into the lagoon to mate. A large group of young men and boys ran through the shallows toward the surf. I watched with Motch, Iti, and Nefaifai as the hunters cut off their prey's retreat to the sea. The men approved this strategy, commenting on who was doing what. I had been peering out to sea for five minutes without even seeing the turtles, let alone what each hunter was doing. Patiently, Motch pointed them out to me, two barely discernible shapes, swimming in the face of the swells. Just then the turtles were surrounded and gaffed. They were dragged triumphantly to shore, flipped onto their backs, and dragged up the beach to lie beneath some low shrubs to await shipment to Satawal.

Piailug remained after the others returned to camp, watching the reclining sun eat away the pool of shadow in which the turtles rested. He called me to help him drag the helpless beasts into deeper shade. Thick, viscous tears streamed down their inverted faces as they sucked great lungfuls of air. He placed a coconut under each turtle's head so it could wait in comfort for death.

Instead of fishing the next morning he ordered me to repair a tear in *Tiger's* sail while he fashioned a new handle for *Suntory's* steering paddle. He seemed tired and walked painfully. The joints in his right hand hurt, too, for he winced as he grasped the handle of his adz.

In the afternoon he took me to bathe. We lolled naked in the azure waters of the northern lagoon. The tight cumulus clouds were lengthening into softer puffs, as the wind diminished and backed into the north. We floated in silence. The ships carrying the commerce of the world were hidden by the folds of the sea, and the world whose trade they carried seemed even farther away, lost in the darkness of the advancing night.

I asked some technical navigational questions, which he answered. Then, after a brief silence, he again lamented that the young men took no interest in navigation. I asked how Maanusuuk had died. He told me that a week after I had left Saipan, he had received word his aunt was ill and returned to Satawal. She had recovered, but then Maanusuuk had gotten dysentery and refused food, drink, and medication. After several weeks he had died. There was no trace of sadness or bitterness in Piailug's voice. Maanusuuk's death seemed wholly in the nature of the world; the old man had simply used up his years.

After bathing, we strolled around the island. Piailug inspected the coconuts on the trees and the condition of the bathing holes, and he watered his tobacco plants. I had brought some ginger root, which he planted to see if it would grow. As he continued his rounds, he sliced away branches obstructing the path with his machete, probed into coconut-crab holes and cleaved coconut husks in half to dry for use as fuel. Finally we wandered back to camp. At sunset, since the weather was clear and fine and the wind was well in the north, he decided we would return to Satawal.

The moon stood straight overhead as darkness swept across the world. The camp stretched into a measured flow of activity. Men packed their sea chests and loaded them onto the waiting canoes. Those with rain gear readied it; others made sure their T-shirts were dry. Others, with only a dry loincloth, carefully placed that aboard the canoes, to change into later when we had cast off. We counted the salted fish drying on racks on the beach, divided them among the three canoes, and packed them into baskets. The two turtles were dragged out of their shelter, flippers pierced with a machete and bound together with strands of line.

Then they were floated out to the canoes and secured upside down beneath the bench. Piailug took me off to a small grove of trees, where he began to dig. Soon he had uncovered seven beautiful conch shells. "Your shells," he announced. My first day on Satawal, the previous year, I had casually mentioned that my wife loved shells. When he had returned from Saipan, he had gathered conch from the lagoon and secretly buried them to await my return.

When the boats were ready, Iti surprised us by ordering *Aloha* to depart immediately. Evidently he was piqued that, despite his head start, we beat him on the sail up, about which Piailug had teased him. The three other crews made a fire on the moonlit beach, ate lobster, and drank coffee. Then *Tiger's* crew wished us well: they would remain another week to hunt turtles. We sailed out of the lagoon, through the channel, and into the sea.

We pointed the bow to Antares, now risen to half the height of the mast. It was a stunning night, Jupiter and Saturn burning through the warm air. *White Horse* ghosted along behind us. As the island disappeared astern, it lay under setting Vega. Therefore Piailug would hold the same course all night.

Assaf, quite sober now, was on the steering paddle; then Piailug took over. I was dying to sit back there and dip my foot in the moonlit sea, but he forbade me at night, afraid I might fall in.

By one-thirty we were almost at *yaw luke*. The moon set; Piailug chanted; no one spoke. The wind was backing to the east. It grew very dark; cigarettes washed the faces in their faint glow. The sail creaked; waves sloshed around the hull; the steering paddle gurgled astern. Rovigno manned the sheet and compass, calling directions to Assaf, who had again taken the steering paddle. Motch occasionally sucked his teeth as he cleaned them with a coconut midrib. It was quiet, the quiet of stellar distances; we couldn't even hear the turtle.

Just after dawn Piailug sighted Satawal, after everyone had searched intently for it for an hour. The other two canoes appeared astern. We breakfasted on pounded breadfruit and the remainder of the lobster, and by mid-morning we had made land and were unloading the turtles in front of the chiefs' canoe house. Men came up to ask how many we had brought but went away disappointed: two turtles would not go far among the eight clans of Satawal.

13

Piailug established me at Nemanong in the low, square tin-roofed hut in which he and his family had been staying. He had expanded the village since the previous year and, clearing the undergrowth from a large tract of beach, had erected a new canoe house. It was smaller than the ones to the south, but the fact that it had been built by an individual and not a clan was revolutionary. In order to give me a hut of my own— a rare luxury, for visiting bachelors are normally quartered in the canoe houses—he had sheathed the open sides of his canoe house with coconut mats and covered the floor with planks salvaged from the fishing boat wrecked on West Fayu. He and Nemoito had moved in with their children Bonefacio, Howie, Carlita, and Marcia (who had just graduated from high school), teen-age nieces Josephina and Insoruun, and grandchildren Atarino and Mauricio, still toddlers.

Their third daughter, Emilia, and her husband, Josede, now lived in the thatch-roofed hut to the north of mine. Since Emilia was close to term, Josede's mother, Tigiri, a stout, energetic woman with a lively sense of humor, had made up her mind to move right in with the couple to midwife the birth and oversee the postnatal care.

To the south of my hut, in a small clearing of its own, a new dwelling house had been built where Nemoito's cousin Nauwan and her husband, Lupomai, lived with their infant daughter and Nauwan's voluptuous teen-age niece.

This year Piailug planned to clear more land around the village and pave it with coral gravel. He contemplated moving the canoe house from the beach to higher ground and permanently converting it to a dwelling house. He would construct a full-sized canoe house in its place. He also planned an outbuilding in which to store fishing gear and tools, and a new cooking shed. I had previously suggested we build a screened-in veranda in which to escape the swarms of flies and had brought a quantity of screening. He incorporated the veranda into his overall design, laying out a place for it next to the site of the new cooking shed.

Piailug's master plan envisioned a complete homestead, clean and proper with its own canoes, dwelling houses, and outbuildings. He even wanted me to help him obtain dynamite to blast a channel through the reef before his canoe house, so he could still launch and retrieve canoes during winter and the typhoon season, when heavy surf closes the island.

Despite these ambitious plans, his immediate priority was to finish the canoe he was building for his own Masano clan in Lepotig canoe house. The keel, which he had begun on Woleai, was now finished and joined to the two bow sections. Several planks had been carved, fitted, and temporarily lashed in place. The crossbeams had been roughed out with the chain saw, but since the wood proved too tough for final shaping by adz, the timbers were buried beneath the moist sand to soften them. The canoe was thirty-three feet long and eight feet high from the keel to the *mas*, or "eyes," at either end. It was to be named *Aninga*, meaning "to decorate," and was the largest canoe to have been built on Satawal in living memory.

Just after daybreak on the morning after we returned from West Fayu, the men gathered before my hut. Josede came over; Uurupa and Rovigno stopped by after harvesting their tuba; fat and lazy Lupomai drifted in from his house. Then Piailug hobbled up from the canoe house. Everyone squatted in my doorway sipping coffee as Piailug gave us our marching orders for the day. Josede would stay in Nemanong to help Nemoito with preparations for the new baby. Lupomai would collect dried coconut fronds in the woods and weave them into thatching material to repair the roof of Emilia's hut. Uurupa would gather the rest of the members of Ropitiu to take them to Lepotig canoe house to work. Piailug instructed me to get out his chain saw, see that it was in good working order, and, with Rovigno, fell a large breadfruit tree growing on Masano land in the southern part of the island: he needed timber for *Aninga*.

As we prepared to depart, the third bell of the morning sounded in the main settlement to the south. As every morning now, all the women except Emilia strolled down the path to church, to offer a rosary for Nemoito's sick mother, Kata, who everyone said was close to death.

The tree was very tall and wide and was supported by many thin, blade-like legs at which a handful of men chopped desultorily with axes. Piailug commanded them to move back as the chain saw roared into life, exhaling blue clouds of smoke. I traded cutting with Rovigno, who had learned to operate chain saws on Truk while clearing the devastation wrought by a typhoon. He handled the heavy machine like a toy. Piailug limped about, fiercely directing us to cut various sections of the legs until a cut through the backside sent the forest giant crashing to the ground, shattering the upper limbs and smaller branches. White sea birds fled their roosts in the surrounding palm trees as sunlight flooded into the clearing.

By then it was noon and very hot; Piailug halted work. Rovigno and the rest of the men went to cut their tuba. Piailug led me to the men's pool at Neunemeuyang, where we lolled in the cool, green water. He was satisfied, for three men with a chain saw had accomplished in one morning what usually took six men more than a day.

The next morning he was up before first light, raking the sand beneath the palm trees around his canoe house. I took him a cup of coffee and we sat, without speaking, on a log on the beach. Big cumulus clouds glowed pink and gray in the dawn. A heavy dew covered everything. Carlita drove the three young boys, Howie, Atarino, and Mauricio, into the sea to bathe.

We returned to the log. Rovigno and I trimmed the legs and branches from the trunk, which was about six feet in diameter and thirty feet long. As before, Piailug directed us with tersely barked commands. Though the rest of the men gathered, they could be of little help since they could not run the machine. Inaiman tried but handled it timidly. Piailug soon became impatient and roughly ordered me to take it back.

A feeble breeze had sprung up but waned by noon, and the day became as hot as the one before. Piailug called me from my perch atop the log, where I was trimming a branch, showering myself with sawdust and milky breadfruit sap. As the others went to tend their tuba trees, Piailug took me to the men's pool, where he showed me how to remove the sticky sap with masticated coconut. I was proud to show my teacher I could work hard and use a chain saw skillfully. Surely, I thought, I must be measuring up to his standards. I felt close to Piailug now, as I had the afternoon we bathed in the lagoon at West Fayu. Yet I was always waiting and watching, like an adolescent hanging awkwardly around his father, hoping for some word, sign, or gesture that would answer all my unvoiced questions and concerns.

The next morning I rose early. The coconut trees at the far end of the courtyard were still rooted in beds of darkness. As I sipped a cup of coffee, Carlita suddenly appeared in my doorway, paused with a shy giggle, and slipped inside. Her body formed a lithe brown curve as she kneeled to get rice from a storage bin in the corner. She smiled over her shoulder, then in a shiver was gone—a beauty in a dream. From across the courtyard Nemoito called the dogs with a trilling sound: "*Kurrr-uuuu! Kurr-uuuu!*" Tigiri called the pig: "*Honk! Honk! Honk!*" Emilia emerged from the dark cooking shed with a kettle of steaming water. In a depression in the coral stones next to her hut, she laid a scrap of rubber salvaged from a life raft, filled it, and began to bathe, the steely light shining on her brown skin.

There was no wind and the air was heavy and still. I remembered a similar morning in the Galápagos, just before my future wife was to return to the States and I was to set sail for the Marquesas and Hawaii. We had anchored my boat in a small cove on Barrington island. A low swell hissed against the rocks behind us, while the deserted island warmed in the sun. Then we'd snorkeled along the rocks, with the seals darting up, peering into our face masks, and doubling back, only to do it again and again. We'd seemed on such a far facet of the world, a patch of earth washed only by the sun and the converging currents of the northern and southern Pacific Ocean. I'd imagined living in such a place with my wife, raising children, making a life amid the great, surging forces of nature—the endless sheets of blue sky, the white, shimmering sunlight, the cry of seabirds, the rasping bark of seals.

Thereafter, the image had burned as a greater dream than I ever really acknowledged. Now, on Satawal, I was, in effect, testing its viability. For this was just such a place, a far facet of the earth, undiscovered, washed only by sea sounds and the light from the vast fields of stars.

By now it was lighter. Josede sat in his doorway rolling a cigarette, then crunched across the coral to borrow matches. Uurupa, knife and coconut-shell containers in hand, squatted in my doorway for a moment, the glow of his cigarette pushing the blue light from his face, then continued to harvest his tuba. A chicken nesting behind my camp stove cooed contentedly, her newly hatched chicks peeping beneath her. Emilia sat in the doorway of her hut, tapping grubs from a rotten log onto a short plank. Then she took her pet chick from its basket and shielded it from the dogs while it hopped about eating the grubs.

I was rereading a letter from my father, which had reached Satawal after I'd left the previous year. Uurupa had placed it in the wooden chest in which he kept his few treasured belongings and had forgotten about it. When we had returned from West Fayu, he'd remembered and retrieved the roach-eaten missive. My father had written it on Father's Day, just after a round of long-distance telephone calls to the rest of my brothers and sisters. By then my parents had separated, and the reality of his marriage's dissolution seemed to make him more vulnerable; he sought real contact with his children. He'd written: "We all share a common feeling of pride and awe at what you are doing and where you are doing it. One thing that reaches me always is the certitude that what you are after—and will accomplish—is a valuable contribution, something unique and human. I am touched with a sense that there's some kind of rhythmic extension of my own self, mind, and feelings going on in you, out there in this quest. What a real Father's Day feeling that is!"

The letter touched and buffeted me in different ways. As I had read it through the first time, the previous afternoon, I had steeled myself not to believe it, to keep my shield raised. But now I knew he was voicing his true feelings; he had no veiled wish for my failure. It seemed an important letter, maybe even key to what I was trying to do. That it had just missed me the previous year also seemed significant, as if the letter had been content to wait for a more sympathetic audience.

But if I understood this much, I was not ready to see the corollaries: that perhaps I could carry out a quest he hadn't been able to; that my failure or success would be his as well. Nor was I ready to admit that, ultimately, I would have to make peace with my own father and not Mau Piailug, a surrogate. Increasingly, I would cast Piailug in the role of my father and seek from him something neither man could give me: that sense of myself, in Conrad's words, as a "free man, a proud swimmer striking out for a new destiny."

What I did tell myself was that I had returned to Satawal to finish my studies with Piailug and record as much of the old lore as I could. I had a book to write, and I didn't exactly know what it was about. I thought that if I cast my net wide and collected everything, I would get what I had come for. Accordingly, I had drawn up long lists of questions about navigation, the spirit world, medicine, divination, and the origins and histories of the clans. I had a list of questions about Piailug, too. I wanted to flesh out my biography of him, to get him to reminisce about his childhood and his relationships with his grandfather, father, and sons.

We worked on the log again that morning, and in the afternoon Piailug came to my hut for the first of a series of interviews. The hard sunlight shot through the loose weave of the mat walls, spraying diamonds of light across the dark interior. Hollow blows of the stone breadfruit pounder rang across the burning courtyard as Nemoito and her daughters prepared dinner. He wore a flower lei Emilia had made for him, and with a look of forbearance seated himself on the floor by the doorway, leaning against one of the house posts.

I asked if he remembered any anecdotes about his grandfather, explaining I wanted something charming and instructive to put in my book. He said he'd been thinking since I first mentioned it several days before, but could remember very little:

"I only remember him teaching me the stars," he explained patiently, "when they rose, their relation to one another. He taught me to watch the sun, because each day it rises and sets in a different place. He told me to be aware of the path the sun travels: that of Mailap, Paiiur, or Uliul. He taught me about the shapes of different clouds at sunrise and sunset and explained the meanings of the colors, white, black, red, yellow, all the colors." His voice rose in an expression of gentle explanation as he smoked dreamily, staring through the open door. Then, as often when recalling the past, he summed up the present, speaking carefully but with a tinge of sadness: "But now it has changed. Navigators don't seem to teach the kids. I don't know why, maybe they are stingy or afraid or weak inside. I don't know."

I questioned him about his *pwo* ceremony but he couldn't recall anything more than he had on Saipan. Then I spent some time double-checking biographical details, the names of the canoes he had sailed and the islands he had visited on his annual voyages to Puluwat to see Angora. He answered these trivial questions graciously.

As I approached the end of my list of questions, I suddenly changed subjects. Casting for a more poetic answer, I asked again why he had become a navigator. He answered immediately, his voice firm and patient, as if instructing a well-intentioned youth on some matter for the last time:

"I wanted this because I went with my grandfather and my father. I saw what they did at sea and I wanted to be like them. I could have no respect for myself if I wasn't a navigator, so I went to them to learn."

"But why?" I pressed. He answered quietly, in the same tone of voice.

"I wanted to learn because if I had sons I would teach them; I would instruct them as did the navigators of old. I would teach navigation."

"How does it make you feel now," I asked, aware of intruding, "now that you are older and respected as a *palu*, how does it feel that your sons don't come to ask about navigation?"

"Oh, very bad," he said matter-of-factly. "Very bad. I feel bad in my very meat." Then he tumbled into anger. "Do you know why it is bad? All the people of Satawal, Puluwat, Lamotrek, and Woleai know my reputation; they know I am a navigator and they think that my sons also hold the *palu*. But they don't. It is not inside them." His conclusion was grim and fierce.

I asked if they were unaware of its importance.

They knew navigation was important, he answered, and they weren't lazy. Sometimes they asked if he would teach them, but didn't return for lessons. I suggested perhaps they were afraid of him.

"Why, because I speak harshly?" he asked.

I nodded.

"Maybe that is it," he said, seizing this as a viable explanation.

"Maybe they are afraid. But you know, Steve, I speak harshly because I don't like laziness. Take today. All those young men sat there, watched me, told stories, fidgeted—*aaaaak*! I don't want that kind of man with me. I want to finish work before I sit and talk. That's why I'm harsh."

"Is there anything you can do to change that now?" I thought that if he only knew the talk of light he would control his own anger and communicate with his sons.

"I don't know. I just don't know. I think if they have problems with my anger they should come talk to me about it. I would tell them I'm angry because they aren't learning navigation. I've told them to bring their tuba here so we could discuss navigation at night. They came once or twice but no more. They prefer to drink with people like Iti, eh? People who joke and lie: '*Ca, ca, ca, ca, ca.*' They don't care. It disgusts me and that's why I am angry at them. You, you are from America and you want to learn navigation. But they are people of Satawal, they are my sons, and they don't care." He settled back against the house post, composed himself, lit another cigarette, and popped open a beer. He thought for a moment and then asked, as if testing this theory: "If you think they are afraid of me, then why don't they go to Uurupa? Uurupa is a navigator, too, and he doesn't speak harshly."

"I have watched," I announced. "I think they are afraid because you are often harsh. For me it doesn't matter, because I—I'm a man. I'm a bit older than them and I'm strong."

"Oh?" he asked, as if the scales were falling from his eyes. "How old are you?"

"Thirty-one," I stated proudly.

"Ah, all of thirty-one," he mocked.

My voice faltered: "Yes."

The next night was *poongen uur*, the "night of pulling," when the setting sun appears to pull the full moon from the eastern sea. Big cumulus clouds glowed far in the distance, cut in half by the horizon. It was still and hot. The beach filled with people escaping the heat of the *pwogos* and cooking sheds. Young women in groups of two or three stood waist deep in the shallow *lealulu*, rubbing their long, black, glistening hair, their arms, breasts, and torsos with coconut oil. One by one they tilted their heads back to let their friends rinse them with buckets, the thick ropes of water twisting slowly, striking their foreheads and parting into many rivulets, glowing like fine glass beads in the sun. Mothers scrubbed their children with grated coconut and released them to play in the water. Then they snared their pots and pans, floating around them in squadrons, cleaned them with sand, and slowly washed themselves, chatting with their companions. Finally they rose, sloughing off streams of water, collected their pots, pans, and children, and migrated back up the beach to their villages.

The men smoked their after-dinner cigarettes in the canoe houses. As the red glow of sunset faded, *Tiger* appeared on the horizon, returning from West Fayu after a two-day passage in light wind. Uurupa, Weneto, and two other men set out in the island's sole motorboat to tow the canoe the last few miles, lest they miss flood tide on the reef and have to anchor offshore until morning. The children made great piles of dried coconut fronds on the foreshore and set them blazing in the darkness between the fading of twilight and the rising of the moon above the palm trees. When the canoe arrived, about fifty men gathered to heave her up the line of palm-frond skids to the chiefs' canoe house.

The moon climbed higher. On the beach before each canoe house sat a circle of men, smoking, drinking tuba, and laughing. In the village, the women gossiped in the courtyards while the younger women strolled along the silvered pathways, holding hands.

The moon climbed through the zenith. Josede, Eguman, and I paddled a canoe up to Pegifung to dive for sea urchins. A dozen canoes flecked the shimmering waters, some rafted together while the men talked and smoked, others drifting empty while their owners dove, hooting as they surfaced. The beach lay like white bones beneath the dark, glistening palm trees.

When our canoe was filled, we paddled back to Nemanong, where Emilia, Carlita, and Josephina smashed the shells to remove the gizzard-shaped creatures. The urchins would be simmered in coconut milk to cut their acidic taste, and served for breakfast with roasted or boiled breadfruit.

The next night was *poongen litu*, the "night of going down," when the coconut crabs leave their holes in the forest and skitter down the beach to lay their eggs in the water. The women stay up late to trap the crabs, prized for their taste even above lobster; they barbecue them over coconut husks or boil them in coconut milk.

The third night after the full moon is called the *poongen kilai*, or "night of begin," the beginning of the moonless period. The waning orb rises later and later at night, shrouding the evening in a blackness pierced only by the stunning fields of stars. The older women do not venture forth on these nights, for they are afraid of the spirits, said to love the darkness. Even the dogs, which on most evenings crunch through the coral courtyards barking at all intruders, real or imagined, now stay close to the doors of their masters' houses, as if they, too, are awed by the cold power of the stars. But the young men love these nights, despite any danger of ghosts, for they are not easily detected as they sneak through the villages to wake their girlfriends.

These days of the waning moon were hot and still and cloudless. A young woman in Neyan village gave birth to a healthy boy, and for the next four mornings all work was suspended for *roe*. Since there was no wind to move the canoes, Piailug directed fish drives on the reef.

In the afternoons he expected everyone to work on the canoe in Lepotig, but perhaps because it was *leraak* and there was abundant tuba, or because of the festive atmosphere of the *roe*, only the older men took their work seriously. Some of the young men came; others never showed. Piailug said very little. He complained privately to me that though it was the young men who had most wanted him to direct them in constructing the new canoe, they were the very ones not working.

In the tuba circle on the evening of the second day of *roe*, Josede began a long, drunken story in English about his first trip to high school on Ulithi, which the students call the "Island of the States" because they think it to be just like America. Piailug quickly got bored and began telling me about the first voyage of the *Hokule'a*. The experiment was designed by anthropologist Ben Finney and researcher David Lewis to determine whether the ancient Polynesians could have made round-trip voyages from Tahiti to Hawaii in their double-hulled sailing canoes. Racial tensions developed between the Hawaiian deckhands and the white afterguard. Before they set sail, Piailug asked them all, in accordance with Micronesian custom, to cast away their differences and respect one another as family. The crew didn't follow his bidding. Upon sighting Tahiti, one of the Hawaiians led his fellows on a rampage, beating up David Lewis and Ben Finney. "Almost me, too," Piailug laughed, "but I stayed neutral; between the haoles and the Hawaiians."

At nine, when the tuba was finished, he told everyone to go home quietly and sleep, so tomorrow we could be strong at work. Then he took my hand in his gnarled paw and, hobbling on his gouty foot, had me help him up the broad, moonlit beach.

There were still men in front of Woleatu canoe house, and as we passed by they called for us to join them. Matto, Joseph, Iti, Unghaur (an elder of the Katamang clan), and some of the older teen-agers moved to make space for us on their mats. The Southern Cross had just arced through its upright position and now reclined toward the west.

After a cup of tuba had been passed to all, Piailug pointed to the Southern Cross, which was nearly half-set. Everyone nodded or grunted. "So?" he asked. "What star is rising?" No one could answer.

"Do you know, Matto?" Piailug directed his challenging eyes to the young navigator. Matto nervously shifted his great bulk to look at the constellation, but couldn't answer the question.

"What about you, Joseph?" Joseph fidgeted with his toes.

"Geriger?" Piailug turned to his relative who, when drunk, always bragged he was Piailug's equal. He didn't know either. Piailug questioned the old man Unghaur, who stared straight back at him, his eyes glistening, seemingly ashamed not to know. Mau looked around the circle.

"We will do 'the appearance of the stars,'" he announced with quiet intensity. "When Poop is straight up Mun is rising. When Poop is half-set, Mailap is rising. Otherwise, when one star is setting it faces its part-ner, which is rising; when that star is setting, the other star is rising. It goes like this: with the appearance of Mun, Maan; with the appearance of Maan, Mun; with the appearance of Mailap, Paiinemaanemefung; with the appearance of Paiinemaanemefung, Mailap . . ." He continued through the whole system. Though he paused several times, no one spoke.

"This knowledge comes from Satawal," he concluded. "The old navigators discovered it and we taught it to Puluwat, Pulusuk, Pulap, and Tamatam. The eastern islands learned it from us."

After this, everyone went home. Piailug and I continued up the beach to Nemanong and sat for a time in the courtyard, watching the moon push back the shadows as it filled the stones with light. It occurred to me that he had tonight voiced his ideal of the fully realized navigator, a man who fulfilled the precepts set forth in the talk of light; that he aspired to be the father of his crew, to teach, to serve, to lose his ego. The thought was fleeting, almost subliminal, and I quickly shoved it aside to lunge ahead, searching for some more dramatic answer to the enigma of Piailug.

After the tuba circle the next evening, Piailug, Josede, and I gathered in my hut to drink and talk. Nemoito sat outside, her legs stretched straight in front of her, taking advantage of the strong lantern light to weave new coconut-frond mats for the canoe house. Piailug quietly told Josede I wanted to interview him alone; the young man remained a little longer, then excused himself and crunched off across the courtyard to Emilia, waiting in their hut. The waning moon rose, the lantern hissed out its spray of light, and the coconut fronds whispered softly, shuttling back and forth in Nemoito's hands. It was flood tide, and a gentle swell crossed the reef unbroken to wash the sands before the canoe house.

Piailug was saying that the critical departure from the traditional course of a young man's seafaring education now occurred when he went away to high school. The first group of Satawalese to graduate learned some navigation, the second group less, and the third none at all. For a time he, too, attended high school with his oldest son, Antonio.

"At the time I planned to learn English and everything about America," he said. "I was going to throw away my knowledge of navigation and adopt American customs." But several months into the school year he became discouraged. "The young men learned fast because their heads were fresh, but mine was too old and slow." I asked if he liked high school.

"No," he answered equivocally, chewing on a salted reef fish he had just pulled from his handbasket ("My chaser," he had quipped in English). At first he liked it, but soon it became clear that learning new skills would be a long process. In re-educating himself he would lose his skills and identity as a navigator, and in the end have nothing: his "head and stomach would be dark."

In the ensuing conversation he articulated his concept that "darkness" was ignorance of one's own traditions. He saw two major forces of cultural change, Christianity and Western education, both of which he felt had been forced on the islanders. Christianity was promoted by the chiefs, education by the federal and state governments. Schooling was mandatory through the elementary level and encouraged through the secondary level. What angered him was the unexamined push to have all children educated, regardless of their aptitude and inclination and without considering the impact on the island. He held the chiefs responsible for allowing a generation of youngsters to grow up without skills, values, and traditions the islanders relied upon to live.

He had allowed his own children to go to high school because initially he thought it would be good. When they finished, he expected them to learn navigation, boatbuilding, fishing, and so on: "But I watched them return, and it was not good. They never came to learn from me. This happened with all the kids, not just mine." He attributed this to the fact that students from all islands board together with poor supervision. Away from the calming and disciplining influence of the elders, and the close social strictures of their island, they are not socialized as Satawalese. Nor are they socialized as Americans: they get caught somewhere in between. "I don't know if it is the same in America," he concluded ruefully, "but by the time our students finish high school they are very, very crazy."

After the second group of students returned, Piailug and some other parents wanted to keep their children on the island. But the chiefs told them high school was mandatory, and if they refused to comply they would be locked in jail on Yap. Now, however, he was determined that Bonefacio, who had just graduated from elementary school, would not go to high school at the end of the summer. I had mentioned that, on West Fayu, Bonefacio had told me he much preferred Hawaii to Satawal, which was too small. Piailug and Nemoito discussed this for some minutes, speaking so rapidly I could not keep up. Then Piailug explained that they thought Bonefacio had gotten spoiled on Hawaii. He would not, he reiterated, allow the boy to go to high school with the others this year.

If Western education contributed to the erosion of seafaring skills on the island, Christianity had attacked the taboo system, which once regulated nearly every aspect of life on Satawal. The taboos of people stipulated that women must *aparog*, or bend at the waist in respect to men; men must *aparog* to chiefs. The taboos of the island ensured adequate supplies of breadfruit and timber by allowing breadfruit trees to be cut only in summer; banana trees, which provide fiber for weaving skirts, could be cut only in the month of Uliul, before the new moon appeared in the west at sunset. The taboos of fishing controlled the annual fishing cycle.

An extensive series of taboos regulated sailing activities. One canoe could not leave a fleet; if it was essential to do so, the *palu* drank a magic potion and recited a chant to Anumwerici. It was taboo to repair a broken mast on another island, since the spirit living inside would be offended; if this contingency arose, the whole crew drank a potion while the most revered navigator of the island performed a magic chant. After returning from a long voyage, the navigator and his crew were sequestered in their own canoe house for four days. If the *palu* had to leave, he took a "medicine of the meeting" enabling him to encounter women and children before the ritual period of separation had expired. The *palu* could never go to the menstrual house or perform work on that structure. The taboos of the navigator gave him power, status, and respect, but also held him responsible to his crew and his island. The taboos of voyaging bound the crew to the navigator and kept a fleet together. The ritual period of confinement after a sailing trip eased the transition from sea to land, slowly releasing the crew's bonds to one another and their leader. Perhaps it also helped to restrict navigational information to the members of a canoe house, for sailing directions and the locations of islands, reefs, and *epar* were closely guarded. (There was another motive for keeping sailing information secret. Sorcerers wielding "bad magic" could reportedly destroy a canoe at sea through "stabbing," a ritual wherein the magician drew an effigy on a coconut tree with red-clay dye and uttered a deadly chant mentioning the seaway on which the canoe was traveling. For this reason both the names of the seaways and the destinations of canoes were tightly guarded.)

Piailug explained that the taboos functioned as a legal system, governing social and ecological behavior. He felt that without them, and without the status and authority granted to the chiefs, navigators, and elders to enforce them, the island and its leadership was falling into confusion. "The chiefs in the old days were wise," Piailug said without malice; "they watched over the sea, the island, and the people to make certain all was good. But now they no longer do this." In the 1950s, for example, the chiefs eliminated the taboo on fishing Wenimung, until then a fish reserve. Even when, several years later, fish stocks on the reef became dangerously low, the taboo was not reinstated. He concluded: "The taboos kept both the sea and the island healthy, kept them alive."

Now it was very late. Nemoito had finished weaving and sat atop her pile of new mats, smoking and listening to our conversation. Piailug and I had finished the bottle of tuba Josede had left for us, and since it seemed a special occasion I broke out my single bottle of Chivas and we sipped it slowly from coffee cups. He and Nemoito talked about the next day's activities, and after a minute or two, seeing that I was leafing through my notebook, he nodded his head as if to indicate he was ready for my next question.

More to get the conversation going again than anything else, I asked, "So you wanted to become a navigator because of the advantages of the taboos of the navigator—so you could have the status of a chief?"

Piailug answered clearly, definitively, and reassuringly, as if to a deserving son:

"You must understand, Steve, if a chief sails with me he is considered a member of the crew and not the leader. When we arrive at an island, *I* will go ashore first. The chiefs of that island will wait for *me* in their canoe house, will listen as *I* tell them of our voyage and give news of other islands. Our chief must stay on the canoe. Why? Because the chief is of the *land*, but the *palu* is of the *sea*." He paused and went on:

"In our custom, the canoe is the mother; it holds the food, holds the crew. The navigator is the father because he distributes the food to his sons, the crew. At sea, the *palu* is the chief, the father, the elder.

"To be a *palu* you must have three qualities: *pwerra, maumau,* and *reipy* (fierceness, strength, and wisdom). Did Maanusuuk teach you this? If you are fierce you are a *palu*. If you are not fierce you are not a *palu*: you will be afraid of the sea, of storms, of reefs; afraid of whales, sharks; afraid of losing your way—you are not a *navigator*. With fierceness you will not die, for you will face all danger. *Maumau* is almost the same. It means 'strength directed by thought'; strength in your meat.

"The knowledge of navigation brings all three: fierceness, strength, and wisdom. Fierceness, strength, and wisdom, Steve, that is a *palu*: a *palu* is a *man*."

14

The moon waned to a sliver that rose late at night and hovered over us by day. We finished the first *roe*, began a second when another baby was born, then a third when Mesailuke's wife had a son. There was little wind, and the sticky heat was soothed only by the rainsqualls creeping slowly across the sea and island. We fished the reef by morning and worked in the canoe house in the afternoon. Progress on the log came to a halt when we ran out of gas and oil for the chain saw. Piailug said our voyaging plans depended on the wind and the condition of Nemoito's mother.

Meanwhile, Emilia was coming to term. Taumuan, the irascible master of medicine who had married into the Katamang clan, determined it was time to perform the *enas*, a magic ritual to protect the mother and child from the evil spirits of the sea, which inhabit all floating things: sticks, nuts, logs, even plastic bottles and cast-off zoris.

One morning before daybreak the old man woke me to watch him make the potion he would later administer to Emilia. He had gathered a variety of leaves and small twigs, which he now minced and tied into two medicine balls with a burlaplike sheath of palm fronds. Around the balls he tied young coconut shoots to form the arms of human effigies. The large one, about the size of a baseball, represented an adult, he said; the small, golf-ball-sized one, a child. Then he wanted me to make him coffee before the ceremony began.

Shortly, all the members of the Katamang and Masano clans began to arrive in Nemanong. Emilia, along with several other pregnant women and their children, and the rest of the women sat on the grass around the canoe house. The men milled around on the path behind them. Taumuan had Piailug's sons pour the juice of twenty coconuts into a large stewpot and he added the medicine balls. He chanted over the pot for a time, then pronounced it ready, instructing the expectant mothers to suck some juice from the large medicine ball and rub it on their stomachs. Their children were to suck juice from the small medicine ball and rub it on their foreheads. After this, the pregnant women each drank two cups of the brew. The rest of us were given one cup each. I took mine anticipating some gruesome taste, but found it very cool and refreshing, like mint tea. During the entire ceremony, Piailug weeded his lawn with his characteristic intensity: he drained his cup in one gulp, then returned to his weeding.

That evening Taumuan repeated the entire process, whereupon he declared the mothers safe from spirits. Despite the *enas*, however, Tigiri forbade Josede to fish at night, for fear that the sea spirits would follow him home to eat Emilia.

During this time I had been asking Taumuan about various aspects of the spirit world. In particular I was curious about *katoepaipai*, the magic chant to call to the island floating logs and the abundance of fish that school beneath them.[*] He chanted while placing packets of special leaves and grasses under coral heads on the reef. The chant was very powerful, he cautioned, and I should never repeat it; he would teach me only because I had been adopted by Piailug.

I transcribed the chant and, with Josede's and Piailug's help, translated it. When I asked to whom it was addressed and why it was effective, Taumuan only squirmed and said again that it was to call the

---

[*]Tuna tend to school around floating logs. Even modern tuna seiners equipped with helicopters and electronic fish-finding gear will mark logs with radio transmitters and continually check for fish.

logs. At this I looked disappointed, so he said he would tell me a story that would enlighten me both about *katoepaipai* and about the function of the *enas*.

He told a very long story about the evil spirit Sauwenima, "master of all things that float at sea," who lived beneath a log on Satawal's beach. When a pregnant woman came down to bathe, he "ate" her child, after which the woman sickened and died. One day the chief's beautiful daughter came. Sauwenima couldn't bring himself to harm her, for he was in love.

When they married, he left his log to live with his wife and her parents. The first time he saw her roasting fish in the fire, he asked why they fed their child first, for he thought the fire was their son. He tried some of the cooked fish and even ate some pounded taro, and for a time he became a real human. He provided well for his family; each day his wife would find their fish by the water's edge.

But one day Sauwenima stopped calling fish, for doing so made him homesick. When his wife complained they were hungry, he became angry. He took the chief's canoe to sea, tied his arms with young coconut shoots, and uttered a chant. Soon the sea was filled with drifting logs. "Logs, give me fish!" he demanded, and the logs did so. When the canoe could hold no more, he announced he was leaving. But first he taught his son a chant to call the floating logs, though cautioning him never to call his father, or he would die.

Later, to aid Nemoito's mother, Kata, Taumuan would perform another medicinal ritual called "basket of spirits." For this procedure he first donned a coconut-frond headband with two antennalike fronds projecting in front as protection against the spirits. Then he collected red coral, dried seaweed, and pepper leaves in a basket, heated small black basaltic stones (called *fairon*), nestled them amid the ingredients, and placed the smoking basket under a sheet with the old lady. His eyes transfixed, still wearing his spirit hat, he wafted a leafy branch over her while uttering a chant. When the basket stopped smoking, he declared the spirits to have been frightened from her body. I asked if the medicine would keep her from dying. "She will still die," he answered thoughtfully, "but little by little."

Kata did get better, although it is difficult to say whether her recovery was due to the "basket of spirits" or the course of antibiotics she received from Epailuk the medic.

After Emilia's *enas* ceremony I spent many afternoons quizzing Piailug and Uurupa, but mostly Taumuan, about the nature of the spirit world. In the past, at least, the metaphysical world of the spirits was so integrated with the physical world of humans that scarcely a distinction could be made between them. Virtually all fields of human endeavor—navigation, canoe building, cultivation, fishing, even birth and aging—had associated magical rituals that were considered essential.

One afternoon I tried to get Taumuan to explain exactly who was who in the spirit world. When I pointed out the contradiction in Rongerig and Rongelap's being the sons of Palulap, founder of navigation, and at the same time being Fanur and Wareyang, sons of Anumwerici, Palulap's son, he just shrugged, squirmed, and claimed he didn't know. This perplexed me until he said that all he knew came from the old stories. There was no fixed organizational chart of deities, I finally realized—only a collection of stories. After this, I gave up asking structural questions and spent a number of afternoons with Taumuan and Josede, and sometimes Piailug, recording and translating the folk tales.

One of the most beautiful of these stories I heard first from Piailug. On Yap I had been told that dolphins and whales were sacred creatures. One clan on Puluwat was even said to have come from dolphins. When I asked Piailug about this he just nodded and said there was a story, which he told, watching me guardedly.

On Puluwat is a fresh-water pool called Galigi. Late each night, while the village slept, dolphins would come from the sea, slip out of their skins to become women, and bathe in the pool. As the dawn rose, they took their skins, walked back down the path, and returned to the sea.

A man named Analungifir noticed grated coconut floating in the pool each morning. He wondered who had been bathing there. One night he hid himself and beheld the dolphin ladies. While they bathed he stole one of the skins and hid it. Dawn came and the dolphins had to return to the sea. But the one whose skin was missing was left behind, crying.

Analungifir took her for his wife and they had two children: a boy, "Fin of Dolphin," and a girl, "She, Fin of Dolphin." After a time, the man took a lover. One day the dolphin lady noticed a bundle suspended from the rafters of their house—her skin—and she knew she had been stolen from the sea.

She bathed her two children in Galigi, powdered them with turmeric, and spread the powder on the posts and beams of the house. Some claim she took her children with her; others say she left after teaching them the lore of the dolphins, to call her back when they wished. No one knows which ending is true, but there is still a clan on Puluwat that believes it came from the dolphins. With the lore of the dolphins, it is said they can divine the future and forecast the weather. When a dolphin dies, they know one of their own will soon die, too.

Now it seemed that at every opportunity Piailug discussed navigation. At the tuba circle one evening he explained weather signs. Some of the young men listened; others talked and laughed among themselves. As it grew dark, someone asked about Pookof Woleai. He obliged by repeating the sequence of birds and fish, stopping to describe them when questioned: Taimeang, a pod of small dolphins between Ifaluk and Elato, bearing rising Maragar from Woleai; Uulegool, one green leaf of the *gool* tree, bearing rising Mailapellifung from Woleai; Paiiroro Parowa, a *pwe* of birds forty or fifty miles north of Woleai. ("Parowa was a navigator who became very sick," Uurupa added. "As a gift of thanks to those who nursed him, he revealed this *epar*, a *pwe* of thirty or forty birds, brown, with black on the feathers.")

When Pookof Woleai was complete, Piailug cleared his throat to speak formally: "All right, we have done Pookof Woleai and that is good. Yet—I don't know how the others feel on this matter, Assaf, Uurupa, Motch, and Napota [the older men in the circle]—I am afraid. I am afraid because there are those who learn some navigation but don't sail. Others don't even learn, they just sit. I am afraid that after Rewena, after Ikimai, after Muanirik and Regaliang, after me and Uurupa, there will be no more navigators here. Then who will sail to catch turtles and fish? Who will sail to other islands so we can be with our relatives when they are sick?"

The older men were flattered, because Piailug had courteously included them in his address. The younger men cast their eyes down; some nodded in agreement.

"In the old times," he continued, "we worked during the day, and when we took a break to smoke or drink a little tuba, we questioned our masters about navigation. In the evening tuba circle it was the same: we always asked about navigation. But now it is not like that, and that's why I am afraid."

Assaf, drunk, began to flounder through *aroom*, naming the stars and their reciprocals until he lapsed into a confounded stupor.

"Good! Good!" Uurupa said sarcastically.

"That is not *aroom*!" Piailug scoffed. He repeated *aroom* very fast until he, too, made a mistake. Uurupa laughed his deep, rich laugh and teased his older brother: "What is this, Mau? Next you will have the Fuesemagut partners with rising Mailap!" This broke the tension and everyone laughed, including Piailug.

When things settled down, Uurupa urged everyone to start learning the talk of the sea. Piailug backed him up. I made a speech in which I sought to dispel the misconception that Western navigation was somehow easy since it used charts and instruments. Yes, I admitted, some aspects were easier, but one still had to study the techniques on land, then master them at sea. In the end, a person could know all about navigation yet would never become a navigator unless he put himself to the test of finding land. Western navigational techniques and tools might be different, I said, but the test was the same.

Piailug proclaimed my remarks to be true. The young men nodded and vowed they would learn. As the last of the tuba was passed around, Piailug went over the work schedule.

"Tomorrow morning," he said in a rich, almost sentimental voice, "we will fish for *roe*. At noon we will tend our tuba trees. In the afternoon we will work in the canoe house. We will drink a little, work, perhaps discuss navigation. That way it will be good; we will further our work as one crew. That is how it used to be." He concluded in a mellow voice filled with melancholy.

For the next week the work proceeded well, and in the evenings Piailug, Uurupa, and their sons and sons-in-law gathered at Nemanong to drink tuba and discuss navigation. One evening there were nine of us: Piailug, Uurupa, Josede, Lupomai, Mesailuke, Inaiman, Rovigno, Paul's brother Eddy, and me. Piailug discussed star courses from Truk to the surrounding islands. He claimed the course from the northeast pass of Truk Lagoon to Pis island was halfway between Sarapul and Tumur. Others disagreed. I suggested we could check it easily on my charts. Eddy and Rovigno urged me into my hut to show them. I spread the charts out on the mat floor, and for the next hour the two young men asked questions about the chart's compass rose, the use of the dividers and parallel rules, the significance of latitude and longitude, how to translate a course on the chart to one on the compass, and magnetic variation.

Meanwhile, the drinking circle broke up and the men went home to sleep. The next day Rovigno told me he had been too interested in our discussion to notice the others had left. Piailug asked me bitterly, "Why will Rovigno spend his time learning your navigation and never ask me about mine?" A subliminal voice told me I'd made a mistake, but I ignored it.

The next night, Piailug tested Mesailuke's mastery of Wofanu Gaferut. Mesailuke knew it well. Next Piailug grilled him about the sailing directions for the voyage from Lamotrek to Olimarao, but disagreed with his answers. Mesailuke, who had made the passage, finally convinced his father, who had not, that his sailing directions were correct. Piailug rocked back on his crossed legs with pleasure: "All right, Mesailuke, you have learned well!" Mesailuke glowed momentarily in his father's praise.

Then Piailug said: "Steve wants to learn the talk of sailing by going to Pikelot and Puluwat. I want you and all my sons to come here at night to learn. Then I want you to sail. You and Inaiman have told me you are ready to make your first voyage. I have waited and waited; when will you sail?"

Mesailuke avoided a direct answer. I anticipated an attack from Piailug, but instead he sat back, slightly out of the circle, as if to remove himself from the arena of potential conflict. The talk veered off into other subjects, and at last he closed the evening with a discussion of the following day's work schedule.

Later that week the *Microspirit* returned and all work stopped. The men began drinking as soon as they had collected their morning tuba. By noon everyone was drunk. Piailug bought a case of beer and a bottle of vodka and ordered one of the young men to go fetch the chiefs: "Tell them to come drink with me," he roared, "drink my vodka, drink my beer!" Finally Rewena came to drink and sing voyaging songs with him and the rest of the men.

Next morning I asked him when we could talk again. He said that aside from the talk of the skies, which we had been working on in the mornings and evenings, there was little he had left to teach me. Then he upended the bottle of tuba he carried, chugged half of it, and walked away.

A chill had crept over our relationship that was all the more disappointing because it came at the end of our lessons, when I expected warmth. If Piailug was the father I wished I had, I was the son he wanted. "You are a tenacious and dedicated student," he had told me one afternoon, "while my sons are apathetic." If he was the navigator who held the lost secrets of old Oceania, I was the child of the modern West who, as a navigator myself, could record and preserve his legacy in the very culture that would supplant his.

But I was not from Satawal, nor he from the West; I was not his son, nor he my father. Our relationship had, inevitably, to confront this, which would mean the fiction we'd both enjoyed would collapse. Neither of us wanted that to happen now. As long as he had more to teach me, and I had more to learn, we could both postpone the reckoning.

That he aspired to an ideal of manhood which fused together the three pivotal qualities of fierceness, strength, and wisdom completely escaped me. I was certain he didn't know or care about the *itang*, which both puzzled and disappointed me. Yet I could not allow my cherished image of him as a hero to be tarnished—nor would I admit that my program might be failing because I was trying to force him into a role of my own casting, one that he had no intention of playing.

By mid-afternoon the captain, having finally succeeded in getting all his passengers aboard and the drunken islanders ashore, raised his anchor and steamed away. The glowing accounts in my journal and the letters I had just sent off to my wife via the ship were full of evasions.

15

Next morning, my alarm woke me before dawn. I stumbled into the bushes behind my hut to urinate, then went to wake Piailug. The dogs sleeping outside the canoe house pulled their noses from beneath their tails to sniff.

He slept in the doorway, Nemoito beside him. Kids lay heaped upon one another like puppies. Carlita and Marcia slept in the far corner.

"It's four o'clock, Mau," I said, leaning over the dogs to shake him. "Let's go watch the stars." He sat up, scratched himself all over, and took a drink of water from a teapot resting on an upturned bowl by his mat. One of the small children woke, whimpered, and fell back to sleep. Then Piailug struggled through the doorway and stood, putting weight cautiously on his foot as his toes felt for their place in his zoris. Together we staggered down the dark beach, our feet sinking in the soft sand. The dogs scampered ahead to sniff each crab hole still unmolested by the tide, then doubled back to snarl and play at our feet until Piailug hissed them away. The beach curved around to the east, where the last crescent of the waning moon cast a thin, mournful streak on the sea. The Pleiades twinkled like the lanterns of distant fishing canoes.

"Maybe we won't see Ul," he said, referring to Aldebaran, the fighting star now active. Scrutinizing my star book in the beam of my flashlight, I said I thought it would rise. He dragged some palm fronds from the bushes and told me to sit with him to wait. The stars making up Cu shone in a delicate string high overhead, with Cassiopeia at the dolphin's tail and Alpheratz at its dorsal fin. I identified other stars, Alimatau, Piing, Sepie, and Ceuta, pleased with myself for how much I'd learned.

Just before five, he pointed to a star glittering on the horizon, through a gauzelike sheath of clouds. "There," he said, "I think that is Ul. Now it is finished storming. Next is Uliul. When the new moon is coming up from the west at sunset, Uliul will be beneath the sea at dawn. Then Uliul will fight."

A light wind springing up from the northeast swept away the smells of the taro swamp and salt pan, replacing them with the fresh scent of the sea. The wind's touch was so light I shivered.

"A little wind from rising Vega," I observed. Piailug pointed to a big, flat, dark bank of clouds in the northeast and speculated there was wind inside it. Perhaps this afternoon we would have good wind from the northeast. I asked about a similar bank of clouds, now glowing in the dawn.

"Those clouds mean good weather," he answered patiently. "The light that appears to float on top of the water is a sign for good weather now." A brilliant, spear-shaped hole in the clouds was left over from the rain of the last few days, he said, as was a large cumulus with an anvil-shaped top.

I asked if the moon fought as well as the stars.

"No," he answered without scorn, "it does not fight. But we must now wait for it to rise from the west at sunset. Then for five days the stars will fight a little. But between the fighting of Ul and Uliul and the waning and waxing moon, we will have good weather. Good weather for sailing to Pikelot," he added as an afterthought. "Maybe I'll ask the crew. If they agree to go, we'll leave this week. Next month the wind will come from the west, bringing big, big waves on Pik and Satawal. Now Nemoito's mother seems a bit better, so it's a good time to go."

Apinallay, the seaway between Satawal and Puluwat, began to shimmer in the dawn. Though the sun was still beneath the horizon, our morning was finished.

We arose early again the next morning. On the walk up the beach,

Piailug stopped to squat in the darkness. A large, dark cloud was about to engulf the island, and he casually asked if I thought it would rain. I scrutinized the cloud carefully, wanting to give the right answer. I could feel a wave of cool air against my chest as the cloud approached, but if it was going to rain, I reasoned, this wave would be even cooler and would be followed by a distinctive smell. I said it wouldn't rain. He grunted approvingly and washed himself in the sea, and together we teetered up the dark beach. The skinny end of the moon hung in the sky. Above it poised the delicate Maragar, and underneath, the reddish Ul.

"Uliul is still beneath the sea," he concluded after some study. "I think it will rise later than the sun." After a silence, he said, wistfully, "In the last two years these stars fought very little, even in winter. We sailed whenever we wanted." I asked if the stars were getting less powerful, and he admitted that maybe they were. Then I scanned the southern sky, asking the names of Capricornus and Fomalhaut. They had no names, Piailug said, they were just two among the stars, the "people in the sky."

The evening gatherings at Nemanong had ceased since the visit of the ship, and as before, we met on the beach in front of Ootenap canoe house to drink tuba. Piailug said little that evening, the tuba ran out early, and we went back to Nemanong. Back in my hut we summed up the essential criteria by which forecasts are made from the clouds.

"Bad weather always comes from the fighting stars," he reminded me. "If a star is fighting, then you must keep that in mind when you observe the clouds. Watch carefully for signs of bad weather."

But with respect to the clouds themselves, he said, first priority is given to their color. Deep red in either morning or evening warns of rain. Pink or rose indicates good weather. The blue of the ocean means wind or squalls, whereas blue lighter than that of the sky is benign. The presence of cumulo-nimbus at sunset or sunrise indicates bad weather; spear-shaped strato-cumulus mean wind. A massive cumulus is called an *imwelliyang*, a "wind house," and is thought to store the wind. If one sees a "wind house" at dawn or dusk, one can expect the wind to blow from the direction in which it lies.

Second priority is given to the height of the hazy band on the horizon, a band of "smoke." If this band is high and descending quickly, strong wind is the forecast; if low and descending slowly, light or variable wind is forecast. Clouds on the horizon may be used for this test also: if they descend quickly, stronger wind is anticipated; if slowly, lighter wind is anticipated.

Piailug suddenly changed the subject to turtles, for he had called a meeting with the chiefs for the next day to discuss reinstituting the taboo on taking small turtles and eggs. He remembered some pictures he had seen of islands in the western Caribbean covered with turtles. I showed him these islands on a map. Once it had been the same on West Fayu and Pikelot, he said: each night fifty or sixty turtles would crawl up on the beach to lay their eggs in the sand. He wanted me to come to the meeting with him to explain that in the United States it is taboo to hunt turtles, and to urge the chiefs to reopen the turtle hatchery on West Fayu.[*]

The conversation wandered to other subjects. Eventually I asked if he had remembered anything else about his grandfather.

"No," he said gloomily. "No one asks me about this, so I've forgotten a great deal." His voice lost its harsh edges, becoming soft and dreamlike.

"Sometimes I try to remember what he taught me," he went on, seemingly lost in a stream of recollection. "I would be very wise if I could remember it all. But because I was so young I have forgotten—the knowledge has gone dark inside me. . . . No more now," he concluded decisively, seeming to shake himself from sentimentality. "It has *changed* here! My generation was taught that *palu* was the highest goal; to be a *palu* was to be a man. We strove to learn it. And now, nothing." He lowered his voice confidentially: "Remember when we sat before Ootenap? Uurupa and I said that someone must learn *sennap* and *palu*—when we die someone *must* hold the skills. But nobody said, 'Yes, I will learn,' or 'I want to hold the knowledge of *palu*.'"

"Are you afraid for your sons?" I asked.

"I'm afraid for everyone's sons," he answered. Then, as he went on, his voice broke and his eyes glistened: "I want my sons to sail. I don't know when I will die. Yesterday I talked to Mesailuke and to Inaiman. I said I wanted them to sail while you were still here, so you could write in your book that my sons are navigators. They claim they are ready to sail, but I wonder, I wonder if they really can."

---

[*]This meeting resulted in setting a fifty-dollar fine for anyone who took small turtles or eggs. I was flattered that Piailug had taken me with him as an expert witness.

He was very sad, as if he had said it all to me before but it still hurt to say it. I asked if he thought Bonefacio and Howie would learn, or if they would want to leave the island also. Piailug answered in a tired, resigned voice, as if he had probed his heart for me again and again and now there were no more recesses into which to look, nothing left to say:

"I know you are concerned about my kids, like you are a father or a brother to them. Maybe someday they will—I don't know— maybe they will look inside your book and say, 'Steve wrote this book and . . . and my father knew all this.' I want you to do your book, but I would rather they learned from me. I want my sons to learn so they will have a name. If they have sons they will teach them so they will know. From the first father through all the fathers, navigation has come down to me. When I am dead, I want it to go on. If after me there is no more, it will be as if the navigators have died. My name will die, and the names of my fathers."

I woke at three in the morning, shivering. The metal roof of the shed sucked the heat into the stars. I was dreaming of a fishing camp; brown, tough men slept on the coarse coral stones of a distant island. I slept next to a leathery navigator, a harsh and gentle man. Maybe it was Piailug or his father or grandfather. I was a young kid, naked, like Howie. I wrapped myself tighter in my sheet and fell back to sleep.

At four I woke again, when my alarm went off. I got Piailug and we stumbled up the beach. The last of the moon had not yet risen; Maragar and Ul, Mun, Mailap, Sepie clung to the thick, clear air like gems to blue velvet. He pointed out the moon in the east, a tiny sliver called *arefu*, "shape of star." He said tomorrow it would be gone. Some spear-shaped strato-cumulus clouds had expanded into smoky ellipses, which he said signified bad weather would come next week, when Uliul fought. Several shooting stars burned through the sky; then a satellite appeared under Sepie, sped along the base of Ceuta and away. He said that when the first satellite appeared only a few men from Lugarig canoe house saw it. The next day they asked their friends if they'd seen the stars move. More people watched the next night, and still more the night after. Soon the whole island waited for the stars to move. Some said that in Christian teachings such a star would cause great change. Others thought it portended the death of Satawal.

"Is this true?" Piailug asked, very seriously.

"No," I assured him. But it was.

With oil and gasoline obtained from the *Microspirit*, we resumed work on the log for *Aninga*. Piailug strode around in his characteristic manner, jaw set and teeth grinding, conversing only to bark orders. The log, easily weighing five tons, had to be rolled one way, sliced down the middle, and then rolled the other way to complete the cut. I proposed an intricate system to increase the mechanical advantage of our single, half-ton-capacity chain hoist, like those used in garages to lift engines from automobiles. Piailug snapped at me to set it up. The ropes strained and the log teetered. Most of the young men sat in the shade, refusing to help. Piailug told me to stop.

"This method is good," I protested, wanting to try again.

"Enough!" he roared. "We will use two ropes and two chain hoists." He sent groups of the younger men off to various canoe houses to fetch the requisite material. When it arrived he worked in an impatient fury, dismantling my system of ropes while cursing his gouty hand. As the physics of his plan unfolded, I had to admit it was better than mine. Still, I had tasted the bitter rebuke some of the young men must feel when they have done their best and still not measured up.

When all was ready, he sent those still squatting on the sidelines flying into motion with barked insults of "Penis!" The log trembled and rolled gently into its new position. He ordered me to begin slicing it down the middle with the chain saw.

At noon, a young boy brought us a bowl of rice. Piailug told me to eat, so I picked out the ants and gobbled it. Then I busied myself trying to remove a hangnail with the tip of my mechanical pencil. He put on his reading glasses, seized his machete, and threatened to cut off my foot. Then he laughed and delicately shaved away the offending toenail.

I spent the rest of the afternoon cutting the log. At three-thirty he called me off, saying it was time to drink tuba. I collapsed on the carpet of palm leaves in the shade, rising only to drink. The forest, delivered of the roar of the machine, echoed with the hoots and guffaws of the men teasing one another. Big vertical cumulus clouds scudded across the hole in the forest canopy, lidding it with brilliant white one moment, pelagic blue the next. Piailug sat alone, drinking and smoking.

When the group broke up to cut their evening tuba, I wandered over to examine the log. He followed and we discussed the series of cuts that would produce two fine, strong planks for the new canoe.

Mau had seemed cross with me, and now it had passed. I assumed he was just impatient with progress on the log. I continued to ask him to reveal his most intimate feelings, and he continued to do so, honoring his original pledge to teach me whatever I wanted to learn. I offered little of myself in return. It never occurred to me that I might learn what I wished about him without battering down the delicate barriers that protected his dignity.

In the morning, Uurupa said he would soon leave for West Fayu. These were the last weeks before the onset of the west wind, and I was worried that I would not be able to complete my sailing program. I urged him to postpone his voyage and urged Piailug to take the canoe to Pikelot, so I could observe the navigational procedures to reach that island. Uurupa graciously agreed. Piailug—although Pikelot lay sixty miles directly upwind, making it a much more arduous passage than to West Fayu—agreed as well, and would do it without compass or timepiece (although he would carry them as a backup) to demonstrate navigation by stars, waves, and birds. We would take *Aloha*, for *Suntory*, in need of a new hull plank, was temporarily out of commission.

16

Squalls swept the island that night. At four in the morning rain was still clattering on my roof when I woke Piailug to look at the clouds. He said it was unnecessary, told me to go back to sleep and to meet him at six to cut coconut-frond skids for the canoe. I overslept; by the time I got down to Ropitiu, *Aloha* and *Rugger* were already anchored at the face of the reef. *Rugger* would be sailed by Iti, who had decided the night before to accompany us. The weather had cleared and a light wind blew from the southeast.

By nine the canoes were loaded and both crews waited in Lepotig. Men from all the canoe houses brought their morning tuba and began to drink with the crews. Anxious to take advantage of the fair wind and disgusted by what I considered a lack of discipline, I refused my cup when offered. Everyone got drunk. Testily I asked Piailug how they could drink and then go to sea. Very quietly he explained it was their custom: "This is the time to be happy and to drink with our master, for he will remind us of the star above the island, of the birds and fish of *pookof*, and of our reference island, the *lu pongank*. It is a ceremony to say goodbye. We cannot know; maybe we will never return." Then he added in English, "Wait! Maybe Chief Rewena or Regaliang will want to talk to you."

Shortly thereafter, Regaliang, who, with Piailug, flanked me as we sat on *Aninga's* half-completed outrigger, told me to pay attention as he placed his hand palm up on my knee.

"Pikelot lies under the rising Cassiopeia," Regaliang said, pointing to his middle finger. "It is flanked by four star points [pointing to his other fingers]: rising Vega and rising Pleiades to the south; rising Big Dipper and Little Dipper to the north." He looked up to see if I was following and went on: "Now the wind is from the south, so you will hold a more southerly course, under the rising Vega. In this wind you will reach the island under rising Vega. Do you understand, young man?" I said I did. Then he tested me by laying on the canoe-house floor a cigarette pack, a piece of Styrofoam, and a few wood chips and asked me to name the stars they represented. I named them correctly.

By noon it was raining again, a short, lazy squall. The younger men were drunkenly singing a popular Yapese song. Some babbled in English. By one, all the tuba was finished. Rewena stopped the talking and led everyone in an old voyaging song, then took us to church, where we kneeled in prayer. He told us to pray each morning and evening at six o'clock. On Satawal they would do the same, to ensure our safe return.

Finally we swam out to the canoes, presented the sails to the light wind, and got under way. Assaf had gotten so drunk he'd fallen asleep and missed the boat. As we ghosted along the beach he appeared, standing at the end of the tide-exposed reef with his meager bundle of possessions: a gaunt, forlorn figure etched in black against the dazzling sand. Piailug ordered us to heave to while two young boys paddled him out in a small canoe. Besides Assaf, Piailug, and me were Rovigno, Joseph, Paul's brother Eddy, and two young men from Ootenap, John and Peter. Piailug had also brought Howie and his grandson Tom, who slept on the outrigger platform with us.

By late afternoon we had sailed around a point offshore of Wenimung. Piailug aligned the eastern and southern tips of Satawal to establish the course to Pikelot. If the wind increased we would continue, he said; otherwise we would be forced to return.

In the evening a light wind sprang up, nodding the heads of the cumulus clouds toward the west, where rainsqualls glowed in the setting sun. Piailug scrutinized the swells, clouds, and the island, still visible in the distance.

"The sunset looks good," I offered. "There is no smoke, a clear red sky, sharp clouds, no haze: no more rain." He glanced at the clouds and agreed—just to be rid of me, I thought. The cumulus clouds became smaller and more compact, which in my experience had heralded the return of steadier tradewinds. I ventured this prognosis to Piailug, adding that I thought the wind would back into the northeast, but he just yawned and said we would wait to see. At twilight he announced we would pass over the deep-sea reef Orraire-par later that night, uncoiling his trolling line as he did so. Evidently we were to continue. A brown booby (*ama*) flew up to investigate, circled, and headed back to Satawal. Howie and Tom, silent until then, suddenly jabbered, "*Ama! Ama! Ama! Ama!*" A dolphin jumped across the bow, squeaked, and vanished with the coming of the first stars.

Tom fell asleep; Howie crooned to himself; the rest of the crew was silent. Piailug sailed closehauled, steering rising Cassiopeia. Since that constellation was not visible, he kept Vega just off the starboard bow.

During the night the wind steadily backed to the northeast. We made long tacks to remain within the arms of the imaginary fish weir. By about nine, as the Southern Cross set and Altair rose, we steered between rising Cassiopeia and the Big Dipper. Piailug kept the rising Vega off our starboard bow. I asked which stars we would use later, when Vega was too high to steer by. He pointed to two faint stars in the constellation Draco, Nodus II and X Draco. The first followed the path of Cassiopeia, he said tersely, the second the path of the Big Dipper. Later, when clouds obscured the stars in the east, he steered by Polaris and two extremely faint stars near the star Alfirk, which he kept over the outrigger platform.

Around midnight the wind dropped, then began a maddening cycle, veering slowly from the northeast to the east, only to die and suddenly spring back from the northeast. Once we almost lost our whole rig—mast, sail, and booms—overboard when the wind suddenly switched directions. Once under way again, I asked what stars we were steering by. Without answering, Piailug stretched out on the very edge of the outrigger platform and went to sleep. Both boys slept, too. I watched the night.

I remembered a similar night in the northern Pacific, sailing from Hawaii to San Francisco. Then, too, the wind had done pirouettes, occasionally backwinding the sails, jamming them into the mast and rigging. It was frustrating sailing, made tedious navigationally by our constantly changing course. But I had a watch and a compass; I merely had to determine an average course each hour and plot it on the chart. Even if I was in error, I could correct my position with sextant sights the next day. Besides, I was on a long passage, where a single night of shifting winds made little difference. Now I wondered how Piailug could keep track of his position in the shifting wind and an unknown current. He, of course, would have no way to verify his position in the morning; the test would come when Pikelot either appeared or did not appear. Also, it was a relatively short passage, on which an unnoticed shift in the current would have a great impact. Yet each time I'd asked him Pikelot's bearing, he'd replied without hesitation.

At perhaps two in the morning, dolphins played with the canoe. Piailug was awake again. The wind blew lightly from the northeast. We sailed east-southeast, with Cassiopeia rising over the outrigger to guide us. Everyone was quiet; most slept. In an hour we tacked north again, steering Little Dipper; that asterism not being visible, Piailug used a small star that I was unable to identify.

At sunrise we hove to, to wait for *Rugger*. Piailug removed his hat to lead us in mumbled "Our Father"'s, then remained squatting on the edge of the outrigger platform to watch the swells. The largest swell, which I could easily identify, came from the direction of rising Vega. Smaller swells also came from the directions of Polaris, rising Altair, and rising Antares. The latter three were difficult to identify, however. Had I been navigating, I would have been very nervous.

In response to my question, Piailug said he was using both the swell itself and the knots tied by the swell systems' interacting; but added, with no trace of anxiety, that the sea was very confused and difficult to read. I calculated we were only at Satawal's *etak* of birds. Piailug agreed, adding that we should arrive at Pikelot's *etak* of birds this evening and Pikelot by morning.

By mid-morning the sea became so jumbled by shifting winds that I could hardly tell the swell under Altair from that under Vega. Piailug only grunted when I tried to discuss it, still sitting on the very edge of the outrigger platform. Joseph spotted a school of tuna in the distance, which we tried to intercept but missed, to our great disappointment. It became unbearably hot. No one talked. I had a splitting headache. Soon we sailed through another school of tuna and caught two. *Rugger* caught nothing. "Too much masturbating, Iti!" someone teased as the canoe maneuvered alongside to receive half a fish. We ate raw tuna and pounded breadfruit, our first food since the previous noon.

By midday the sun had burned any thought from my head. Piailug covered the sleeping children with a spare loincloth. It cooled late in the afternoon; the boys woke to play in the shade of the mainsail. The appearance of a bird produced a burst of jabber: "Frigate bird! Frigate bird! Frigate bird! . . ."

"That's not a frigate bird!" Rovigno said. "It's a booby."

"Oh!" the boys exclaimed. "Booby! Booby! Booby!" Rovigno told me his son loved to be at sea; when Piailug had sailed to Gaferut to salvage the newly wrecked Japanese fishing boat, Tom had tried to stow away. Rovigno discovered him under some palm-frond mats. He refused to be put ashore, and Rovigno had to trick him into staying behind.

The boys then pointed to my camera's viewfinder and cried, "Teevee, Teevee, Teevee, Teevee." Everything became a television—a hole in a coconut, my sunglasses. Piailug silenced them with a hiss. Tom began a nonsense song; Piailug chanted a song of navigation. Massive cumulo-nimbus clouds appeared in the south, and by sundown rain-squalls swept the sea. The setting sun struck *Rugger*'s sail, a small, brilliant triangle beneath the foreboding sky.

Soon we started sighting birds flying toward rising Vega, evidence that we had reached Pikelot's *etak* of birds. We stopped to wait for *Rugger*, prayed, then sailed on in wind constantly shifting with the squalls. A sliver of the first quarter-moon hung in the western sky; Uliul was fighting. Later it struck me that Piailug assumed I was aware of this when I had asked him to make the passage.

Darkness hooded the sea like an oily rag, obscuring the stars and the jumbled waves. Piailug felt there was a current but could tell neither its speed nor its direction. He ordered us to drop sail. We would heave to until dawn, when he hoped that birds flying out from the island to fish would give us a bearing to our objective.

All night the wind and rain swirled around the canoe; lightning flashed in the west. Piailug tucked the naked children beneath an old plastic tarp and told them to sleep. After baking under the sun all day, I was shivering. Unashamed, I crawled under the tarp with the kids. Soon Piailug did the same, but the tarp was old and full of holes and we got soaked anyway. The crew took turns trumpeting a conch shell to ward off the rain. Although we couldn't know it, on Satawal Emilia was giving birth to a son.

Dawn that Sunday broke to a dark and leaden sky. The rain stopped momentarily as the wind veered into the north. We could not be sure how far we'd drifted. No birds were visible.

We prayed and made sail. The sun, rising into a pair of huge cumulo-nimbi, sent shafts of pink light raking across a higher fan of cirrus—all signs of bad weather. For the next hour everyone searched for birds, without success. The eastern sky was choked with clouds. "No island," Piailug told me almost apologetically in English. "We cannot see it because of the clouds." He decided to make for West Fayu, about fifty miles distant but well screened by reefs that made it a big target. Rovigno moved aft to allow the canoe to run more easily as we slid down the face of the swells. The compass was unshipped; men strapped on their wristwatches. I was disappointed but too weary really to care.

At eight someone sighted a lone tern. Piailug, who had been sitting glumly on the outrigger platform, scrutinized it closely, then ordered a change of course back to Pikelot. Fifteen minutes later a flock of terns appeared, flying toward us from the northeast. Since the sky to windward had cleared somewhat, Piailug decided to search for the island.

By noon we had seen nothing. If we had been on Pikelot's *etak* of sighting, or even its *etak* of birds, I calculated, we should have seen the island by now. Growing worried, I took out my battered plastic sextant, which on my own boat I had kept in the liferaft, and began to adjust it. (Foolishly, I had left my good sextant at home, for fear of damaging it.) No one commented. In an hour I told Piailug I would try to establish our position if he wished. Tersely he commanded me to do so.

It took quite a while for me to shoot three sights through the overcast. When I had finally succeeded, they placed us south of Pikelot. In several hours I could take additional sights for a "running fix," an accurate plot of our position, but for now my estimated position placed us to the southwest of Pikelot. Piailug thought this was right. At midday I shot more sights, but the plastic sextant was apparently expanding and contracting in the heat, for no two were even close to each other.

Meanwhile, the crew scanned the horizon. Shortly, Eddy spotted swells to the southeast, the sign of a reef. We altered course toward it, and as we sailed back and forth across it, I took more sextant sights. Now, according to my sights, we had sailed past Pikelot and were on a reef called Wonipik. Piailug grabbed the chart to look. I had an uneasy feeling the sights were in error, but when I tried to shoot more, the sun refused to emerge from behind the clouds. Piailug reasoned we were on a reef called Moen, about sixteen miles west of Pikelot.

As the two canoes sailed back and forth to check the reef's shape, the sun came out. The day grew cooler, and I carefully took three more sun shots, worked them out, and plotted them on the chart. To my relief, they placed us on Moen reef. By this time, Piailug, Eddy, and Rovigno had identified the reef by the shape of some channels in the southern end. Nonetheless, Piailug was satisfied that my conclusions agreed with theirs. He ordered us to sail halfway between rising Altair and Beta Aquila. The two canoes slid quietly through the calm water. Contented in the knowledge of our position, we dined on pounded breadfruit and red snapper caught on the reef. At sundown Eddy sighted the island.

The wind died and a light rain swept the sea. We paddled in the drizzle and by three in the morning approached the dark island. Piailug barked orders as he piloted us through the low surf. Suddenly the beach loomed out of the darkness, and our bow struck the sand. Everyone scrambled to hold the canoe in the waves. Piailug fell as he tried to stand, cursing his foot. It had taken two and a half days to cover the sixty miles to Pikelot.

Once we had dragged the canoe up the steep foreshore, we signaled to *Rugger*. She did not approach, evidently preferring to heave to offshore rather than negotiate the tricky approach in total darkness. Piailug sent me with Assaf to look for turtles. I followed the skinny old man, stubbing my toes against the coral stones in the darkness, as he zigged up the beach. Soon he came across a wide, shallow track, as if something heavy had been dragged across the sand, and we followed it into the bushes. A big turtle was ponderously scooping out her nest with her front flippers. Even the beam of my flashlight did not interrupt her life's task. Terns cackled in the trees, and the sweet, unmistakable odor of guano drifted out from the heart of the island. I wanted to sit down, to watch her lay her eggs and make her way back into the sea, but we were there to hunt and I, too, was hungry for meat. Before she had laid her eggs, I grasped her tough flippers and tried to heave her over. She struggled, her viscous eyes opening wide; then she seemed to give up, and as I rolled her onto her back she sucked ponderous breaths of air, as if to prepare for her last dive. We left her that way, the early-morning rain falling from the black holes between the stars.

At first light, I was awoken by swarms of flies feeding on my eyes and the corners of my mouth. I crawled from the crude shelter to survey the island in daylight for the first time. Our camp was in the middle of the wide beach. Rovigno, Eddy, John, and Peter had dragged the turtle up and were burning it. All around us, rotting, half-eaten turtle carcasses littered the sand, interspersed with piles of human shit. On the higher ground behind the beach, a large turtle had been abandoned on its back to die, and now lay in a puddle of its own putrescence, jaw and tail eaten away by maggots and hermit crabs. The coconut trees were stripped of nuts. The island looked as if it had suffered repeated visits by some crude and unprincipled hoard. Only the small mariners' chapel in the woods was untouched, plastic flowers arranged neatly before a statue of the Virgin Mary, the sandy courtyard clean and freshly raked. Piailug hobbled around on a stick, surveying the waste.

"This was done by the people of Puluwat or Tamatam," he spat in a fury, "by crazy, stupid people—not people but pigs or dogs. Don't they see that if we do this we will soon have no more turtles?" He buried the remains of the turtles in the sand. No one else offered to help. Later we found a youth's name and "Puluwat" carved into a palm tree near the chapel, dated several days before we had left Satawal.

Pikelot is a tiny island, less than two hundred yards wide and four hundred long. Like West Fayu, it is not large enough to support a freshwater lens and, except for several brackish puddles on the beach, is dry. Limited supplies of water for drinking and washing are held in steel drums and replenished by rain running off the tin roof of the chapel. But unlike West Fayu, Pikelot does not enjoy a lagoon, and its shark-infested reef lies close to the beach. Here one has the sense of being a castaway on a distant island, a small speck of sand vulnerable to the sea's great power.

Again like West Fayu, it belongs to Lamotrek, Elato, and Satawal, but the people of Tamatam, Puluwat, Pulap, and Pulusuk often make the easy passage here to hunt turtles. Piailug has visited Pikelot many times since he was a small boy, first with his grandfather, then his father and his uncle Eguwan. Once, two canoes were sailing from Satawal to West Fayu when they were becalmed, then swept off course by currents. For two weeks they searched for land. Finally they were caught in a typhoon that drove them east. Late at night, after nineteen days at sea, they came upon Pikelot. The wind had diminished but the surf still beat wildly on the reef. Both canoes foundered and sank while attempting to negotiate the reef pass, but all eight crew members, including Piailug, swam safely to shore. Stranded, they survived on sweet tuba and turtle—so well that by the time they were discovered by canoes from Puluwat seven months later, none could fit into his loincloth. When they returned to Satawal, the people thought they were fat spirits—indeed, they had given them up for lost.

We remained on Pikelot for four days, hunting turtles at night and spearfishing the reef by day. We dined often and sumptuously on turtle, fish stew, fish tripes and octopus stewed in breadfruit leaves (very delicious), and on *afour*, the strange cucumberlike fruit. Piailug drew into himself, speaking only to command or briefly answer direct questions. He limped badly and told me he had a sharp pain in his stomach. Both morning and evening I tried to get him to continue with our cloud studies, but he showed little interest.

On the second day, in the hottest part of the afternoon, I sat with him in the shade while he killed flies with a palm-frond swatter. I told stories about sailing in the Atlantic, Pacific, and Caribbean. It had become a beautiful, tradewind day (it was the fourth day of the waxing moon); a steady wind blew from the southeast, and big, puffy cumuli lolled in the sky. Their tops dazzled like snow-clad mountain peaks, while their bases glowed a dark and brooding purple. I said I missed life at sea; perhaps in several years I could buy another boat and return to the Pacific. I asked if he'd like to come, but he said he'd be dead by then.

On the evening of the third day, someone sighted turtles mating along the northern reef. About ten of us plunged through the glistening surf with a log, a coil of line, and a gaff. Once past the breakers, we swam along the shore, fanning out above the deeply striated reef. We sighted the turtle, a female with one of her flippers chewed off by a shark; the male had fled. Quickly we surrounded her so that everywhere she turned to flee she encountered a picket of hunters. The reef was too shallow for her to dive. She skittered along the line of swimmers, pumping the water hard with her flippers. Then John darted out with the gaff and sank the hook deeply into the soft flesh behind her flipper. She was reeled in, manhandled to the log, and tied, as if crucified. It all happened very fast. We dragged her to the beach and left her on her back under the trees. We had taken eight turtles by this time, seven females and one male. They were warehoused in a low thatched shed near the canoes, periodically flapping in unison in desperate and futile attempts to right themselves.

The next morning, our fourth on the island, dawned still and windless. Piailug had hoped to return to Satawal today, but we were forced to wait. The male turtle was dragged from the shed and roasted for breakfast.

We spent the morning swimming around the island hunting turtles, sighting only one, which quickly dove beyond our reach. We passed the afternoon spearfishing. After a big supper under the palm trees on the northern beach, we wandered back to camp to shower and change.

It was a picture-postcard sunset, the fat, cumulus clouds glowing pink in the swelling evening, drifting before the light northeasterly that had sprung up in the mid-afternoon. The moon, six days old, sailed among the clouds. Piailug collected turtle shell in an old rice sack for the women of Eauripik, who fashioned it into beautiful women's belts.

He searched for the shell with his characteristic fierceness, demanding from the sand its bits of shell, stuffing them into his sack, then limping to the next spot. He embodied such contrast, I reflected. I doubted that anyone ever asked him to collect the shell; he just knew the women of Eauripik needed it, and Pikelot had it in abundance. The code of the navigator held that one should care for all the people of one's island. Piailug, it seemed, had extended this notion to include all the Carolines and even Saipan and Hawaii, anywhere he was recognized as a *palu*. Yet he could be so severe, so unapproachable, so harsh. My initial impressions of him were only reinforced over time.

I interrupted him to ask if we could watch the sunset. Without answering, he shut the neck of the sack, limped over to a log, and sat down. I decided to let him initiate the lesson, instead of prompting him as I usually did. Five minutes passed in silence. I studied the clouds, trying to account for all the signs he had taught me. Finally he asked for my forecast. He used the same tone of voice—light, patient, but firm and definitive—as when, on the *Microspirit*, he had told me to come to shore with him. It implied that one would do his bidding, or simply be passed over. He seemed to use it at decisive moments.

I said there would be a good wind tomorrow, because the hazy band was descending steadily; it would blow from the northwest, like today. It would be a good wind for sailing back to Satawal.

"Any rain?" he asked.

I checked the clouds again. There was no red in the sunset, so I answered that we would just have light showers beneath the largest of the cumulus clouds. He nodded.

After tomorrow, I added, I thought the wind would die. Frowning, he demanded an explanation. The only cloud sign I could point to was that the cumulus clouds had grown long and thick, not a sign he had taught me. As a yacht skipper, I had noticed that when the trades increase, the cumulus clouds grow small and compact, like shellbursts; when the wind moderates or dies, the clouds grow very thick and lazy. Besides this sign, the wind just *felt* as if it would die. I couldn't explain it, I told him, except that I had seen the same pattern before in both the Atlantic and the Pacific.

Piailug listened impassively. When I finished I asked what he thought the weather would do. He just shrugged and said he had no idea. Then he gazed at the clouds a few moments, fidgeted with his sack of turtle shell, and asked if I was finished. When I nodded, he rose, limped over to our shelter, ordered Howie and Tom to bed, and crawled in after them.

Morning dawned according to my forecast. The crews began to eat a leisurely breakfast before leaving for Satawal. I found Piailug to tell him I thought the wind would die at sunset, and we should hurry to leave. He scanned the horizon and demanded to know how I knew this. Again I had no hard evidence, other than that it just felt as if the wind would not hold through another night. He called me a liar, perhaps thinking I was trying to make a fool of him, but stomped off to whip the crews into action. In short order, the canoes were slid into the water, the turtles dragged from their shed, flippers pierced and bound, then floated out to the canoes and stowed aboard. A large pot of rice had been cooked for breakfast, and Piailug now divided it between the two boats. Then he took us to the chapel to pray, as Rewena had instructed. By eight o'clock we were away.

The day made the sea seem benign. The wind was from the east at twelve to fifteen knots, veering to the southeast and becoming lighter in the afternoon. Light rain in the shadow of the biggest cumulus clouds provided cool relief from the hot sun. Piailug sat by himself on the outrigger platform, speaking to no one. The rest of us ate rice and turtle and told jokes. Someone asked me to tell the story of how I killed the rooster the previous year, and the whole crew guffawed as I told how I had brained it.

By five-thirty we sighted Satawal. We had been so confident of Piailug's course that no one had bothered to look for it until Joseph nonchalantly announced it was on the horizon. We were already well past the *etak* of sighting.

The island loomed larger and larger. Then, as the sun set, the wind lightened and died. We paddled until midnight, when we anchored on the reef.

It was a stunning night, the massive cumulus clouds in the west backlit by the setting first-quarter moon, Scorpio and Sagittarius wheeling overhead. Our two voyaging canoes calved a dozen paddling ones as men bottom-fishing in the calm night came over to talk and smoke. We had missed the tide and would wait for morning.

As the stars climbed through the summit of the night, the men in the paddling canoes left for shore. Piailug went with them, along with Assaf, the kids, and Rovigno. I was offered the option but turned it down, preferring to spend one more night, perhaps my last, on a canoe at sea. I felt close to the young men. I reflected that if I could stay on Satawal and mold myself to their customs I might even become one of their leaders. But I knew I could not stay.

My relationship with Piailug seemed terminated; my hero had failed me. The word "fail" revolved in my mind. I had suffered similar (if not worse) navigational embarrassments in much better sea conditions, I reminded myself, and, like him, I had still found my destination. Besides, I doubted he was ever really lost. If we had not sighted Moen reef he would probably have run downwind to intercept the wide reefs of West Fayu—he had not really failed, I reflected. Perhaps what had occurred was that in using my sextant, and later correctly reading the clouds, I had demonstrated I was already a navigator and thus didn't need him. Maybe he thought I had been disingenuous in my desire to learn his navigation, collecting bits of knowledge from him to pin them on a board, like dried bugs. I felt bewildered and somewhat abandoned. I didn't know how to patch the widening cracks in my image of Piailug. But at the same time, it was a relief to be away from his brooding presence on such a brilliant night.

Meanwhile, someone had left us with a bottle of tuba, which Eddy, Joseph, John, Peter, and I shared as we told stories and laughed softly. The island behind us was dark and quiet and the wide sea so calm that the clouds gazed at their own reflections in the starlit water. Peter made a fire in the oil pan and we drank coffee as the dawn and the tide rose.

After we had brought the canoe through the reef pass and pushed it up the beach to the canoe house, we shouldered our sea chests to return to our own villages. The fragile moment of our camaraderie rolled away and was lost, like the thin wake of a canoe at sea.

Piailug had been drinking all night. He met me on the path to Nemanong to demand my whiskey. He wanted to keep drinking, he roared, then run about wildly, causing trouble. When I said the whiskey was gone, he threatened to burn down my house, then laughed as if it were a joke. I was alarmed at the undercurrent of violence, directed for the first time at me.

After bathing at Fanagoon, I found him sitting on a log talking soberly to Nemoito. He asked for two beers, drained the first, and sipped the second. He had called a meeting with the chiefs and elders that afternoon to discuss the carnage on Pikelot, to be followed by a radio conference with the chiefs of Puluwat and Pulusuk. He again expressed alarm at the recent decline in the turtle population. As he rose to leave, I asked when we would again talk about navigation. He said we were finished; he had nothing further to teach me.

17

The newborn boy created ripples of new activities in the stable patterns of life in Nemanong village. Josede's mother, Tigiri, bustled about her self-appointed child-care tasks. As I lay down to sleep on the coral-stone floor of my hut, or when I was awoken early in the morning by the chill rising from the ground, I would hear her chanting to the baby as she rocked him in her arms or in his little hanging crib.

Emilia looked tired, but was hauling water from Fanagoon and performing her other chores. Her skin turned yellow from continual application of turmeric, and now she always wore a turmeric-dusted cloth over her breasts as further protection from the spirits. She avoided the woods. Tigiri still prevailed upon Josede not to go night-fishing.

Each day the women of Asugulap came to Nemanong to bring food and help with chores. Some evenings they would babysit so that Tigiri and Emilia could go to the clearing before the dispensary to watch "teevee." One of the University of Guam students had returned for the summer with his VCR, on which, powered by the asthmatic town generator, he was showing *Oh, God, Flashdance,* and *Hill Street Blues* to his fellow islanders, few of whom understood English.

One Sunday the chiefs called an island-wide meeting in Lugarig. The women and their infants squatted in the landward half of the canoe house, while the men sat on and beneath the chiefs' canoe, *Tiger*, to seaward. Then the chiefs promulgated a seemingly arbitrary set of new rules, culminating in the banning of alcoholic tuba.

Thureng opened by exhorting everyone to attend church and make a contribution of money: "Before we had magic to bring our fish," he said; "now we just have God." Then Rewena announced that married men could not visit their home villages after ten at night, in order not to catch young men trysting with their girlfriends, the married men's sisters. He reminded women not to take turtle eggs: it was now taboo. Uliso, seemingly in contradiction of Rewena, told the young men *not* to creep around at night looking for "women's things," and not to wake their mothers and aunts to ask for food. Thureng reminded the high-school girls they must *aparog* to the men.

Then one woman voiced her fears: "We've seen boys walking around at night with steel bars [reinforcing rods from the building sites of the concrete houses]—we're afraid they'll break into our homes and put cloths in our mouths, like we see on the TV."

Rewena scoffed at her: "Women have been making up stories and exaggerating! They shouldn't do this, for it creates problems between people."

An old woman from the Council of Elders proclaimed that the three chiefs were the "outriggers of Satawal, our canoe. We, the people, are the sailors. . . ." Rewena cut her off, too, by abruptly commanding all the women to go prepare the evening meal. They rose slowly and, still crouching in deference to the sitting men, waddled up the low rise to the villages.

Weneto then announced that, since there was so much work— rethatching canoe and dwelling houses, drying copra, building canoes— making tuba should be banned. His brother, Rewena, vigorously disagreed, but Weneto had the backing of the other two chiefs. The initiative for the ban, it was whispered, came from the Council of Elders. Rewena had no choice but to agree, and the rest of the men had no voice in the matter.

The meeting was closed. Auhror vowed he would take the next canoe to Lamotrek. Piailug complained bitterly that the *telap* and the Elders had never been consulted on this matter—a clear violation of the traditional decision-making procedure.

Then, with the moon waxing, we entered a period of very calm weather. At night the paddling canoes hovered around the island like fireflies to fish the dropoff on the face of the reef. Nemoito's mother took a turn for the worse and was moved from her own hut to Uurupa's house in Asugulap. Nemoito, Piailug, the three young boys, and the teen-age girls all slept in the house with her, in case she should suddenly die. Nemanong was empty except for Josede, Emilia, Tigiri, and the dogs, who now moved up to my courtyard, where their barking, crunching on the coral stones, and gnashing of tin cans and bits of garbage woke me at odd hours of the night.

In the mornings a heavy dew lay on everything. Condensation dripped from the tin ceiling of my hut onto my typewriter, books, and cameras. I woke very early, chilled to the bone. I saw Piailug rarely now; by day he devoted his energies to the new canoe, and at night, since there were no tuba circles, he returned directly to Asugulap, ate, and slept. Josede and I finished recording, translating, and transcribing Taumuan's stories and I was at a loss what to do next. Then, by chance, I met the blind and crippled navigator Mwaramai.

There was a story of the origin of Satawal island that no one seemed to remember. Piailug thought he'd once heard one but could not recall it. Josede asked his uncle Regaliang, who couldn't recall it either but suggested we ask old Mwaramai, who stayed in Anatiu village, now that his wife had kicked him out of the house. We found him sleeping in the corner of a hut, curled up like a child, clutching a filthy sheet. When I called his name he opened his eyes, looking around in confusion; he didn't flinch in the brilliant tide of light from the open door.

I identified myself and told him why I'd come. He asked why I wanted to hear such stories if I was studying navigation. Americans were interested in these things, I said. He asked for a cigarette, smoked part of it, then told the story:

Two sisters, Nigaupoop and Alimung, were on their way from Truk to Woleai to build a new island there. But while they were crossing between Puluwat and Lamotrek, Nigaupoop's basket slipped and the earth it held spilled into the sea. Since it was impossible to recover, she tried to pile the dirt into a mountain, and in doing so crushed her sister's little finger. In turn, Alimung smashed Nigaupoop's little finger. Both spirits abandoned the new island: Alimung swam away to become a mangrove crab, and Nigaupoop stayed to become a small crab near shore. Both species now have flattened legs as a result. If a mangrove crab is ever seen on Satawal, it is a sign that someone will soon die.

I was pleased with this story. Mwaramai smiled toothlessly and said they told many like it in the old days. I asked if he still remembered them and he answered that of course he did. Emboldened, I asked if he knew the chants to Anumwerici. "What?" he asked indignantly. "How could you think otherwise? Can't you see that my head is white and my beard hairs grow down long? I am an old man, I must know such things!"

Quietly, I asked if he would teach me some. He didn't answer at first, but asked me to light another cigarette for him, which I did and then guided it into his quaking hands. Through his father he was related to Nemoito's clan, he said; therefore he could consider Piailug and Uurupa his sons, and me a son as well. Thus he could rightfully discuss such things with me. In previous years he would never have done so, but "now I am an old man and have waited and waited—I have a pain in my head, I've waited so long for someone to come ask me about these things. Now you have come. I will tell you everything correctly, for that is our custom. What else can I do, take my knowledge into the sky with me when I die?"

Nearly every day for the next month, I went to his hut. I took my tape recorder and typewriter and induced Josede to help translate. We would record the old chants, then translate and transcribe them, line by line. It was exhausting work that required absolute concentration. Mwaramai would frequently drift into reverie, forgetting the line and even the chant we were working on. Most problematic was the language of the chants, a formal and arcane dialect as similar to contemporary Satawalese as Middle English is to Modern English. Neither Josede nor any of the younger men could understand it without extensive explication. There were many phrases Mwaramai didn't even understand; he had simply learned them by rote.

We worked every day, from nine in the morning to four or five in the evening, when Josede and I went spearfishing to try to catch dinner. Mwaramai and Josede were willing to work as hard as I wished, and, feeling the press of time, I pushed myself to the limit. After nearly a month of this punishing schedule, Mwaramai pronounced us finished. We had assembled a body of lore the West had never seen.

The general function of the chants was to enlist and maintain the favor of Anumwerici, in whose especial care the initiated *palu* resided. According to Mwaramai, Anumwerici "heats the navigator's words to make his magic hot," thus giving his magic the power necessary to prevail against fate and evil spirits.

Magic was needed for every aspect of a voyage. To gather his crew together, the navigator enlisted the offices of Farepuey, the spirit of gathering. The *palu* made his entreaty with a great blast on his *sawie*, his conch-shell trumpet. ("We used the *sawie* like a walkie-talkie," Mwaramai said. "It carried our words. Now we no longer use it, because we have walkie-talkies.") As the crew brought the mast and sail to the canoe, the navigator chanted to Anumwerici and the spirit of the mast. As they raised the sail, he chanted again, asking Anumwerici to give him a clear head and protect his crew at sea. When sailing away from the island, the *palu* used the *sawie* to greet the spirits of the four schools of navigation, the island's navigators, and the island itself. He asked Anumwerici to "pull his canoe from the mouths of the spirits and the mouths of the people"—i.e., to protect them from the chants of evil sorcerers and from evil brought by spirits in response to malicious gossip. Then the navigator may do several chants to protect the canoe against bad weather, death, and evil. At sea, after tying young coconut shoots around his arms, the navigator may chant to Anumwerici asking to be taken into the aura of his care, to be sailed as his canoe.

During bad weather, the navigator performed a cycle of chants to ward off the "spirits of the middle heavens": Nainearh, the spirit of the white squall or waterspout; Nitar, the spirit of the swells beneath these disturbances; Olaipemwar and Olaisettmwar, spirits of the black, spear-shaped alto-cumulus clouds, which, when viewed at sunrise and sunset, signify strong wind; and a host of other spirits.

Once having reached his destination, the navigator had a set of chants to test the edibility of food presented to him and his crew, for it was not unknown for a host to poison his guests with the lethal spines of the scorpionfish or lionfish, in order to steal their canoe.

Chants covered every exigency of voyaging. There were chants to remove certain taboos, such as stepping over anchor lines or having one canoe leave the fleet, chants to counteract sickness on distant islands, even chants to soothe whales threatening to destroy a canoe. (Mwaramai said he used these once to calm Yoliwa, the killer whales near Lamotrek.) I found several of the chants very beautiful. Certainly, I reflected, they must have been intended to go beyond the function of propitiating the spirits to honor them with the melody of their language. Mwaramai felt similarly. "When the Christians came, everyone threw away their knowledge," he said, "but I couldn't forget, for I knew these words too well."

"Opening the sea" is addressed to Anumwerici and Laousourer, the master and mistress of the sea. The metaphor of floating logs in the first stanza stands for storm waves, and the breadfruit-laden bough signifies storm clouds. During certain seasons the leaves of the *oomah* tree turn bright yellow, the color of the sky before a storm.

> *When the floating logs come*
> *And breadfruit-laden bough,*
> *On the tide pool sea,*
> *And leaves of the* oomah *tree,*
> *He will open*
> *The door of his house,*
> *The house of the Master of the Sea.*
>
> *It will open,*
> *It will spread,*
> *It will spread,*
> *It will open,*
> *And it is opening there,*
> *On his land,*
> *And I come in.*
>
> *I penetrate that Forest of the Sea,*
> *That Sea of Smoke,*
> *Sea of Smallness, Smallness; that*
> *Sea of Shortness, Shortness.*
> *But this is not a sea!*
> *But She of the Flower!*
> *Mistress of Goodness, Goodness;*
> *Master of Goodness, Goodness.*
> *"We have opened, we have opened,*

That sea of, that sea of, that sea of,
Of Laousourer! Of Laousourer!"

Another beautiful chant is a greeting of respect to Sagur, the legendary chief of Pulap. Sagur resides in bamboo floating at sea. If a canoe was lost, her crew starving and thirsty, they would find a length of bamboo. The navigator would stop to *atirro* Sagur, to greet him with solemn respect—to ignore Sagur would be suicidal. He would take the bamboo from the water, place it next to him on the outrigger platform, and begin to cry, for he had missed Sagur. After he chanted, he dove into the water with the bamboo and, two fathoms down, released it. If the bamboo surfaced parallel to the canoe, they would spend just one more night at sea. If it surfaced at a right angle to the canoe, it was also auspicious, for it signified a skid for sliding the canoe up the beach. But if the bamboo surfaced at an oblique angle to the canoe, it meant more days at sea, lost and starving, burning in sun and freezing in rain.

The chant begins with a yelp: *"Ai eeee hoo hoo!"*

Do not navigate, do not navigate,
And do not steal, do not steal, do not steal.
I see you, see you, Sagur,
Atirro, atirro, my chief,
And mother of turmeric, you are the mother of turmeric,
Sagur.
Take my canoe to the beach of the island, O Sagur,
Anchor it on the reef.

I speak over the fleet:
I speak with your voice, you speak with my voice.
You speak with my voice, I speak with yours;
Our voice is one, for we are both sons of Wareyang.
You are Revelation, I am Obscurity,
You are Obscurity, I am Revelation.
The leaf of the banana tree will be our lei,
You will wear one side, I will wear the other.
A single coconut will be our drink;
You will drink some, I will drink some.
With a single piece of copra we will wash ourselves,

You will rub your skin, I will rub mine,
So I will have knowledge of navigation.

*Lelillio, Lelillio, whose son is he, Sagur?**
He is tired of wandering at the end of the sea-of-
  shortness;
In the sea-of-weeping, at the end of the sea-of-shortness.
He will Lelillio, Lelillio be.
Oh! Not Lelillio!
He will swim toward, swim if
You are Sagur, you Sagur.
I carry you from the ruung,† *that* ruung, *my* ruung
  Wareyang;
You are tired of floating, weeping in the middle of the
  sea;
You will give me knowledge of navigation.

Now I will swim with Sagur,
I have wasted to just backbone,
Like paddle of my canoe.
Now I will swim with Sagur,
I have wasted to just backbone,
Like paddle of my canoe.

One day of voyaging, Sagur,
And one night,
One day and one night
Be with me, Sagur,
On the beach of my island.
Be with me, Sagur,
On the beach of my island.

In addition to sailing magic, Mwaramai also recorded the chants for *katomai*, "calling breadfruit," and *katonu*, "calling coconuts." These two song cycles appeal to the spirit Saurhewon, master of Iur, an island

---

*Mwaramai thought Lelillio was a spirit, but the syntax suggests it is the name of the navigator performing the chant.
†*Ruung* is a taboo area. Here it refers to the outboard end of the outrigger platform, where, it being closest to the outrigger, the residence of Yaleluweii, only the *palu* was entitled to sit.

floating above the southern horizon, to bring fecundity to the breadfruit and coconut trees.

"Bad magic" was also practiced before Christianity. With the most powerful chants a sinister practitioner could destroy a canoe at sea or bring sickness or death to his victim. Although one was free to use the dark side of magic, it was a Faustian bargain: if the sorcerer killed with his power, Anumwerici would take one of his relatives in exchange.

It has not been that long since "bad magic" has been performed on Satawal. Two incidents occurred within living memory and are held to be true. In one case a man was seen performing magic as a canoe was launched. The canoe never returned. Sometime later, he was caught kicking the skids of another canoe. Then he was followed and observed making magic. That canoe, too, disappeared at sea. The man's relatives gave permission to kill him, and he was hunted down by men with spears. One spear penetrated the small of his back to emerge below his testicles, but he merely bent the spear in half and continued to run. A second spear to his testicles brought him down for good.

A second incident entailed the rivalry between two magicians, Erai and Melosar. Late each night, Melosar would creep into Erai's village to make magic in the ashes of his fire. Erai tried to protect himself but slowly went insane. He took two sea spirits for wives, rejecting his human wife. Finally he jumped from a breadfruit tree. When they found his body, the rats had already gnawed away his toes. Many people were crazed with the fear that sea spirits still inhabited the villages, and would not return to their homes. They stayed in the canoe houses instead.

This event struck close to Mwaramai. Erai was his fellow initiate in *pwo*; Mwaramai's only son was the first to discover the body. He thereafter fell ill from the fright, it is said, and died.

Mwaramai had no idea how old he was, but simply asserted he was the oldest man on Satawal. He recalled that when "Sanny Ferto," the first white man anyone remembers, came to Satawal on a sailing vessel, they thought he was an evil ghost. But Sanny gave them rice and took copra in return. He married a woman of Satawal, and one of his great-granddaughters is still alive. Next came Lewis, "a big man with many hairs," who sailed among the islands in his schooner. Mwaramai thought he was not a person, "because he had hair coming from his eyes all the way past his nose to the middle of his chest!" (This was probably Evan Lewis, a Welshman, a resident trader on Lamotrek from 1880 to 1900.)

Then came the Germans, who were interested only in copra. They divided Satawal with a road, taking half the island for themselves and leaving half for the Satawalese. After them were the Japanese, who shot all the Germans. Japan, too, made the Satawalese collect copra, and later impressed men into labor gangs to work the fields on Yap and the phosphate mines on Fais and Palau. The Japanese beat the men and raped their wives. No one has fond memories of them. One afternoon I asked Mwaramai if things were better under the Americans. He grew reflective.

"Under the Japanese and Germans, there was much sickness. The ways of America are better. They take care of Satawal. Now there are doctors and plenty of houses made of wooden planks with tin roofs. Made by America. This is good.

"Before, each clan stayed on their own land; we were hostile and suspicious of each other. People would try to beat us if we walked in front of their canoe house. Now we all eat together, and people even eat with chiefs. When the blackbird finds a ripe breadfruit it makes a sound, 'shushushu,' and all the blackbirds come to eat. It is like this on Satawal now; long ago it was not.

"Yet, in the old days, we still had our magic. We called the bread-fruit and coconuts; we called the logs, the tuna, the herring and the fish of the reef. There were more fish then, because we called them. Now there are few because no one calls. We can say it is a new age now, the age of the Christians. Our magic no longer lives."

He drifted into reverie, beholding, perhaps, the sparkling island of lur, floating in the south.

"What about the spirits?" I asked, startling him. "Are they still around? Is Anumwerici still around, or has he left or died because of the Christians?"

"Yes," he said, brightening, "the spirits will not leave—Anumwerici will not leave. He listens for the songs we used to sing to him, and waits for us to sing them again. Then he will come."

He taught me one last chant in the cycle of calling breadfruit. It was a simple chant, sung by a student while sliding a small canoe on the chest of his dead master. If the ritual was performed, Saurhewon came to transfer the master's knowledge to his student. If it was not performed, Saurhewon took the knowledge back to Iur, where the good was preserved and the evil thrown into the pool of the sea to be devoured by sharks.

18

One morning a light wind sprang up from the east. Piailug suddenly set sail for Lamotrek to fetch some things Mesailuke needed for his baby. He told me to stay behind to complete my work with Mwaramai. After a week on Lamotrek he radioed he was leaving for West Fayu to hunt turtles. There the wind died, stranding him.

Each evening the sun sank into a clear, hard horizon that knifed off the bottoms of the distant cumulus clouds. The palm trees did not stir, as if the breathing of the earth itself paused at the cusp of the season for the wind from the west. Each night the paddling canoes slipped out to fish the reef, their lanterns etching trails of brilliance across the black, moonless pool of the sea. Catches were poor, not even enough to feed the men's own families. As the sun baked the island, people grew hungry. Nemoito's mother had recovered now, and the family moved back to Nemanong. There was no one to fish for them, since Piailug was away with the rest of the crew and I had conscripted Josede to help me, so I provided canned mackerel bought from one of the island's three small stores. After we ate, the hungry dogs licked the stones beneath our feet and fought over the discarded tins.

I caught the flu and would wake in the middle of the night bathed in sweat. I dreamed repeatedly of spirits. Once I walked down the street of a city resembling Rome, arm in arm with my wife. Then she changed into a different woman, dark, tawny, smelling of smoke and sweat. I spoke a strange European language mixed with archaic Satawalese. That vision faded, and I was flanked by two dark spirits. I woke in terror, feeling powerless. I had to tell myself I was awake now and had been dreaming. I was Western, I didn't believe in spirits; my wife had not been transformed—she was in Boston, waiting for me. I stumbled outside, vomited in the bushes, and crawled back in my hut, shivering. I wrapped myself in a plastic tarp and fell back to sleep.

The next night I went fishing with Uurupa, Weneto, and In-aiman in Weneto's Fiberglas skiff. The wheezing outboard motor pushed us past the coral heads exposed by the low, spring tide, past the twinkling fires in the villages, and along the northern beach, where the tall breadfruit trees crossed the starlit sky in lacy patterns. Finally we arrived on a deep reef to the north of Wenimung, killed the motor, and drifted. The others began working their hand lines to catch bait fish. I waited, since Uurupa didn't want to loan me one of his hand-tied lures, knowing I would probably lose it. I peered through the halo of the gas lamp toward the dark silhouette of the island. Uurupa and Weneto told stories about the spirits on Wenimung.

I tried to "invert my thinking," as I put it in my journal, to perceive this world through the mind of the pre-Christian navigator, a world mysterious, feminine, impenetrable, illogical. Desiring to submerge my growing feeling that Piailug had cut me loose, and in some important way my program had failed, I derived reassurance from pondering the condition of the natives like some Victorian gentleman-scientist. "I cannot know what this world was like," I concluded bombastically in my journal—forgetting that I *had*, in a sense, glimpsed it through my nightmare, and been terrified. "Old Satawal has gone the way of all cultures and all individuals and all worlds. It has died a natural death. If vestiges of it live at all, they live only in the seaways of memory."

There was a peculiar mood of waiting and resignation. People began to think of the return of the ship that would, in a few weeks, take the high-school students back to Ulithi. I would be leaving, too, and everywhere I went people asked me if I would return, if I would bring my wife, and if I would then have children.

The wind was still, the days hot, the sea empty. A grim industry possessed the place, markedly different from the heady days of summer, when the wind fed the island and a man could drink tuba and grow fat. Now, after fishing all night, the men would take their wives and children into the woods to make copra. The children would collect the fallen nuts while the men and women hacked them apart and removed the meat to dry. World copra prices had been falling steadily for the last several years, and a forty-kilo sack, representing perhaps three days' to a week's work, was worth less than ten dollars. Yet this was the only source of cash most families had, cash to buy kerosene for lanterns, fishing hooks and line, cotton for men's loincloths, powdered baby formula, and cotton thread for the women to weave into *turrh*. "Now money comes into our island," lamented Uurupa. "Before we used to make everything we needed: fishing line from hibiscus bark, hooks from turtle and clamshell; we used to roll our own tobacco in the bark of the banana trees. Now we work to buy these things."

When not drying copra, men made repairs to their houses, paddling canoes, and canoe houses. In the center of town two new houses were going up: of a hybrid design, they incorporated cement beams, posts, and floor with the traditional thatched roof, which can be lifted from the posts and set on the ground in case of a typhoon. Several of the richest families, whose sons worked for the state or on one of the government field ships, were putting up all-cement, pillbox-type houses. These structures required a great deal of time and money to build: the eighty-pound sacks of concrete were shipped from Yap, lightered ashore, and carried by hand to the site, then laboriously mixed with coral gravel collected in baskets from the beach at low tide. Even the fresh water with which to mix the concrete was hand-carried in buckets from wells in the woods. When it was time to pour the floor and the roof, all the men of the island were summoned to help, some mixing, others pouring, and still others spreading and smoothing. The family building the house fed everyone and, of course, distributed ample cigarettes and tobacco. Yet, despite the expense, many families hoped to construct these squat, ugly structures, which have become a status symbol.

When the flu swept the island, I had a steady stream of requests for aspirin. Nemoito caught it and sat one night on the stones of the moonless courtyard, moaning. Tigiri massaged her back and shoulders with long, firm strokes. Josephina came to massage her breasts and stomach. Soon Uurupa's wife and her sisters arrived from Asugulap to lend their advice and company. I was oblivious to the crisis, sitting in my hut listening to music through headphones, swilling the last of my Scotch and reading, until Tigiri burst in to demand medicine.

I took Nemoito's temperature, then, reasoning her illness was some combination of flu and menstrual discomfort, began a set of questions vaguely designed to find out when her period would begin. After squeamishly trying several oblique approaches, I settled down to basics:

"Tigiri, what is it called when blood comes to a woman?"

"It's called 'blood.'"

"When will the blood see Nemoito?"

"When will it see you, Nemoito?" Tigiri asked.

"Soon," she answered, pointing toward the western sky. "When the moon starts to rise from there." The first-quarter moon would appear the next evening.

"I think both flu and blood see Nemoito at the same time," I stated. Tigiri looked puzzled. "The *meselipic* and the *cha* come together to make her sick—both come at the same time." Tigiri listened with a puzzled expression. I told her to give Nemoito aspirin every four hours; she nodded deferentially, then pulled the wraithlike patient to her own big, warm, fleshy body as if to suck away her pain like a living sponge. I squatted there, feeling awkward, as she continued her massage, the other women crowding in close to observe. Nemoito moaned with each stroke, occasionally coughing a low, rasping cough.

As more women arrived from Asugulap to sit straight-legged in the courtyard, I escaped to my hut. Their murmuring blended with that of the feeble surf. The stars blazed overhead. Nemoito's moaning died away as the aspirin took effect, and the women talked about illness and death and the hospital on Yap. As Orion and Scorpio climbed through the sky, a light wind sprang out of the west, making the palm fronds "shushu," like the call of the blackbirds. Tigiri helped Nemoito to the canoe house to sleep. The women talked a little longer, then rose in groups of two and three to crunch across the courtyard back to their villages.

The next evening Piailug returned, reaching across a light westerly that later backed to the north and died. He brought eight turtles, which were immediately burned, cut apart, and distributed.

That day a troubled Mwaramai had sent for me. One of his nephews had overheard the chiefs talking in their canoe house. I was a thief, they were reported to have concurred, and should pay Mwaramai for his efforts. He was afraid to talk to me any more, for fear of angering the chiefs.

Disturbed, I went immediately to Piailug, who speculated that the nephew, a cunning fellow, was trying to con me by manipulating his old uncle. Piailug took me to see Chief Rewena, who categorically denied the rumor and criticized the nephew for being such a troublemaker. I went to the other two chiefs and received the same answer. Just to smooth things over, I took Mwaramai a gift of cigarettes, bed sheets, a new towel, and some T-shirts. He was very happy that the chiefs were innocent and beamed when I described the gifts. I was troubled by the whole incident, for I didn't know whom I could trust. But in the end I was satisfied of Mwaramai's innocence and the chiefs' honor, and thereafter eyed the nephew with suspicion.

With plenty of turtle, a spirit of levity briefly returned to the island. Since tuba had been banned, some men brewed two big pots of "yeast," a vile mixture of bread yeast, sugar, and water, in a remote spot in the woods and invited all the men from Ropitiu, Woleatu, and Ootenap, along with Chief Rewena, to drink. We sat on coconut fronds in a wide circle under the trees. Josede squatted in the middle, serving the sweet, milky brew. I arrived late and was given the place of honor between Piailug and the chief.

Everyone was drunk and getting drunker. Rewena wanted to sing songs of navigation. Half the circle joined him with gusto; the other half talked among themselves. He kept time with a leafy branch he used to swat flies, turning occasionally to beat time on my head. Someone cranked up the volume on the ghetto blaster, drowning the navigation song with the latest Palauan pop hit. The other half of the circle started singing along with the pop song. Rewena, still directing with his branch, laughed and joined them. "I just want to sing and be happy now!" he roared, dusting me, then Piailug, then me again.

Someone turned the ghetto blaster down.

An old man was telling Piailug that outboard motors should be banned. I interrupted to declare they were good, if used as auxiliaries on sailing canoes, since that would make the canoes more versatile and help to keep canoe building alive.

But there was no money for gas, oil, or spare parts, the man countered.

Soon, under the terms of the Compact of Free Association, I explained passionately, they would build airstrips, water-catchment systems, and on some islands harbors and roads. There would be more government jobs, which meant more money. I pointed to the example of a Satawalese who worked for Yap Memorial Hospital. He had recently built himself a cement house, and would soon take delivery of a new, four-thousand-dollar fishing skiff with a powerful outboard motor.

"That is the fault of the hospital," Piailug sneered, "ruining us with their money."

"But there will be more things like the hospital!" I claimed drunkenly. He listened while I explained that under the Compact, Micronesians could freely emigrate to the United States to live and work. Paul told me that many young men planned to go to Hawaii or Guam. Piailug just nodded, then cleared his throat. The conversation quieted.

"We should all learn some of the talk of our fathers," he announced. "We will do Wofanu Satawal:

> "I stay on Satawal, I go Mailap up east on Truk.
> I stay on Truk, I go Mailap down west on Satawal.
> I stay on Satawal, I go Paiifung up east on Puluwat.
> I stay on Puluwat. . . ."

The buzz of conversation steadily resumed as the drinkers turned back to their own conversations. Rewena lay down his branch and moved his arms as if to beat time to Piailug's recitation of the star courses. "Penis!" he yelled at selected individuals. "You listen!" Then he picked up his switch to dust me and Piailug. As if this were a signal, the ghetto blaster started again, drowning Piailug's *wofanu*. Rewena waved his branch to the music.

"Everyone is too drunk," Piailug said resignedly; "it is no use trying to talk about anything now."

Then Mesailuke turned the stereo down. He recited Wofanu Satawal and Wofanu West Fayu. Piailug sat cross-legged, his eyes closed,
visibly moved. "Uh-huuuu!" or "Mmmmmmmmmmm!" he encouraged
after each star course. Mesailuke finished without interruption: "All
right, that is all," he concluded, embarrassed.

The stereo blasted; Rewena cheered at the renewed merrymaking,
then beat me soundly with his branch. The drinking circle was out of
control, and this chief, who was supposed to care for his island as a
navigator cared for his crew, or a father for his children, was encour-
aging anarchy. This somehow chafed away the last strands from which
dangled my fiction that a purer world existed outside my own culture and that a truer sort of man upheld that world: heroes were not
Heroes, and fathers not Fathers. My reaction was peevish, childish
anger.

I stuck my hands into the folds of Rewena's belly and tickled
him mercilessly. Howling with laughter, he desperately tried to fend
me off, but I got to my feet, grabbed his ankles, and hoisted him
upside down. "Let's throw the chief into the pot!" I gaily shouted, glancing around the circle to share the enjoyment of my prank with the
others.

But their faces, I noticed, were ashen gray, frozen in various
attitudes of horror, disbelief, and anger. A ghastly silence fell on the
circle. It dimly occurred to me I'd made a grave mistake. I set the chiefly
feet back on the ground and resumed my place. Polite conversation
began immediately. Rewena regained his composure with astonishing speed and launched into a spirited song. Everyone sang with
gusto.

"What were you doing?" he asked under his breath once the song
was under way.

"I don't know, maybe I was crazy," I answered lamely, feeling
dizzy.

"That is not possible," he said with deadly seriousness. "You are
a *navigator*."

Protected thus far by shock, I became nauseous.

"This is not good, Steve," Piailug whispered in my ear, shaking
his head: "Not good, not good, not good." After the song, guarded
conversation resumed.

Rewena ordered the second pot of yeast distributed and after several rounds sang "Pistol Packing Baby," which he pronounced "piston." He became very excited about this song, jumping around in his place like an off-balance washing machine. I thought it would be a dandy time to recite some of the *itang* and so whispered a stanza into his ear. He shouted with pleasure, grabbed me around the neck, and pulled me head-first into his lap.

Things degenerated as the second pot of yeast was consumed. The stereo played at full volume and everyone sang rowdily, except Piailug, who remained self-contained and expressionless, smoking cigarettes. Soon the younger men wanted to brew another batch of yeast and drink all night. Rewena held his hands forth in a gesture for silence. He began the song of Saipweric, one of Satawal's great navigators, a peer of his own father. The song, a lament, was composed by his lover, Aouani:

> *We live south of the white people,*
> *On low islands, reef elbows.*
> *Oh, I am sad,*
> *For that man cannot hold himself from the sea,*
> *Like a shark in winter.*
> *I, Aouani, I have a pain under my reef.*
> *I walk wearily, I dream of before,*
> *Of your talk, a tune so sweet.*
> *This is the first year of his voyage;*
> *He is far away and we are far apart,*
> *Like the green arms of the coconut tree from its trunk.*
>
> *He squats to hold his sheet,*
> *Driving through the sea of salt spray,*
> *He relies on his crew, and his arms,*
> *Strong as the* langit *plant.*
> *Go on, attempt any passage!*
> *I will rub my hands with turmeric,*
> *So my love will fill you.*
> *This year, the first of your voyage,*
> *In the north sea, the sea of Saipan.*
>
> *As you stand under the flapping sail and shroud,*
> *Pick up and look at*

That adornment of ours,[*]
Place it tightly in your hair knot,
Carefully, ours, inside your hair knot,
Knot of the eastern islands,
Hair knot of Truk,
Tightly so your crew won't see,
Strongest one.

Make magic against the rain,
For that's your custom when voyaging.
Slack the sheet in the gusts,
Under the falling rain.
You cannot break the aura of your care,
Barracuda lying
On the surface of the sea.

"We will leave now," Rewena announced when the song was over. "We will cut our sweet tuba for our children, then return quietly to our villages, eat, and sleep. We have all drunk well."

Slowly the group wandered off. Rewena attempted to stand, fell down, was hauled to his feet again, and, with Mesailuke and Joseph steadying him, made his way down the path. Piailug and I walked to Fanagoon, washed in silence, then wandered back to Nemanong.

In the morning I found Piailug bathing in the sea in front of the canoe house. He flashed angry glances at me as he rubbed himself with seawater. I went down the beach to defecate, then returned.

"Are you angry with me?" I asked.

"I am angry with you," he answered fiercely.

"Because of what I did to Rewena? I'm sorry, I didn't know. In our custom I could have done that with my own father. We can play like that." I hoped to gloss over the underlying issue, which was that I was peevishly enraged at Rewena for not being the wise chief my script called for. Piailug sensed my disingenuousness immediately.

---

[*]"Adornment": when a man left for a long voyage, his lover shaved her pubic hair and wrapped it in a small packet as a keepsake.

"Maybe in America," he said doubtfully, "but never here on Satawal. Never. It is very bad, very bad."

"So what do I do now?" I asked hopefully.

"It's up to you," he said, shrugging. Clearly, I had gone too far and was on my own. There was nothing he could or would do for me.

"They plan to kill you," he added, almost casually. I thought it was a joke but he was utterly serious.

"Oh yes, Steve!" he added, reading my thoughts. "Kill you!" He drew his hand across his throat. "Joseph, Eddy, and Mesailuke talked about it last night. They vowed to kill you for what you did to our father, the chief."

Alarmed, I pictured myself getting ambushed on my way to the bathing pool, my throat slit with a machete, like a pig. They wouldn't really kill me, I reassured myself; the consequences would certainly deter them. But, clearly, I had gotten myself into serious trouble. The only way out now was to go to the chief, the very man whom in my childish anger and drunkenness I had regarded with contempt, and ask him to forgive me.

"I must find Rewena," I said almost dreamily. "I must take him gifts and *atirro* him."

"That would be good," Piailug replied. Then he gently, almost paternally, told me to have breakfast and go to Rewena.

The chief sat alone in his canoe house, rolling coconut fibers into rope on his thigh.

"*Atirro*, I greet you with solemn respect, chief," I said as I entered, bending at the waist in the *aparog* position. I placed the paper bag containing cigarettes and coffee on the ground next to him.

"What's this for?" he demanded.

"For yesterday, when I pulled your feet. I bend with respect to you. I forgot the ways of the island. I was drunk. On my island it is not as strict; I could have done such a thing to my own father. I was playing around and only afterward did I see that I was breaking the custom. *Atirro*."

The chief scrutinized me carefully, as if weighing his right and power to banish me against my desire to be forgiven—leaving aside, perhaps, the doubtfulness of my excuse.

"I forgot the ways of the island," I entreated. "I only meant it as play. I am very sorry. *Atirro*."

The chief's eyes, dimmed by cataracts, remained fixed on mine until I looked down at the wood chips at my feet. I sat cross-legged before him like a small boy.

"We will throw it away," he finally said. "We will simply throw it away."

Piailug came to me early the next morning to tell me he was leaving. He had been asked to lead a turtling expedition to West Fayu and, according to custom, could not refuse. I couldn't go, for the *Microspirit* was due to arrive in less than a week, and if the wind died again I would miss it. Besides, he had not invited me. The fair east wind held through that day and evening. At dawn the next morning he radioed he had reached the island.

On Sunday the chiefs announced a taboo on picking coconuts and entering the woods. A conch shell would be blown at six each morning, at noon, and at four in the afternoon, at which times we could shower, harvest nonalcoholic tuba, and pick breadfruit. Each afternoon men were to spend several hours clearing their coconut plantations to make the trees more productive. Men from the high clans were appointed to patrol the woods for violators.

In the past this would have been the occasion for the *umau*. Masters of calling breadfruit and those who call coconuts, reef fish, logs, octopus, and tuna would have performed their magic to make the island rich with food and fish. At night the people would have danced to the songs of *umau* and refreshed themselves with new sexual partners. But now everyone was to report to the chiefs' canoe house each evening for a head count.

The wind that had taken Piailug to West Fayu died, and for over a week did not stir. The air was suddenly filled with dragonflies. The boys, trimming enough of their wings to let them fly but not gain altitude, played catch with the creatures on the beach.

The ship was delayed leaving Yap and a new schedule had not been set. But the school year began in September, and the students would have to be transported to Ulithi before then. I began to conclude my project. Josede and I had finished translating Mwaramai's lore, and Josede returned to his duties in Nemanong. I spent several days reviewing the material and double-checking details with the old man. Thereafter I visited him every couple of days to give him cigarettes and to chat. Then I began the last task on my list of research objectives, to interview some of the young men to get their perspective.

I spoke with Battista, Piailug's son, who was planning to return to his job on Yap, now that his grandmother was recovering. Several years before, when both his mother and Bonefacio required hospitalization, he had taken a job as a stevedore to pay their medical bills. Soon he was promoted to warehouse manager and asked to stay. Now he had second thoughts about returning to his job. He was proud of his father's reputation and wanted to learn the old arts. But all the young men give lip service to that, I countered, and no one seemed to learn. He admitted that he had been lazy in this respect.

He feared great changes in the next few years, as the elders passed away. His generation had not acquired seafaring skills, and, consequently, imported food and a cash economy would predominate. He didn't know what he would do in the future. He didn't hold himself responsible to the island (in contrast to the code of the navigator), although he was responsible to his relatives. In the worst case, he thought, he could move them to Yap and provide for them there. His generation's greatest loss would be the talk of wisdom, he said. For without it the normal tensions of close living on a small island would find release in fighting and discord.

The other young men I talked to all felt similarly: Rovigno, Josede, and Mesailuke all sensed themselves on the precipice of fundamental cultural change. Rovigno, who was from Ulul island in Truk state, had seen the future of Satawal in the presence of Truk: "Like them," he said, "we will throw away how we live. It is not good on Truk and Saipan." Although he thought he would enjoy a traditional life style, he foresaw that his son would grow up in a changed world. We talked early one morning when he had stopped on his way back from his tuba trees.

"But is there anything you can do now to influence the future condition of Satawal?" I asked.

"I don't know, Steve," he answered, swirling the dregs of his coffee and tossing them through the open door, "I just don't know."

Bonefacio, now fifteen years old, had not yet begun to think about these things. He would remain home from high school, because that was his father's will. He wanted to learn navigation, he said, so he could see all the islands of Micronesia. He was studying and taking notes. He didn't like Satawal, because it was dirty and small: "You walk up and walk back and you are still in the same place." Hawaii, in contrast, was very big, with good stores, many automobiles, and bright lights.

Josede had just begun to think of the future with the birth of his son. He had attended technical school on Palau after graduating from high school. There he experienced the phenomenon of purchasing what he ate, which formed his conception of the future on his own island: "I know we will not do as we do now—when someone comes along, to freely offer him food. We will make him pay to eat. This is not our custom." I asked if there was any way he could influence the future. He answered dreamily, as if thinking about it for the first time: "I don't know what we will do when Piailug and the others pass from us. I just know this island will change unless they impress us with what we are to do."

Mesailuke had thought much about these issues. He had been an infamous troublemaker in his youth, fighting and stealing chickens. As a teen-ager on Yap, he recalled with a laugh, he had once thrown a policeman in the harbor. He became bored with high school and dropped out to work on a ship, then went off to Saipan. Eventually he returned to marry. Now he was studying with Rewena and Piailug during the portions of the year he resided on Satawal. He kept notebooks, which he reviewed each evening and on Sundays. He assured me he would soon be ready to sail—it was his firm intention to become a navigator and canoe builder. But he worried about his son. Responsibility for the children's education was increasingly being turned over to teachers, he observed, and the link between father and son was broken.

Paul had just graduated from high school this year. When I had seen him on the *Microspirit* he'd exuded confidence: "I'll be going out to learn about the outside world," he stated; "my brothers will remain home to learn navigation. When we meet we will exchange information." He had visited Satawal for several hours, before returning to Ulithi on the ship, to attend summer school. Next year he would go to college on Guam, and hoped eventually to transfer to the University of Hawaii. He would pay for his education with government loans, but was unsure how he would repay them. On Hawaii, Ponape, and Guam, I had seen a number of boys who had done the same and after graduation had stayed to work. They had rented apartments, bought cars and stereos, sometimes borrowing more money. Whether they wanted to return home or not, they were forced to stay to service their debt. Paul didn't know how he would solve this problem.

The press of time seemed to nag at him, too. He had not been able to see Maanusuuk before he died. "I felt there was something else I was supposed to ask him," he said, "something very secret that only he knew." He halted, then asked himself: "What if Uurupa and Piailug die when I am away at college? Dying is in the corner of our eyes, always in the corner. We cannot say, 'I plan to die at this time, so I must teach you this beforehand.'"

In several days I had completed my interviews and come to the end of my prepared research program. There were still some last-minute details I wanted to check with Piailug if he made it back in time, but essentially I was finished.

One evening I mixed my remaining one-third bottle of gin with the juice of about twenty limes, exchanged my loincloth for a pair of shorts, took my lawn chair and Walkman down to the beach, and sat, drank, listened to jazz, and watched the sunset. The incident of the chief's feet had chastened me, and I was no longer angry at Piailug; but neither did I have a sense of resolution, of closure. Our relationship just hung there. In a way it was a relief, for I was free of the constant mental pressure of justifying his actions with my prearranged script. I wished that our relationship had been closer, but was resigned to the fact it wasn't. Even though he had faithfully transmitted his knowledge, I had no sense of him as a master, one to whom I could return year after year for wisdom and strength. My original dream to apprentice myself to a master of forgotten knowledge still seemed worthy, albeit naïve. As I refilled my coffee cup with gin gimlet, I snorted at the puerility of it all. If I stripped away all the romanticism of the Pacific-island setting, the outrigger canoes, the leathery, tattooed men and bare-breasted girls, all I really had was a dozen notebooks full of notes, some tape recordings, and photographs. Piailug could have been a house-builder in Milwaukee who had learned his craft from his father. His sons and sons-in-law seemed more interested in his craft than he gave them credit for. If he had known the talk of light, perhaps it would have been different. But perhaps not. I didn't know. Somewhere in all my notes might be the answer. In them, too, might be the answers to my original questions (whatever they were) and the wisdom of old Oceania (if there was such a thing). Just then I didn't particularly care; I had played my hand; I was spent and would leave on the next ship. Whatever fire had driven the engine of this quest was quenched, and that was a relief. Soon I would be home and I could figure it all out there.

19

When the moon began to wane, a light wind sprang up from the west, gentle at first, but building steadily. Hot, salty air moved in slabs from the sea through the canoe houses, cooking sheds, and dwellings. Jupiter, Saturn, and Mars throbbed so clear and distinct that one could almost visualize the tracks of their orbits. Soon it clouded over and there fell a warm, salty rain.

Piailug rode the favorable wind home. Children playing on the beach first spotted his sail, a small delta beneath a blood-red sunset. Nemoito began to prepare a dish called *sooahsoo*, a delicious mixture of sweet taro and coconut milk baked in an earth oven. As I headed from Nemanong down to the beach to wait, I paused by the cooking shed. Nemoito sat on her folded legs, holding a lighted torch in one hand. The other held a clamshell, with which she swirled concentric rings in the surface of the *sooahsoo*, as if arranging the frosting on a cake. The torchlight flowed across the hollows of her cheeks, across the feline repose of her shoulders, to shadow her withering breasts. She seemed mesmerized by the movements of the clamshell on the glistening food. It could have been an image from a thousand years ago: the only light in the world was the light of her torch, the only task the one at hand, making a dish to welcome her husband home from the sea. All around her was darkness and the slanting lines of rain.

That night I drank yeast with Piailug and the rest of the crew. I asked some last questions about the fighting of stars and phases of the moon and listened to stories about hunting turtles on West Fayu. I turned in early, but Piailug drank all night.

The next day was Assumption Day. Thureng had declared an island holiday, celebrated with Mass, a procession, dancing, and a feast. As I sat outside the church waiting for Mass to finish, Piailug wove through the churchyard, shouting. Spots of lipstick were painted on his cheeks and forehead.

"Who decorated you?" I asked.

"Me," he proclaimed, pounding his chest, "so I can drink and make trouble!" Then he tacked north to rejoin his fellows.

After Mass, the procession issued from the church. On a flower-covered float at its head bobbed a plastic statue of the Virgin Mary. Four teen-age boys carried the float, followed by Thureng and the entire female population of the island. The men were conspicuously absent.

As the procession moved along the main path, women rushed up to kiss the effigy and splash their children with holy water from the cup before it. At Ropitiu the procession turned down to the beach, made its way in front of the canoe houses and back to the church.

Then the turtles Piailug had brought back from West Fayu were burned and distributed. The girls did traditional slap dances before the chiefs' canoe house, singing teasing songs to the chiefs, who, in a traditional gesture, threw whole packs of cigarettes into the crowd. Squealing children rushed after the prizes, snatching them from between the feet of the dancers.

The next morning Piailug rose early, and worked all day on the new canoe. The ship was now scheduled to arrive on Sunday, and he told me he had planned a going-away party for me tomorrow, Friday, for which he had saved one of the turtles. He would invite the chiefs and the elders along with the rest of the Masano and Katamang clans. I bought yeast and sugar, and with Rovigno's help brewed two big pots of "yeast."

Late that afternoon, however, an old woman came from the chiefs to inform Piailug he would be fined for drinking on the morning of the procession, and was now prohibited from further drinking. He told her he was a man and would drink like a man, any time and any way he wished. He told her to repeat this to the chiefs. I had never seen him so angry. Evidently two of the chiefs, after hearing complaints of Piailug's sacrilege, had decided to single him out for punishment. None of the *telap* had been consulted beforehand, a clear violation of tradition, and no announcement of the new rule prohibiting drinking before noon had been made. Piailug was charged *ex post facto*. Worse was the insult: the chiefs sent a woman to tell him instead of doing it themselves.

I asked if there wasn't perhaps some misunderstanding. After all, I reasoned, when I had gone before Rewena he had responded generously and reasonably. Why couldn't Piailug do the same? I never considered there might be years of rivalry between him and the chiefs, that they might be jealous of his fame, his ability to cross freely between the worlds of Micronesia and the modern West, might envy his fierceness, courage, and skill. I still believed that Piailug brought many of his problems on himself through some vital character flaw. For some reason I insisted he acknowledge this.

"There is no misunderstanding," he explained bitterly but tolerantly. "That woman came directly from the chiefs. Everyone knows exactly what is going on here."

That evening all the men from Nemanong and Asugulap gathered before Ropitiu to drink the yeast intended for my party. Piailug spoke bitterly and rebelliously against the chiefs, and we excitedly declaimed the injustice. Later, when a rainsquall forced us inside, he lapsed into brooding silence. Some men talked quietly; others stretched out to sleep on the big sailing canoe or on the fat coils of rope and fishnet. The waning moon rose to wheel through the tropical Pacific night. As it was poised above the sea, I left him.

Just after sunrise, when I came down to bathe in the sea before Nemanong, he was still drinking. Inaiman and Jesse slept in the sand, Jesse resting his head against the stewpot containing the remainder of a third batch of yeast. The turtle lay on its back near-by, beating its flippers helplessly. Then it took a deep breath and waited.

"You run off to sleep!" Piailug taunted me, spoiling for a fight. "Some Americans are of strong meat, just like us. But you, maybe you are made of a woman's meat, or a child's!" He had teased me plenty of times before but never cruelly, never insulting my manhood as I had seen him do to others. I thought of several retorts, but since he seemed on the brink of rage, all I said was "Yes, maybe." He laughed and slapped my chest with his callused paw.

"If you wanted me to drink with you, why didn't you say so?" I asked.

"Oh? You want to drink now?" he taunted again. "Then go bathe and change your loincloth. You and I, Steve, will get *drunk!*"

When I returned, Mesailuke, Joseph, and Geriger had arrived and hacked off the turtle's left hind flipper, pulled out its intestines, and were roasting them over a fire. Piailug made me sit on a mat next to him and ordered me to drink. Joseph placed the roasted tripes on a small piece of driftwood, then retreated to pile dry coconut fronds on the turtle and set them alight.

"Eat, Steve," Piailug commanded. Then he drained another cup.

"I'm going to drink and drink and then I'm going to kill all the people here," he vowed bitterly.

"Who?" I asked. He looked at me challengingly.

"The people!" he pronounced fiercely.

"All of them?" I rattled on, getting scared. "Like the ancient warrior Saiow?"

He switched momentarily to English: "I want to fight the chiefs. I will drink and keep drinking. I want you to go back to Boston and bring me a machine gun so I can kill all the chiefs on this island!" His lip curled in rage as he blasted them with his extended forefingers.

"Don't you think it's just a misunderstanding?" I asked. Something in me seemed to push for a final confrontation. "Maybe the old woman didn't understand the chiefs' message. Maybe if you talked to them it would be cleared up."

"Do you think the chiefs speak the language of America or our language?" he lashed back, his face compressed in fury.

"Your language."

"Of course! And was that a woman of America or a woman of this island?"

"A Satawal woman . . . but . . . maybe she didn't understand. . . ."

"The chiefs sent that woman to tell me I will be punished and you think there is no problem? I took my canoe to West Fayu to hunt turtles for their feast. I got stuck there two weeks with no wind. Even as they ate my turtle, they ruled I'd be punished, then sent a woman—a woman!—to tell *me*, a *navigator*, I'd be punished for drinking like a man!" His voice was clear now and as hard as a bitter wind. "You tell me to go talk to the chiefs! You must think you're a chief, Steve!"

I offered a lame excuse: "I thought maybe she didn't understand. I've seen how rumors spread on this island and . . ."

His anger rushed forth in a torrent: "Did you come to this island under the name of the chiefs or the name of Piailug?"

"I want to tell you why I said that about the woman—I . . ."

"You want to tell me? What do you have to tell me, Steve? No, you listen to me. You came to this island under the name of Piailug. You stay here under the name of Piailug. You are protected by Piailug. You *live* because of Piailug! Lately you have left me to talk to others, even though last year I told you not to. You have given them gifts and sat in their houses. You even talk to the chiefs on your own. You forget that you are under my name."

He had known I was talking to Mwaramai, I tried to protest, but Piailug just raised his voice and leaned so menacingly close that I shrank back.

"When the ship comes, take all your things and leave. Take your gifts back with you! I don't want them! If you ever return, return under the name of the chiefs. You are no longer under the name of Piailug!"

"But why?" I gasped in disbelief. He had just turned against me. Deep down, I had to admit he was justified, for I had betrayed his loyalty by questioning his mastery; I had left him, seeking knowedge elsewhere; I had tried to tread a line between him and the chiefs. But to say I was no longer under his name was the ultimate rebuke. Now was the time in my studies when I should be graduating with his blessing; instead, I was being sent forth, a pariah.

Mercifully, it started to rain, warm and soft at first. The coals around the expired turtle hissed and guttered. A low surf nibbled at the reef. I sat at his feet like a small boy.

Then the squall bore down upon us, driving hard, cold raindrops across the sea and island. The others helped Piailug to his feet, and he turned away from me and limped toward the canoe house.

20

I sat on my mat as the rain streamed down my face and bare chest and formed spots on my eyeglasses. I didn't know what to do. Uurupa couldn't help me, because he wouldn't go against his brother. There was no one else in the whole clan I could turn to; Maanusuuk was dead. No one would go against Mau. Maybe the chiefs would shelter me in the dispensary, but that would be the final break. They would delight in my defection, and my project—my real project—would have failed.

I suppose I rebelled against Piailug in a way I had never done with my own father. After we returned from Pikelot, Piailug had left me on my own. This was as it should have been, for once I had proved I could navigate, it was time for me to command my own canoe. Then, over the months and years, I would return to ask more questions, as Piailug himself had done with his masters.

But I had wanted more from him, something I had no real right to ask: I had wanted him to explain himself to me, to give me reasons to admire him. I had wanted a father's indulgence. That went far beyond our original deal.

Before reaching the canoe house, he turned back to me: "Come, Steve," he coaxed in English, "come in from the rain." I obeyed.

Inside, he motioned for me to sit next to him. I felt very strange and flushed, as if everything still hung in the balance.

We all sat in a circle now, drinking the watery yeast that had been brought in. The others talked quietly; then some went to finish butchering the turtle. Piailug drank in silence, staring out the door to the rain-washed sea. He didn't really mean to blast me, Joseph reassured me in English. "I know him. Yesterday he said he was angry that the chiefs accepted your gifts yet still wanted to charge you for Mwaramai."

Piailug demanded to know what Joseph was saying. He responded rapidly, in Satawalese. I cringed in anticipation of another outburst, but he just asked for another cup of yeast, downed it, lit a cigarette, smoked it for a time, then spoke:

"My anger means nothing," he said soothingly, "for the earth which belongs to Piailug also belongs to Steve. We can argue and it must come to nothing. You are my brother. But chiefs will cast you onto the sea, without an island, without a canoe."

Time passed and the rain slackened. I followed him up to the cooking shed, where he served me a bowl of turtle stew and roasted breadfruit. The sun was out, and the world seemed kinder. Casually he told me that Rewena later admitted that the chiefs *had* met to assess a fee for Mwaramai. Rewena had denied it because I spoke Satawalese, he said, and would have understood. If Piailug had gone alone, he would have told him the truth.

I was incredulous. Had each chief unabashedly lied to my face? I'd been warned of this on the *Microspirit*, before I ever set foot on the island. Piailug reminded me: "I told you all they want is money! They don't care about *you*, Steve."

For the rest of the day he kept me at his side. We drank more yeast amid tough, defiant talk. Geriger wanted to leave immediately for Lamotrek, there to wait for the ship. Others wanted to camp on West Fayu. Piailug said the chiefs wanted me to leave, now that my work was finished. They thought I was a potential troublemaker, with my opinions and ideas.

We drank until the early evening, when the yeast was gone, then dispersed to shower and eat. There was another pot fermenting, though, and I was told to show up at Geriger's house that evening. Piailug was not there; he had fallen asleep in the canoe house and Nemoito forbade anyone to wake him. We drank quietly, out of his fierce aura. I discussed books with Jesse; Geriger boasted of his plans to make his village as clean and orderly as Piailug's; Josede sang songs. Later, Joseph recited some *itang*. Perhaps there was hope after all, I reflected. Perhaps these young men were learning more than Piailug thought, and would keep enough from their own heritage to smooth the path into the future. They seemed to open up like sea anemones when away from the jabbing fingers of his anger.

Toward midnight, Josede and I wandered back up the path to Nemanong and stood in the courtyard to talk. He advised me to forget Piailug's anger: he was just like that sometimes, and it would all blow over. The sky above us was soft with clouds and the air very still. Occasionally a breath of wind would stir the forest, shaking big drops of water from the coconut trees to crash softly on the undergrowth below.

Early the next morning, Piailug sent for me. I went down to the canoe house prepared for another blast. Instead, he was sitting happily, drinking with Jesse. "These are your last days on Satawal, and I wanted the chiefs, the *telap*, and all the navigators to come to your party," he announced, smiling. "But the chiefs ruined the feast, so today we will do it ourselves. We will eat turtle, drink, and be happy. Soon you will leave us."

All morning we ate turtle and drank the sweet, muddy yeast. Later we sang Ulithian love songs and listened to tape recordings of Piailug singing navigation songs on the ghetto blaster. I composed doggerel (in Satawalese) about Jesse's nocturnal antics in the woods with partners of various sexes and species. The young men howled with laughter, hissing at me to keep my voice down so the women wouldn't hear.

As the sun slid off into the west, we all danced. Piailug and I were great pals again, and as we danced I hugged him and he laughed. I recited the Prologue to the *Canterbury Tales* in Middle English. Piailug sang a song bidding me farewell and telling of my forthcoming journey. I said I was American but part of me belonged to Satawal; I knew I would return. As the sun swooped low, a despondency fell across the circle. Piailug's recorded *wofanu* now played on the stereo.

Josede asked questions about it, provoking angry words from Piailug: "Are you going to learn from me, or are you going to wait until I die and learn from Steve's writing?"

Then Mau fell asleep and the partygoers wandered home. The stereo played a chant about a young navigator's first voyage, which moved like a chilly gray wind through Nemanong:

I sit and sit
On the beach near my village
To tie the knots of pwe.
It is good, the good spirits have come.
And I set sail.

We will use that stone for muir,
Put it in the center of the island,
So we sail straight under Mailap.
Sailing down, we meet birds under Ul.
And what bird is this?
Maybe the one that flies!
The epar *called Arrolpurrosso.*
I know now to gybe,
On the albatross called Lissingor,
To sail Mailap down west.
We will hold that course
To the reef of Onari;
And we've finished,
Our voyage,
As men.

I left the circle to eat turtle by the fire in the cooking shed. Nemoito sang along with the tape as she grated taro for *sooahsoo.* Piailug woke and played gently with Mauricio. As the chant finished and the tape ended, he took the child down into the sea to bathe. The sunset sky was a deep blood-red, and later there fell a gentle rain.

Piailug was sick the next day, Monday. On Tuesday we received word that the ship was again behind schedule and would arrive in several days. I told him I wanted our relationship to be like that of master and student: we would rise together, eat together, work together, spend the evening together. He said he wanted that, too. That afternoon he went down to the settlement to see how great a scandal we had caused. When he returned he told me to remain in Nemanong for several days.

Later in the week the west wind started to blow and soon built to a near-gale. Waves crashed on the reef in front of the canoe house, and a fine salt mist coated everything. The Southern Cross was setting in the evening, Piailug reminded me, and it was a new moon. He predicted the wind would last until the fifth or sixth day of the moon's cycle. The *Microspirit* was directed to Woleai to wait for better weather.

Uurupa and I spent one whole day with my charts. He would ask me the course between two islands, I would find it in compass degrees true, convert it to degrees magnetic, and finally to the star heading. He copied the courses and mileage in his notebook, painstakingly making sketches of the islands. "Now I am happy," he said when we finished; "I know these courses are good—for we have taken them from the chart!" When Piailug heard about it he scorned his brother: "Why does Uurupa even worry about your way of navigating? We have no money for charts and sextants, or all those books. We have no place on our canoes to do all the things you must do!" But his anger seemed spent.

The wind blew harder, driving rain through the mat walls of my hut. Piailug and I tied down the ridgepole of the canoe house to prevent it from being carried away. The heavy surf washed all the way up to the canoe house. All work stopped on the island.

We spent the days lounging in my hut, drinking coffee. I told him how once I had been caught in a dense fog off Cabo Finisterre on Spain's northern coast. I could hear ships everywhere, but could see nothing. We had neither radar nor radio. Soon the fog scaled up a bit and we counted thirteen ships around us—we were directly in the center of the shipping lanes.

Mau related how as a young man he had been sailing with Eguwan. Late at night they spotted what looked like a floating log, but before they could determine what it was they collided with it. They tried to tack but found themselves out of the water—on the back of a sleeping whale! Slowly the whale submerged, leaving the canoe floating once again.

By Sunday the rain had stopped but the wind continued. Since we were out of food, I bought canned mackerel from Thureng's store. The chief greeted me cordially, making no reference to the past week's events, which evidently had been struck from the record.

That afternoon Piailug again reflected that previous chiefs had been wiser: "They looked after the island, the fish, the turtles. They watched and did things that were good for the people. Maybe it's because we don't have to be as careful these days. We know we can eat food from a can or a jar or a bag [pointing to these articles around my hut]. Maybe they think that Yap, Ponape, or America will take care of us. But I have been to Hawaii, to Saipan, to Guam, to Tahiti, to Los Angeles. Don't they see that soon, very soon, change will crash on this island like a wave?"

The wind roared in the palm trees. He said that some of the chiefly clans wanted the government to build a landing strip on Satawal so they could fly back and forth to Yap for meetings. "They want to make this island like America, to force change upon us. Maybe they have a way to get money to buy their food—those of the chiefly clans—but I have none. In Nemanong we have to grow our food, to bring it from the sea.

"Now the chiefs have placed a taboo on making tuba, but one of them still sells yeast and sugar. When the ship comes, he will sell beer and vodka. How can they put a taboo on liquor we make ourselves but not on liquor we buy? Now they've placed a taboo on the woods, we care for the coconut trees so they will be productive. But I believe the chiefs did this knowing we would make much copra to sell to the ship. Then we will have plenty of money to buy beer and vodka from the chiefs. That's what I think; write it in your book, I don't care. I am afraid of what's happening to my island.

"I think money will break this island. Now on Woleai, Lamotrek, Pulusuk, and Puluwat, too, people fish in their motorboats and ask for money when they divide the catch. This was never our custom. In our custom everybody eats, not just those with money."

There was no rage in his remarks, no bitterness, no sentimentality. They seemed to tumble out in a clear stream of recognition that change on Satawal marked the end of his tradition.

That night, the fifth day of the new moon, the wind began to diminish and a few stars struggled through the rushing air. By the next day it had fallen away completely, but the big swell continued to crash on the reef. I walked about freely; if my relations with the chiefs had ever been strained, none now alluded to it. I visited each one to thank him and bid farewell.

Over the next few days the sea calmed, and the ship left Woleai to complete its rounds. I packed my books, my cameras, and my gifts: a beautiful scale model of *Suntory* Uurupa had carved for me, a dozen banana-fiber *turrh* from the women of Nemanong and Asugulap, Piailug's shells. I gave the rest of my things to Piailug, and was ready to depart. We stuck close. In the mornings we worked in the canoe house and in the afternoons cleared his coconut plantation with machetes. Then we bathed at Fanagoon, rubbing ourselves with grated coconut. In the evenings we sat on the benches near the cooking shed to eat and talk.

Then I said goodbye to Mwaramai, thanking him for what he had taught me, but he refused to accept my thanks. "It is I who should thank you," he said. "No one came to me until you did, and if you hadn't come I would have forgotten all I knew. You made me remember, and—oh!—I am sorry you are leaving us."

"Eesh!" Josede sighed as we walked back up the path to Nemanong. "If I was from another island, like you, and Mwaramai said those things to me, I would feel sorry, I would feel really bad here." He placed his fist on his chest.

On my last night on Satawal, Piailug said he had been thinking about Bonefacio. Perhaps he would send him to high school after all, but not on Ulithi. Maybe he would put him in school on Hawaii that winter. That way he would learn English and other subjects, and at night still learn navigation. Piailug asked me if this was possible, and I told him how to go about it.

The waxing moon had set early, abandoning the sky to the light wind and the shining stars. I couldn't sleep. I lay on my mat listening to the launch of the space shuttle on the Voice of America. When it had blasted off, I got up to watch the stars. I heard the ship arrive, growling up the eastern side of the island, and anchor in the lee of the northern reef. Orion, Scorpius, and Sagittarius sailed overhead. I took back my own stars. The tiny island on which I stood seemed to hover in time, while my own culture spread itself across the nighttime sky. I was convinced Piailug was right: in one year, in five years, all would be different. I remembered how I felt upon setting out from the Canary Islands as a young and inexperienced skipper of a yacht bound halfway around the world—that I was crossing lines never to be recrossed, traversing a watershed in my life. Now I felt *that* era was coming to a close, the era in which I had sought fierceness, the first level of manhood. Then I thought about seeing my wife soon and becoming a father.

At five-thirty I took Piailug a cup of coffee. We sat together on the log by the canoe house as the ship steamed around to begin unloading cement and lumber. Josede and Bonefacio took my gear out to the ship while I walked along the beach to bid everyone goodbye.

Once aboard, I bought a case of beer and retreated to my cabin with Piailug, Josede, and Bonefacio. I wanted to sum up my feelings about Satawal. I told the two young men they were like my brothers or sons. I was older, and in my own country was a navigator. "Now you must decide if you will become men in your own culture. You must learn the talk of the sea; otherwise you will not be considered men. If you are afraid of dying at sea, you must throw that fear away. I am afraid of dying at sea. The only thing you can know in life is that you will die—you might die tomorrow from a coconut falling on your head. . . ."

Bonefacio started laughing, then Josede; then we all laughed. We had downed most of the beer by now, and my Satawalese was inelegant. But then Piailug motioned for us to stop.

"Let's not laugh," he said, "because Steve is right. I, too, am afraid at sea. I am afraid of dying. But we have just a little time beneath the sky. You, Josede, must think about this, for now you are twenty-seven. And you, Bonefacio, I want you to learn because you are my son. I want you to hold the knowledge of the *palu*."

The ship's whistle started to blow and someone was shouting through a megaphone that the next boat would be the last to go ashore. Piailug said they should soon leave.

Then I turned to him, announcing I had something to say.

"What?" he asked with a crooked grin, expecting another testimonial. From Mwaramai I had learned a chant with which a student bids farewell to his master. I had memorized it, because I wanted to say goodbye in a meaningful way:

> *I am leaving behind me the canoe of Palulap*
> *For I will reach behind,*
> *I will reach ahead;*
> *I will reach ahead,*
> *I will reach behind.*
> *And, after my voyage, will you still hold me?*

Piailug began to laugh, perhaps surprised that I had learned it. Then I became mixed up and started to laugh myself, and had to repeat the whole thing over again. He slapped me on the shoulder, telling me in English that I was "no good."

But I repeated the last line, for there is a special answer the master must give. Piailug grew serious, his eyes soft, like the cloudy sky before a rain in the summer season of the west wind. Nodding his head, he affirmed: "After your voyage, Steve, I will still hold you."

And as my eyes clouded over and tears ran down my cheeks, he spoke gently and firmly to me, as father to his eldest son:

"I will still hold you, because my flesh is your flesh; my name is your name; my earth is your earth. And I know that your flesh is my flesh, Steve, your name is my name, your earth is my earth." Tears just streamed down my face; my lip trembled and it seemed just fine. Here a man cries when someone he loves will no longer be with him, through death or the blue wastes of water.

Then, in sheer exuberance, I began chanting the *itang*. He chanted with me:

> *Floating leaf swept out,*
> *Floating leaf swept back,*
> *The leaf of the* tong *tree*
> *(The leaf of our love)* . . .

I was astonished: "You said you never learned that."

"On Saipan you told me you learned a little from Maanusuuk," he said matter-of-factly, "so I knew you knew."

"You learned from Maanusuuk?"

"Of course, he is our father," Piailug shrugged, laughing. "You knew what I knew. If you had learned from someone else, I would have taught you what I know, because it might have been different. But you learned from our father, Maanusuuk; you know what I know."

By now the ship's whistle was blasting furiously. Pandemonium broke out on deck as the high-school boys and girls came aboard, giggling, pushing, helping one another, struggling with their sleeping mats, plywood boxes, bundles of taro, breadfruit, and coconuts. Piglets escaped from a burlap sack and skittered about. An immense sow blocked access to the cargo hatch. The captain started the main engines and gunned the ship forward to hoist the anchor. I followed Piailug to the railing. Bonefacio disappeared. Josede was on the verge of tears. Weneto's boat came alongside to discharge another teeming wave of students. I gave Josede my watch, which he had admired for weeks. Crying openly now, he thanked me again and again as he descended the rope ladder and was lost to my sight.

Piailug was waiting. I turned back to him and extended my hand. He took it, but seized me in his gaze, piercing yet loving.

"Think well," he instructed.

The whistle blew again as the ship backed off. Piailug flashed a brilliant smile and dove into the sea. Then the ship pivoted and rode down the shining path of the morning sun.

APPENDICES

∎

These appendices contain much of the *kapesani serak*, the "talk of sailing." Originally I had thought to publish this material in specialists' journals, thinking it would be of little interest to the average reader. Later, however, I decided to put all the material—the narrative of my quest and the substance of my research—between the covers of a single book. This was partly for aesthetic reasons. Mostly, though, it was to pay a debt I owed to Piailug and his family. Once, when I asked him why he wanted me to do the book, he said, "So my sons, and their sons, can look in it and see what I know." If, in a preceding narrative, I have been fortunate enough to communicate a sense of Piailug's soul, I wish in these appendices to communicate the contents of his (and Uurupa's) mind. To my knowledge, none of this particular material has been published.

Note on translation and the *itang*

I have taken some liberties in my translation of direct quotations, since a literal rendering of Satawalese makes for extremely awkward reading in English. In Piailug's case, an exact translation fails to communicate the force and dignity with which he presents himself. I hope that whatever license I have taken in this regard is justified by the character of Piailug portrayed in the narrative and by the appendices, which demonstrate the breadth and sophistication of his navigational knowledge.

The *itang* is traditionally held secret. Yet after the death of Maanusuuk, the elders of the clan wished me to publish some of the verses—here slightly altered—in order that the young Carolinian men in high school and college could read of the *itang*'s power and beauty and return to their islands to learn it before their fathers and grandfathers died.

APPENDIX 1

Stars and Planets

Satawal names	Western description
Alimatau	Aries, Triangulum, and Alamak
Alung	Beta Canis Major. This is the body of Maan.
Annupo	Rigil Kentaurus and Hadar
Apisarapul (or "Ap")	"Behind Sarapul," Spika
Aremoi	Arcturus
Ceuta	Enif, and Delta, Upsilon, Alpha, Chi Equuleus
Cu	Constellation that resembles a dolphin. Cassiopeia forms the tail, Alphcratz the dorsal fin, Mirach and Upsilon Andromeda the ventral fins, and the faint spray of stars in Andromeda trace the body.
Eech	Gamma Cancer
Egulig	Cassiopeia
Fuesemagut	Polaris: "Unmoving Star"
Ifungunul	Capella: "North of Ul"
Illelligek	Formation in Leo representing the rack on which the warp for *turrh* is strung: Adhafera, Algieba, Nu Leo, and Regulus
Maan	Sirius

Machemeias	See Poop
Mailap	Altair
Mailapellifung	Perkat, Kochab and #5 Ursa Minor: "Mailap in the North"
Maragar	Pleiades
Mesal Arik	Dubhe and Kochab: "Eyes of the Arik," a small crab
Mesaru	Shaula
Mongoisum	Castor and Pollux
Mose	Muphrid: "White Hair" (next to Arcturus)
Mun	Vega
Na	Alpheratz
Paiifung	Gamma Aquila (Tarazad)
Paiinemaanemefung	Procyon: "Northern Wing of Maan"
Paiinemaanemeiur	Canopus: "Southern Wing of Maan"
Paiiur	Beta Aquila (Alshain)
Parrung ai Tumur	Fan of stars above Arcturus: Jabbah, Acrab, Dschubba, Pi, and Rho Scorpio: "Hat of Tumur"
Piing	Theta, #22, Kappa Andromeda: a V-shaped configuration representing the vestibule of a house
Poop	Southern Cross (Crux). It defines five positions: Talup, at rising; Machemeias, at 45° risen; Wuliwulilup, at upright; Machemelito, at 45° setting; Tubulup, at setting.
Roe	Corona Borealis, which is shaped like a dip net
Sarapul	Corvus
Sepie	Delphinus: represents a carved wooden bowl
Tefrhowai	A formation in Grus representing a comb
Tingar Uliul	Betelgeuse and Rigil
Tumur	Antares
Ul	Aldebaran
Uliul	Orion's Belt
Wulego (or Wule)	Ursa Major (Dubhe, Megrez, Phecda, Merak, which constitute the cup of the Big Dipper's ladle)

Planets	**Western description**
Auren Mangar	Venus when the Evening Star: "Light of the Flying Fish"

| Fu Raan | Venus when Morning Star: "Day Star" |
| Weriai Tumur | Literally "see Tumur." Jupiter, at the times of year it is in the constellation Scorpio, is said to illuminate Antares, enabling one to see it. |

CROSS REFERENCE

Western names	Satawal name
Adhafera, Algieba, Nu Leo, and Regulus	Illelligek
Aldebaran	Ul
Alpheratz	Na
Theta, #22, Kappa Andromeda	Piing
Altair	Mailap
Antares	Tumur
Beta Aquila	Paiiur
Gamma Aquila	Paiifung
Gamma Cancer	Eech
Arcturus	Aremoi
Aries, Triangulum, and Alamak	Alimatau
Beta Canis Major	Alung
Betelgeuse and Rigil	Tingar Uliul
Canopus	Paiinemaanemeiur
Capella	Ifungunul
Cassiopeia	Egulig
Cassiopeia forms the tail of Cu, the Dolphin; Alpheratz the dorsal fin; Mirach and Upsilon Andromeda ventral fins; and the faint spray of stars in Andromeda trace the body	Cu
Castor and Pollux	Mongoisum
Corona Borealis	Roe

Corvus	Sarapul
Delphinus	Sepie: represents a carved wooden bowl
Dubhe and Kochab	Mesal Arik ("Eyes of the Arik," a small crab)
Enif, and Delta, Upsilon, Alpha, Chi Equuleus	Ceuta
Grus	Tefrhowai
Jabbah, Acrab, Dschubba, Pi, and Rho Scorpio	Parrung ai Tumur: "Hat of Tumur," a fan of stars above Arcturus
Jupiter (when in Scorpio)	Weriai Tumur
Muphrid	Mose
Orion's Belt	Uliul
Pleiades	Maragar
Polaris	Fuesemagut: "Unmoving Star"
Procyon	Paiinemaanemefung
Rigil Kentaurus and Hadar	Annupo
Shaula	Mesaru
Sirius	Maan
Southern Cross (Crux)	Poop
Spika	Apisarapul (or "Ap")
Ursa Major (only Dubhe, Megrez, Phecda, Merak, which constitute the cup of the Big Dipper's ladle)	Wulego (or Wule)
Ursa Minor (Perkat, Kochab and #5)	Mailapellifung: "Mailap in the North"
Vega	Mun
Venus	Fu Raan
Venus (when the Evening Star)	Auren Mangar: "Light of the Flying Fish"

APPENDIX 2

Subdivision of the *Etak* of Sighting

The *etak* of sighting, which spans the distance from the canoe house to point at sea at which the island is no longer visible, is subdivided into numerous units. (Dictated by Uurupa)

etakidigina	The point at which the island first appears
ngilligenennie	"One Tooth"; the island appears as one point
rongirup	The island appears as several mounds on the water. *Rongirup* is a fishing technique in which several men drag a sweep made from breadfruit leaves through the water causing fish to huddle together, whereupon they are speared.
arlukseson	The whole side of the island is visible but low
arluketakias	The whole side of the island is visible and high
naatipei	*Naat* bushes (unidentified) are visible on the beach (*pei*)
naatserram	Light is visible beneath the *naat* bushes
peiailus	Waves lifting the canoe make the whole beach visible
afarfarnapei	The whole beach can barely be seen

peiaric	The whole beach is visible but narrow
peialap	The whole beach is visible and wide
warigiriginaramas	People are visible walking on the beach
neineinseinematch	Zone off the reef where flying fish are caught, using coconut floats, a technique called *match*
neineinseiachaek	Zone in which needlefish are caught, using a lure suspended from a breadfruit-leaf kite, a technique called *achaek*
neinenassutow	Zone in which bottom-fishing is done
sonamachetch	The zone near the reef where the bottom (*son*) is visible. *Machetch* is a term denoting the sunbeams playing in the water. Presumably, it means here that they shine on the bottom.
mesanor	Face of the reef
aoulong	Place on the reef where waves break
faanaoulong	Behind the *aoulong*
lealulu	Shallow and narrow inner pool
moraisett	Point where the water meets the sand
faanropurup	Steep foreshore
ropurup	"Little mountain": crest of the foreshore
lugunupanipei	Middle of the beach
faannaat	Under the *naat* bushes before the canoe house
mesanoot	Face of the canoe house

APPENDIX 3

Itimetau

Itimetau: The names of the seaways between islands
(Dictated by Uurupa)

Islands	Name of seaway
Oroluke—Ngatik	Winafarsoutu
Namoluke—Lukunor	Metaurigarig
Nama—Namoluke	Ahpong
Nama—Murilo	Winafarsoutu
Truk—Nama	Fainemuh
Truk—East Fayu	Wenoupwenamwear
Truk—Pisaris	Wounupwenegoura
Truk—Ulul	Wonnupwennon
Pisaris—East Fayu	Faannifai
Truk—Pulap	Faasett
Truk—Puluwat	Arrouwan
Truk—Pulusuk	Nuguneewan
Truk—Orrowraan (possibly Onari)	Metauwonurumaan
Puluwat—Pulap	Faaisaup
Puluwat—Ulul	Faainuruwai
Pulap—Ulul	Faainuruwai

Islands	Name of seaway
Puluwat—East Fayu	Neamoureniyang
Puluwat—Pulusuk	Metau Pongank
Puluwat—Satawal	Apinallay
Puluwat—Pikelot	Metauwonimaan
Pulusuk—Satawal	Faanewan
Pulusuk—Pikelot	Fainugasseuh
Pulusuk—West Fayu	Fainumore
Pikelot—Satawal	Metauwonoomar or Metaueuu
Pikelot—West Fayu	Metauwaniamam or Metauwairheim
Satawal—West Fayu	Metau Pongank or Lugunugeurak
Satawal—Lamotrek	Oairek
West Fayu—Lamotrek	Legerhrak
West Fayu—Elato	Faanigarahk
Satawal—Gaferut	Woneorr
Gaferut—Lamotrek	Faanearh
Elato—Olimarao	Metauwonigaisa
Elato—Olimarao— Farailap	Apinimetau
Gaferut—Woleai	Faanigumatorr
Ifaluk—Farailap	Metau Pongank
Ifaluk—Elato	Apileuroop
Ifaluk—Woleai	Faanarama
Woleai—Eauripik	Metauwonipoon (*poon* is the woman's belt for *turrh*; Eauripik is known for its production of these articles)
Woleai—Fais	Apiniamaan
Eauripik—Fais	Faanimughon
Farailap—Fais	Lugunimughon
Fais—Sorol	Metau Pongank
Fais—Ulithi	Metauairhobakh
Sorol—Eauripik	Metauwonikiinimwar ("Sea of Picking Flowers")
Sorol—Gnulu	Metauwonuul ("Sea of Ulithi")
Ulithi—Yap	Metauwairoupel
Yap—Gnulu	Metau Pongank
Yap—Palau	Metaumuan
Yap—Philippines	Metauwoyatinga (Philippines, known as Tause- leata, or "Open Channel")
Palau—Philippines	Apinifaimotau ("Channel of Smooth Stone")
Merir—Philippines	Faanipannaie (Palau)

APPENDIX 4

Pwipwimetau

In *pwipwimetau*, or "brother seas," similarly aligned seaways are grouped together so that if the *palu* forgets the star course for one seaway he can remember it through its brother seaway. (Dictated by Uurupa)

Group I: setting Mailapellifung—Machemeias

Puluwat—Pulusuk
West Fayu—Satawal
Gaferut—Elato
Ulithi—Sorol
Nama—Namoluke

Group II: rising Wulego—Tubulup

Puluwat—Ulul
Ifaluk—Gaferut
Woleai—Farailap

Group III: rising Mailapellifung—Machemelito

Pulusuk—Tamatam
Pulap—Ulul
Fais—Sorol
Yap—Gnulu

Group IV: rising Egulig—setting Mesaru

Pulusuk—Pisaris
Satawal—Pikelot
Lamotrek—West Fayu
Woleai—Gaferut

Group V: setting Mun—rising Tumur

Namoluke—Lugunor
Truk—Pisaris
West Fayu—Pulusuk
Elato—Olimarao—Farailap
Gaferut—West Fayu
Farailap—Elato
Fais—Woleai

Group VI: setting Maragar—rising Sarapul

Truk—Ulul
Namoluke—Puluwat
Puluwat—Pikelot
Ifaluk—Fais
Eauripik—Sorol
Farailap—Satawal

Group VII: setting Paiiur—rising Paiifung

Puluwat—Satawal
Pikelot—West Fayu
Elato—Ifaluk
East Fayu—Pisaris

Group VIII: setting Wule—Taglup

Truk—East Fayu
Lamotrek—Gaferut

Group IX: setting Sarapul—rising Maragar

Truk—Pulusuk
East Fayu—Puluwat
Pikelot—Lamotrek
West Fayu—Olimarao
Gaferut—Farailap
Olimarao—Ifaluk
Yap—Palau

Group X: setting Ul—rising Uliul

Nama—Truk
Truk—Pulap
Pulap—Pikelot
Woleai—Sorol
Fais—Ulithi
Pikelot—Gaferoor (a mystery island northeast of Yap, said to have
    sunk)
Puluwat—West Fayu
Satawal—Olimarao
Ifaluk—Woleai
Palau—Philippines
Farailap—Fais

Group XI: Fuesemagut—Wuliwulilup

Truk—Nomwim
Gaferut—Olimarao
Ifaluk—Farailap
Gaferut—Guam

Group XII: rising Mailap—setting Mailap

Truk—Puluwat
Elato—Woleai
Fais—Yap
Pulusuk—Eauripik
Puluwat—Lamotrek
Gaferut—Fais
Farailap—West Fayu
East Fayu—Magur—Gaferut

5 APPENDIX

Aruruwow

This system envisions an *ura*, or parrot fish, hiding in its reef hole in the channel (*wow*) of one island. The fisherman tries to catch it with a dip net, whereupon it darts out of its hole and swims to the reef channel of the next island. Again the fisherman attempts to net the fish, and again the fish swims to the next island. Eventually the fish returns to Satawal's channel. The system, known only to navigators, is like *wofanu* in that it gives star courses between islands. Since the names of islands are never referred to, navigators use *aruruwow* to discuss voyages in secret. (Dictated by Piailug)

Channel/Island of origin	Star course Ura takes	Channel/Island of destination
Wowulipar/Satawal	Tan Egulig	Wowirwow/Pikelot
Wowirwow/Pikelot	Tana Sarapul	Wowulgar/Puluwat
Wowulgar/Puluwat	Machemeias	Wowulgabur/Pulusuk
Wowulgabur/Pulusuk	Tana Mailapellifung	Wowunmanur/Ulul
Wowunmanur/Ulul	Tan Egulig	Wowunimaias/Magur
Wowunimaias/Magur	Tana Tumur	Wowuligun/Ono
Wowuligun/Ono	Tana Tumur	Wowmarmar/Onari
Wowmarmar/Onari	Machemeias	Wowilipa/Pisaris
Wowilipa/Pisaris	Tana Paiifung	Wowilaput/East Fayu

Wowilaput/East Fayu
Wowunar/Nomwin

Wowfalalu
Wowlikun/Murilo
Wowulik/Truk
Wowulumar/Oroluk
Wowulap/Ponape
Wowisaukoraw/Kusaie
Wowpweripuer/Ngatik
Wowilima/Lukunor
Eaupow/Namoluke
Wowligar/Puluwat

Tan Uliul
Tana Mun

Tana Maragar
Tubulup
Tana Paiifung
Tan Uliul
Tan Uliul
Tubula Sarapul
Tubula Mailap
Tubula Maragar
Tubula Maragar
Tubula Paiiur

Wowunar/Nomwin
Wowfalalu/(possibly
    channel on Murilo)
Wowlikun/Murilo
Wowulik/Truk
Wowulumar/Oroluk
Wowulap/Ponape
Wowisaukoraw/Kusaie
Wowpweripuer/Ngatik
Wowilima/Lukunor
Eaupow/Namoluke
Wowligar/Puluwat
Wowulipar/Satawal

6 APPENDIX

Pookof

The series of sea creatures arrayed about each island. This transcript also includes some *wofanu*. (Dictated by Piailug)

POOKOF SATAWAL

Star course/Range from the island	Name and description of epar
Wuliwulilup/*etakidimaan*	Eguwan, one tan shark making lazy movements in the water
Machimelito/*etakidimaan*	Mesarmeur, two birds, silent
Tubulup/between *etakidigina* and *etakidimaan*	Mesarmeifung, two birds, same species as Mesarmeur, one bird makes noise. Piailug has seen both of these.
Tubula Mesaru/ *etakidimaan*	Ineffitimwar, a *pway* of various species of birds. The name denotes a flower lei made with a variety of flowers.
Tubula Tumur/just after *etakidimaan*	Innanomwar, a ray with a red spot behind the eyes. Many navigators claim to have seen this *epar*.

Tubula Sarapul/halfway between Satawal and Lamotrek	Neagumwuan, a fish. Identified by Piailug as *Gnathanodon speciosus*, yellow ulua.
Tubul Uliul/south of Lamotrek	Lugoisum, tropic bird, red, very old now. Piailug believes this bird is dead. One man on Satawal claims to have sighted it.
Tubula Mailap	Mesalialu, channel between Elato and Toas
Tubula Paiifung	Lamotrek
Tubul Ul	Nothing
Tubula Maragar/near Etakidimaan Lamotrek	Yoliwa, ten to twenty killer whales
Tubula Mun/between *etakidigina* and Etakidimaan Satawal	A swordfish, swimming
Tubul Egulig/before Etakidigina West Fayu	Neamirrh, a *tagu*, or yellowfin tuna, one fathom long. It rises just under the surface of the water but won't jump. Piailug saw this in 1959 or so. He believes I saw it while searching for Orrairepar.
Tubula Wulego/ Etakidigina Pigale	Manirrik, a yellowfin tuna one fathom long that jumps out of the water. Piailug saw this in 1960 or so.
Tubula Mailapellifung/ halfway between Satawal and West Fayu	One frigate bird
Fuesemagut/Etakidimaan Pigale	Uliso, frigate bird bigger than above-named bird, but with tatty wings. Continue on this course to Eiutametau, "reef that stands up in the sea."
Tana Mailapellifung	Orrairepar, a reef
Tana Wule/at *etakidigina*	A swordfish, bigger than under Tubula Mun. Piailug identified *Xiphias gladius*. Next: Moan, reef between West Fayu and Pikelot
Tan Egulig	Pikelot
Tana Mun	Oleipik, reef
Tana Maragar	Orraisau, reef
Tan Ul	Ruat, reef
Tana Paiifung	Puluwat
Tana Mailap/Etakidigina Satawal	Laifanimung, frigate bird flying around in circles. Many navigators from Puluwat claim to have seen this.

Tan Uliul	Uurorran, reef between Puluwat and Pulusuk (Tubula Mesaru from Puluwat)
Tana Sarapul/two to three *etak* from Satawal	Igisapan, a whale with a dolphin swimming around its midsection
Tana Tumur/at Etakidimaan Satawal	Turtle, unnamed, with white spot near tail. Next: Orraisaifitan, reef.
Tana Mesaru	Naifailuke, frigate bird, doing nothing special
Talup/*etakidigina*	A swordfish same size as under Tana Wule. Piailug saw this once.
Machemeias	Nothing

POOKOF LAMOTREK

Course/Range	Epar
Tan Uliul/very distant	Lugoisum, red tropic bird (see Pookof Satawal)
Tana Tumur/*etakidimaan*	Innanomwar, ray (see Pookof Satawal)
Tana Sarapul/halfway between Satawal and Lamotrek	Neagumwuan, yellow ulua (see Pookof Satawal)
Tana Maragar	Yoliwa, killer whales (see Pookof Satawal)
Wuliwulimeifung/ Etakidigina Lamotrek	*Pway of mwerigow*, identified as *Sterna dougallii*, a species of tern. Piailug saw this once when sailing from West Fayu to Lamotrek.

POOKOF WEST FAYU

Course/Range	Epar
Tana Mailap	Eiutametau, reef (see Pookof Satawal)
Tan Uliul	Uliso, frigate bird with tatty wings (see Pookof Satawal)
Tana Sarapul/halfway between West Fayu and Satawal	Orraitufer, reef. Piailug has never seen this.
Tana Mesaru/halfway between West Fayu and Satawal	A frigate bird. Same as the one bearing Tubula Mailapellifung from Satawal.

Talup	Epwinegerik, a pod of small dolphins. Piailug has seen these many times. Once he spotted them and changed course to reach West Fayu.
Machemelito	Manirrik, yellowfin tuna. Same as the one bearing Tubula Wulego from Satawal.
Tubulup	Neamirrh, yellowfin tuna one fathom long. Same as one bearing Egulig from Satawal.
Wuliwulimeifung	Oneipwinik, pod of big porpoise of species *igipowh* (unidentified)

POOKOF PULUWAT

Course/Range	Epar
Machemeias	Pulusuk
Wuliwulilup	Sunkarim, a single brown booby, *Sula leucogaster plotus*
Machimelito	Eu Ponank, a section of reef near Pulusuk:

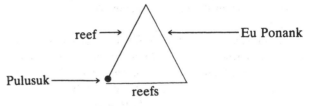

Tubulup	Erimetenmerimeto, reef near Pulusuk
Tubula Mesaru	Orrowrun, reef. There is now a wrecked fishing boat on this reef.
Tubula Tumur	Piailug can't recall
Tubula Sarapul/near Etakidimaan Puluwat	Raulawup, a white tropic bird sitting on the water
Tubul Uliul	Rewena, black whale
Tubula Paiiur	Satawal
Tubula Mailap	Lamotrek
Tubul Ul	West Fayu
Tubula Maragar	Pikelot
Tubula Mun	Apinor, end of Ruat reef
Tubul Egulig/*etakidimaan*	Regaliang, big black whale that slaps its tail on the water

Tubula Wule	Lananannan, deep pool on Ruat reef, near Puluwat. Men from Puluwat often fish here.
Tubula Mailapellifung	Faimoran, big rock on Ruat reef, about ten fathoms deep. You can see it under water.
Wuliwulimeifung	Efailela, end of Ruat reef
Tana Mailapellifung/close to Puluwat, maybe *etakidigina*	Learhumoi, frigate bird that climbs in altitude
Tana Wule	Ulul
Tana Mun	Pulap
Tana Maragar	East Fayu
Tan Ul	Pisanorifung, north end of reef in Truk. Pis is an island in Truk Lagoon.
Tana Mailap	Truk
Tan Uliul	Tunoriur, south end of reef in Truk
Tana Sarapul	Namoluke
Tana Tumur	Kutu, island in the Mortlocks
Tana Mesaru	Can't remember: "Too many birds, too many fish . . . I forget"
Talup	Manerh, an all-white member of the *keachie* species, identified as *Sterna sumatrana*, a black-naped tern, but without the black eye mask.
Machemeias	Pulusuk

POOKOF PULUSUK

Course/Range	Epar
Tubula Mailap	Eauripik
Tubula Maragar	Satawal
Tubula Mun	Pukulielie, place where reef sticks out. *Puku* means elbow:

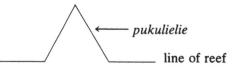

Tubul Egulig	Lulunan, "there far in distance." Next: Ourauron, a reef upon which waves tumble.

Tubula Wule	Piailug couldn't recall
Tubula Mailapellifung	Puluwat
Wuliwulilup	Piailug couldn't recall
Tana Mailapellifung	Tamatam
Tana Maragar	Truk
Tana Mailap	Namoluke
Tana Mesaru	Reef; Piailug couldn't recall name

POOKOF PULAP

Course/Range	Epar
Tan Uliul	Truk
Tana Mailap	Piailug couldn't recall
Tana Mun	Pisaris
Tana Wule	Yapeui, reef
Tana Mailapellifung	Ulul
Tubul Ul	Pikelot
Tubula Mailap	West Fayu
Tubul Uliul	Satawal
Tubula Tumur	Puluwat
Machimelito	Pulusuk

POOKOF PIKELOT

Course/Range	Epar
Tubula Mailap	Pelifaimo, part of the reef on which there appears to be gravel
Tubul Ul	Moen, reef
Tubula Maragar	Orrailar, reef of *lar*, or sea urchins. There are many sea urchins on this reef.
Tubula Mun	Orrailepoap. *Poap* is a species of shark. Something on this reef looks like shark.
Tubul Egulig	Orraitigilimaan. This section of reef is tilted. A bird on the reef cries *tig i tig i tig*.
Tubula Wule	Orraifu. Something on the reef looks like stars.
Tubula Mailapellifung	Orraisaita. *Ta* means "clam." Looks like many clams on reef.
Wuliwulimeifung	Orrailepun. Underwater section of reef looks like lamp (*pun*).

Tana Mailapellifung	Orrailemwar. Underwater section of reef looks like flower lei (*mwaramwar*).
Tana Wule	Tiufatul. Underwater section of reef looks like paddle (*fatul*).
Tan Egulig	Nemaigu. Underwater section of reef looks like hook (*gu*).
Tana Mun	Orrailem. Underwater section of reef is white.
Tana Maragar	Orrailepoopen. Underwater feature of reef looks like black trigger fish (*poop*).
Tan Ul	Sepie Mailuk. *Mailuk* means "outside." This part of Wonipik reef looks like round bowl (*sepie*).
Tana Mailap	Wonipik, large reef
Tan Uliul	Sepie Mailan ("inside bowl") refers to a place inside Wonipik reef:

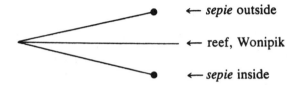

Tana Sarapul	Orraiferh, reef
Tana Tumur	Oognalepar. Underwater section of reef shaped like conical hat.
Tana Mesaru	Rutapinau. Piailug doesn't know description.
Talup	Olimaan, reef
Machemeias	Thurang, reef
Wuliwulilup	Orraisau, reef
Tubulup	Orranik, reef
Tubula Mesaru	Satawal
Tubula Tumur	Orrairepar, reef. Piailug describes as two hundred yards wide and one thousand yards long.
Tubula Sarapul	Wenallute, reef
Tubul Uliul	Pwilenan, reef
Tubula Paiiur	West Fayu

POOKOF WOLEAI (DICTATED BY UURUPA)

Course/Range	Epar
Tana Mailap/between Elato and Ifaluk	Faselos, reef

Tan Ul	Olimarao
Tana Maragar/between Ifaluk and Elato, close to Ifaluk	Taimeang, school of small dolphins
Tana Mun	Rheuminwonipugu, reef
Tan Egulig	Gaferut
Tana Wulego	Farailap
Tana Mailapellifung/ *etakidimaan*	Uulegool, one green leaf of the *gool* tree
Wuliwulimeifung/forty to fifty miles from Woleai	Paiiroro Parowa, thirty or forty *paiiroro* birds, long-beaked, brown with black on feathers, wing span two feet. Parowa was a navigator who became sick, and as a gift to those who cared for him he told them about this *epar*.
Tubula Mailapellifung/ *etakidimaan*	Soueriang, a fat tropic bird, flying
Tubula Wule/*etakidimaan*	Soupuungwa, parrot fish that comes to the canoe and will not be chased away
Tubul Egulig/thirty to forty miles	Igosuuk, small tropic bird
Tubula Mun	Fais
Tubula Maragar	Ulithi
Tubul Ul	Sorol
Tubula Paiifung	Nothing
Tubula Mailap/ *etakidimaan*	Repota, sting ray, very large, with black spots, white stripe around neck, swimming east toward Woleai
Tubula Paiiur	Nothing
Tubul Uliul/*etakidimaan*	Faitoyang, reef
Tubula Sarapul/ *etakidimaan*	Repaghituun, a burned coconut-frond torch (*tuun*) used by people of Falalap, Woleai, floating on the water
Tubula Tumur	Eauripik
Tubula Mesaru	Naweeimai, a school (*wee*) of skipjack tuna
Tubulup	Orraitiinipu, reef. Many herring (*tiin*) on this reef.
Machimelito	Nauwenimar, a school of tuna with a flock of white terns flying overhead
Wuliwulimeiur/ *etakidimaan*	Yaniruun, a tropic bird with red beak and feet and orange feathers
Machemeias/*etakidimaan*	Suuoh, an egret
Talup/past *etakidimaan*	Orrainaiepweou, reef

Tana Mesaru/ *etakidimaan*	Lugunumaat, a booby, flying
Tana Tumur/*etakidimaan*	Merron, reef
Tana Sarapul/forty miles	Orraitaakunumaar, reef named after needlefish (*taak*)
Tan Uliul	Ifaluk

APPENDIX 7

Wofanu

Wofanu, meaning literally "gaze at the island," comprises the star courses between islands. It is repeated in a long chant, such as "I sit on Satawal, I go rising Mailap to Truk. I sit on Truk, I go setting Mailap on Satawal. . . ." In the following lists of *wofanu* for various islands, I give only the star course to the destination. It is understood that the navigator will return home under the reciprocal bearing. It is also understood that the destination may not lie squarely under the star specified in *wofanu*, but to one side or the other. For instance, the course given to West Fayu from Satawal is setting Mailapellifung, whereas the actual course is halfway between the setting positions of Mailapellifung and Wulego. Navigators learn the necessary adjustments from their masters during their long apprenticeship.

The following *wofanu* was recorded by Uurupa on July 8, 1984, at Nemanong. Uurupa reviewed the tape and pronounced it accurate. I did not have a chance to review a transcription with him.

Star course	Destination
WOFANU WEST FAYU	
Tana Paiifung	Pikelot
Tan Ul	Ulul

Star course	Destination
Tubula Mun	Gaferut
Tubula Mailap	Orranagaiusaum
Tubula Sarapul	Olimarao
Tubula Tumur	Elato
Tubula Mesaru	Lamotrek
Machemeias	Satawal
Tana Tumur	Pulusuk
Tan Uliul	Puluwat
Tana Mailap	Pulap

 ## WOFANU SATAWAL

Tana Mailap	Truk
Tana Sarapul	Pulusuk
Tubula Paiifung	Lamotrek
Tubul Ul	Olimarao
Tubula Maragar	Farailap
Tubul Egulig	Gaferut
Tubula Mailapellifung	West Fayu
Tan Egulig	Pikelot
Tana Maragar	Ulul
Tan Ul	Pisaris
Tana Paiifung	Puluwat

WOFANU PIKELOT

Tana Mailap	Wonipik reef
Tan Uliul	Pulap
Tana Sarapul	Puluwat
Tana Mesaru	Pulusuk
Tubula Mesaru	Satawal
Tubula Sarapul	Lamotrek
Tubul Uliul	Olimarao
Tubula Paiiur	West Fayu
Tubula Mailap	Farailap
Tubul Ul	Gaferut

WOFANU LAMOTREK

Tubula Sarapul	Namowiniur (possibly Helen Reef or Tobi Island)
Tubul Ul	Elato
Tubula Maragar	Olimarao
Tubula Wule	Gaferut
Tan Egulig	West Fayu
Tana Mailap	Puluwat
Tana Paiiur	Satawal

WOFANU ELATO

Tan Uliul	Lamotrek
Tana Mun	West Fayu
Tubula Mailapellifung	Gaferut
Tubula Mun	Olimarao
Tubula Mailap	Woleai
Tubula Paiiur	Ifaluk

WOFANU OLIMARAO

Tana Maragar	West Fayu
Tan Ul	Pikelot
Tan Uliul	Satawal
Tana Sarapul	Lamotrek
Tana Tumur	Elato
Tubula Sarapul	Ifaluk
Tubul Uliul	Woleai
Tubula Maragar	Farailap
Wuliwulimeifung	Gaferut

WOFANU IFALUK

Tana Paiifung	Elato
Tana Maragar	Olimarao
Tana Wulego	Gaferut
Wuliwulimeifung	Farailap
Tubula Wule	Woleai
Tubula Sarapul	Eauripik

Star course	Destination
WOFANU WOLEAI	
Tan Uliul	Ifaluk
Tana Mailap	Elato
Tan Ul	Olimarao
Tan Egulig	Gaferut
Tana Wule	Farailap
Tubula Mun	Fais
Tubula Maragar	Ulithi
Tubul Ul	Sorol
Tubula Tumur	Eauripik
WOFANU FARAILAP	
Tana Maragar	Gaferut
Tana Mailap	Pikelot
Tan Uliul	West Fayu
Tana Sarapul	Satawal
Talup	Lamotrek
Tana Tumur	Elato
Wuliwulimeiur	Ifaluk
Tubulup	Woleai
Tubula Sarapul	Sorol
Tubul Ul	Fais
WOFANU GAFERUT	
Tana Mailap	Magur
Tan Uliul	Pikelot
Tana Tumur	West Fayu
Tana Mesaru	Satawal
Talup	Lamotrek
Machemeias	Elato
Wuliwulimeiur	Olimarao
Tubulup	Ifaluk
Tubula Mesaru	Woleai
Tubula Tumur	Eauripik
Tubula Sarapul	Farailap
Tubul Uliul	Sorol
Tubula Mailap	Fais
Wuliwulimeifung	Guam

WOFANU EAURIPIK

Tana Mailap	Pulusuk
Tana Maragar	Ifaluk
Tana Mun	Woleai
Tana Mailapellifung	Farailap
Tubula Wule	Fais
Tubul Egulig	Ulithi
Tubula Maragar	Sorol

WOFANU SOROL

Tana Sarapul	Eauripik
Tan Uliul	Woleai
Tana Maragar	Farailap
Tan Ul	Gaferut
Tana Mailapellifung	Fais
Tubula Mailapellifung	Ulithi
Tubula Mailap	Ngulu

WOFANU FAIS

Tana Mailap	Gaferut
Tan Uliul	Farailap
Tana Sarapul	Ifaluk
Tana Tumur	Woleai
Talup	Eauripik
Machemelito	Sorol
Tubul Uliul	Ngulu

WOFANU ULITHI

Tan Uliul	Fais
Tana Sarapul	Woleai
Tana Mesaru	Eauripik
Machemeias	Sorol
Tubula Sarapul	Ngulu
Tubul Uliul	Yap

Star course	Destination

WOFANU YAP

Tan Ul	Ulithi
Tana Mesaru	Sorol
Machemelito	Ngulu
Tubula Sarapul	Palau

WOFANU PULUWAT

Tubula Mailap	Lamotrek
Tubul Ul	West Fayu
Tubula Maragar	Pikelot
Tana Wule	Ulul
Tana Mun	Pulap
Tana Maragar	Gaferut
Tan Ul	Pisanorifung (reef in northern Truk Lagoon, next to Pis island)
Tana Mailap	Truk
Tana Sarapul	Namoluke
Machemeias	Pulusuk
Tubula Paiiur	Satawal

WOFANU PULUSUK

Tubula Mailap	Eauripik
Tubula Maragar	Satawal
Tubula Mun	West Fayu
Tubul Egulig	Pikelot
Tubula Mailapellifung	Puluwat
Tana Mailapellifung	Pulap
Tan Egulig	Pisaris
Tana Mun	Gaferut
Tana Maragar	Truk
Tan Ul	Nama
Tana Mailap	Namoluke

WOFANU PULAP

Tana Mailap	Pisanorifung
Tana Mun	Pisaris
Tana Mailapellifung	Ulul

Tubul Ul	Pikelot
Tubul Uliul	Satawal
Tubula Tumur	Puluwat
Machemelito	Pulusuk
Tan Uliul	Truk

WOFANU ULUL

Tan Egulig	Magur
Tana Maragar	Onari
Tana Mailap	Ururruh (Ono)
Tana Paiiur	Pisaris
Tana Sarapul	Truk
Machemelito	Pulap
Tubulup	Puluwat
Tubula Sarapul	Satawal
Tubul Uliul	West Fayu

WOFANU EAST FAYU

Tubula Maragar	Magur
Tubula Mailap	Ururruh (Ono)
Tubula Paiiur	Pisaris
Tubul Uliul	Pulap
Tubula Sarapul	Puluwat
Tubula Tumur	Pulusuk

WOFANU TRUK

Tubula Mailap	Satawal
Tubula Paiifung	Puluwat
Tubula Maragar	Ulul
Tubula Mun	Pisaris
Tubula Wule	East Fayu
Tubula Mailapellifung	Apinorenifarr reef
Wuliwulilup	Nomwin
Tana Paiifung	Oroluk
Tana Mailap	Ponape
Tan Uliul	Nama
Tana Tumur	Namoluke

8 APPENDIX

The Fighting of Stars

M orellifu, or the fighting of stars, is a unique calendar and weather fore-casting system comprised of twelve star months. Each month begins when its star is forty-five degrees from the horizon—when to look at it one tilts one's head back and just feels the back of the neck forming a roll of skin. In each star month there will rise one or two "fighting stars," which are said to con-trol the weather. If there is one fighting star in the month, it will fight for five days after the moon first appears in the west at sunset and each evening is higher in the sky—i.e., the first five days of the moon's new cycle. This will coincide with the rising of the storm star at dawn. If there are two storm stars in a month, the second will storm when the moon appears lower and lower to the eastern horizon at sunrise until it finally disappears—i.e., the last five days of the moon's cycle. This, too, will coincide with the rising of the storm star at dawn.

The twelve star months make up two "seasons" or "years" of six months each, *lefung*, the time of impatience, and *leraak*, "the year," the time of plenty.

Star month, Description

Storm star and phase of moon at which it fights

Sarapul (November)
Sara, said Piailug, means "flying around." *Pwen* means "earth." Much dust in the air. Easterly winds returning but light. Time for the turtle eggs to hatch, but no turtles come on the land. Fish on Wuligee and bottom fish. Voyaging begins again.

Roe (Corona Borealis)
Storms at waning moon. Marks beginning of *lefung*.

Tumur (Antares)
Storms at waxing moon

Roe (December)
Roe means "dip net." Last month for sailing and fishing before time of real hunger. Canoes that have voyaged to Puluwat and the eastern islands must return now or risk getting caught by strong winds of *lefung*.

Mun (Vega)
Storms at waxing moon

Tumur (January)
Tumur means "empty." Northeasterly trades strong, no rain. Tuba is not good because of little rain. Trees turn brown, people get skinny, some yellowfin tuna caught along shore.

Mailap (Altair)
Storms at waxing moon. Signals beginning of strong northeasterly winds.

Mun (February)
Gives back some of what Tumur took away: rain, clouds, lots of tuba. Windy, but there is taro.

Sepie (Delphinus)
Storms at waning moon. Sepie indicates rain.

Ceuta (in Equuleus)
Storms at waxing moon. Ceuta means "sweep": the star sweeps the beach clean for the coming turtles.

Star month, Description	Storm star and phase of moon at which it fights
Mailap (March) Breadfruit begins to form on trees. Strong northeasterly winds and rain.	*Na (Alpheratz)* Storms at waxing moon. Signals end of strong northeasterly winds and the end of *lefung*. When Na finishes storming a clap of thunder sounds to mark the beginning of *leraak*.
Ceuta (April) Some breadfruit; more forming on trees. Southeasterly winds. Time for Saipan voyages.	*Cu* Storms at waxing moon. Some strong northeasterly winds while storming. *Alimatau (Aries, Triangulum, Alamak)* Storms at waning moon. Marks season of good winds for voyaging.
Na (May) From *nana*, "plenty." It is said, "In Na many breadfruit form on the trees; in Cu we will bite them." People start to get fat. Waves diminish. Season of voyaging begins. Wind still northeasterly trades but diminished. Beginning of turtle season.	*Maragar (Pleiades)* Storms at waxing moon
Cu (June) *Cu* means "bite." It also means "dolphin."	*Ul (Aldebaran)* Storms at waxing moon *Uliul (Orion's Belt)* Storms at waning moon. No severe weather under either star.
Ul (July) Month for turtles, fishing, breadfruit. Good winds from	*Maan (Sirius)* Storms at waxing moon. Strong winds from east, south,

northeast and east. Wind getting
lighter and lighter all the time.
Month for fishing with fish traps
and bottom-fishing. Breadfruit
begin to thin out. Turtles start to
hatch.

Uliul (August)
Beginning of yang *ilito*, the west
  wind. A little sailing, depending
  on the waves on the reef. Wind
  from westerly sectors. Turtles
  hatching. Lots of bottom-fishing,
  sometimes fish traps. *Yang ilito*
  lasts from the setting of Poop to
  end of the storms of Aremoi.
  Wind strength fluctuates with the
  storm stars and the phase of the
  moon. Winds diminish when the
  moon is in the second and third
  quarters.

Maan (September)
West wind. No fish, some
  breadfruit. Lots of waves on
  reef.

Eech (October)
Same as in Maan. A little
  breadfruit, some fish, a little
  taro.

southwest, and west that last
only half a day because, it is
said, "Eech cuts the wings of
the Maan, [the bird]."

Eech (Gamma, Cancer)
Storms at waxing moon. Eech
  produces small storms (as in
  Pikelot trip).

Poop (Southern Cross)
Storms when star sets in
  evening and at waning moon.

Illelligek
Storms at waxing moon

Apisarapul or Ap (Spika)
  Storms as it is setting and at
  waning moon.

Aremoi (Arcturus)
Storms when star sets in
  evening and at waxing moon. End
  of its fighting signals end of *yang
  ilito* and end of *leraak*.

9 APPENDIX

Kapesani Serak:
The Talk of Sailing

The talk of sailing comprises sets of sailing directions for the commonly made voyages from Satawal to West Fayu, Lamotrek, Pikelot, and Puluwat. These sailing directions enable the navigator to compensate for the current offset observed when taking leave of land. They all involve sailing an initial course to "One Tooth," when the island appears as a single nub of land, at which point the navigator backsights to the island to determine under which star it has "moved," thereby invoking the series of course corrections listed below. Piailug said these were all the sailing directions he learned from his master, Angora. For voyages to other islands, he constructs his own sailing directions.

Note: *Nematch* is a term used to indicate a point halfway between the two star points. *Yaw luke* is the midway point in a voyage.

SATAWAL—WEST FAYU

The reference island or *lu pongank*: Lamotrek

Wind: northeast
Initial course: Tubula Mailapellifung (Piailug says the old navigators used Fuesemagut for an initial course.)
Directions: Sail Tubula Mailapellifung to "One Tooth," backsight, then if:

SAILING DIRECTIONS:
SATAWAL–WEST FAYU

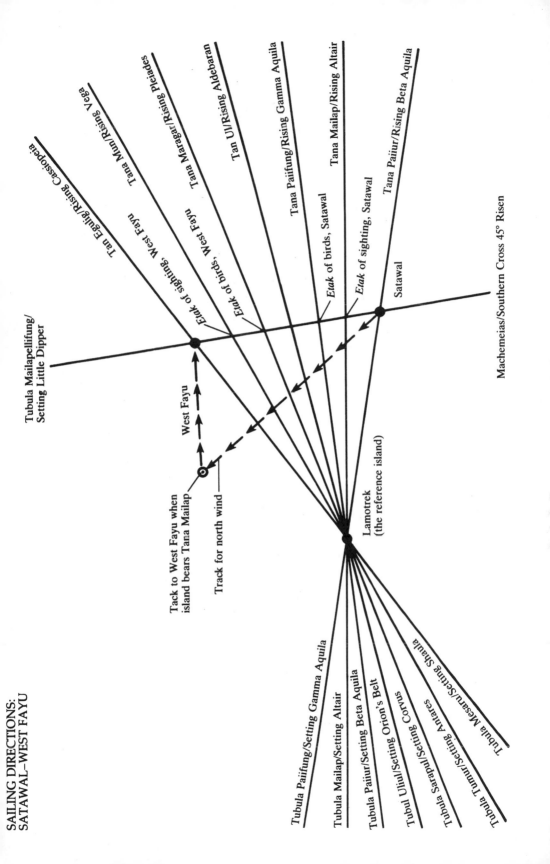

Tubula Mailapellifung/Setting Little Dipper

Tan Emuiig/Rising Cassiopeia

Tan Mun/Rising Vega

Tana Mun/Rising West Fayu

Tana Maragar/Rising Pleiades

Tan Ul/Rising Aldebaran

Tana Paiifung/Rising Gamma Aquila

Tana Mailap/Rising Altair

Tana Paiiur/Rising Beta Aquila

Etak of sighting, West Fayu

Etak of birds, West Fayu

Etak of birds, Satawal

Etak of sighting, Satawal

Satawal

Machemeias/Southern Cross 45° Risen

West Fayu

Tack to West Fayu when island bears Tana Mailap

Track for north wind

Lamotrek (the reference island)

Tubula Paiifung/Setting Gamma Aquila

Tubula Mailap/Setting Altair

Tubula Paiiur/Setting Beta Aquila

Tubul Uliul/Setting Orion's Belt

Tubula Sarapul/Setting Corvus

Tubula Trumu/Setting Antares

Tubula Mesaru/Setting Shaula

Satawal lies under:	Alter course (AC) to/at:
Machemeias (no current)	Tubula Wule at Etakidigina Satawal
Nematch Talup-Machemeias	Tubula Wule at Etakidimaan Satawal
Talup	Tubula Wule at *yaw luke*
Nematch Talup-Mesaru	Tubula Wule at Etakidimaan West Fayu
Mesaru	Tubula Wule at Etakidigina West Fayu
Wuliwulilup	Tubula Wule at Rongirup or One Tooth Satawal
Machemelito	Tubul Egulig at One Tooth
Tubulup	Never Tubulup, Piailug said: Satawal would only move under Tubulup if one were sailing to Pikelot, not West Fayu

Wind: north

If the wind is from the north, Piailug sails Tubula Mun until West Fayu is under Mailap, then tacks. He uses Lamotrek to gauge his progress (i.e., as the *lu pongank*) until West Fayu bears Tan Egulig: "Until I am in the road between Lamotrek and West Fayu. Then I use West Fayu as the *lu pongank*. I think of it moving back to Mun, Maragar, Ul, Paiifung, Mailap; then I tack to West Fayu."

WEST FAYU—SATAWAL

The reference island or *lu pongank*: Lamotrek

Wind: northeast

Initial course: Tana Tumur

West Fayu lies under:	Alter course (AC) to/at:
Tubula Mun	Tana Mesaru at One Tooth. At Etakidimaan Satawal, AC to Talup. Satawal will appear to starboard.
Tubul Ul	Tana Tumur to Etakidimaan Satawal. AC to Mesaru.
Tubula Maragar	Tana Mesaru at One Tooth West Fayu, then Talup at Etakidimaan Satawal

Tubul Egulig	Tana Tumur to *yaw luke*, then Mesaru to Etakidimaan Satawal, AC to Talup, and look for Satawal. If you can't see Satawal, AC to Machemeias.
Tubula Wule	Tana Tumur to Etakidimaan Satawal, then AC to Mesaru
Tubula Mailapellifung	Tana Tumur all the way. Satawal should come up on starboard side.
Fuesemagut	Tana Tumur, but you must think that Satawal will move to the east—i.e., since the current is very strong you may be carried even farther to the west—and thus you might have to tack. If the wind is more from the north, then one can sail Mesaru.
Tana Mailapellifung	Never
Tubula Maragar	Steer Mesaru. At *yaw luke*, AC to Talup. At Etakidigina Satawal, AC to Machemeias.
Tubul Ul	Steer Talup. At *yaw luke*, AC to Machemeias. At Etakidimaan Satawal, AC to Wuliwulilup. Satawal lies under Machimelito.
Tubula Paiifung	Steer Machemeias. At *yaw luke*, AC to Wuliwulilup. At *etakidimaan*, AC to Machimelito. Satawal lies under Tubulup.
Tubula Mailap	Steer Wuliwulilup. At *yaw luke*, AC to Machimelito. At Etakidimaan Satawal, AC to Tubulup. Satawal lies under Tubula Mesaru.
Tubula Paiiur	Never

Wind: northwest

Initial course: Wuliwulilup

West Fayu lies under:	Alter course (AC) to/at:
Fuesemagut (no current)	Machemeias at *yaw luke*. Talup at Etakidimaan Satawal. Satawal should appear to port.
Tubula Mailapellifung	Machemeias at Etakidimaan West Fayu. Satawal appears to port.
Tubula Wulego	Wuliwulilup to halfway between Etakidigina West Fayu and *etakidimaan*. AC to Machemeias.

Tubul Egulig	Wuliwulilup to Etakidigina West Fayu. AC to Machemeias.
Tubula Mun	All the way under Wuliwulilup

SATAWAL-PULUWAT

These sailing directions are slightly different from others, since, with the wind from the northeast, the navigator is sailing as close-hauled as possible. Thus his course is determined by the weatherliness of his canoe and by the exact wind direction.

Upwind voyages are considered navigationally easier than downwind voyages, since the canoe tacks back and forth before the target island many times. Consequently, the sailing directions for upwind passages are much less specific. Piailug visualizes paths radiating from both Pikelot, the reference island (shown on diagram), and Puluwat, the target island. He uses Pikelot to visualize his east-west relative position; Puluwat to visualize his north-south relative position. He tries to tack on the paths radiating out from the reference island. Also he tries to remain inside *yalap* between the home island and the target island.

On upwind passages Piailug judges the current by the speed with which the "island moves" on his initial northerly tack away from land (assuming wind from northerly sectors). If the home island appears to move faster than normal, then the current is from a southerly direction. If slower than normal, the current is from a northerly direction. He verifies this when he tacks, i.e., watches to see if the island moves faster or slower on the new tack. By correlating observations of the relative speed of his canoe with back-sights toward the home island, Piailug can estimate the current's east-west vector. He allows for the current's strength and vector when reckoning his *etak* plot and compensates for it by adjusting the distance he sails on each tack.

Reference island, or *lu pongank*: Pikelot

Wind: northeast

Current: none

Initial course: Fuesemagut (or as close-hauled as possible)

A: When Pikelot is under Tana Mun, Satawal will be at Etakidigina	Tack to make course of Tan Uliul. Piailug says it is inadvisable to cross the *yalap* between Puluwat and Satawal.

SAILING DIRECTIONS:
SATAWAL-PULUWAT

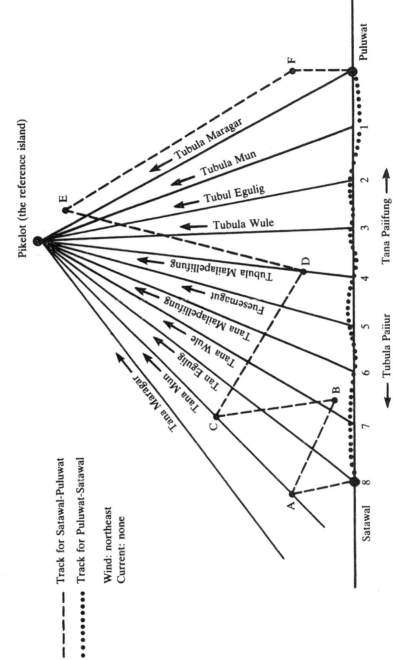

— — — Track for Satawal-Puluwat

•••••••• Track for Puluwat-Satawal

Wind: northeast
Current: none

Pikelot (the reference island)

Puluwat

Tubula Maragar

Tubula Mun

Tubul Egulig

Tubula Wule

Tubula Mailapellifung

Fuesemagut

Tana Mailapellifung

Tana Wule

Tan Egulig

Tana Mun

Tana Maragar

Tana Paiifung

Tubula Paiiur

Satawal

A B C D E F

B:	Pikelot has moved under Tana Wule
C:	Pikelot has moved under Tana Mun or Tana Maragar
D:	Pikelot under Tubula Mailapellifung, Puluwat lies under Tan Uliul.
E:	This point is near Etakidigina Pikelot
F:	This point is to windward of Puluwat. The reason for over shooting the island is to anticipate the wind veering to the east, which commonly occurs here.

B:	Tack to make a course of Fuesemagut
C:	Tack to steer Tan Uliul
D:	Tack again, sail Fuesemagut
E:	Tack to steer Tan Uliul
F:	Reach off for Puluwat

PULUWAT-SATAWAL

On this passage, Piailug no longer tracks the movement of Puluwat after he has passed *yaw luke*.

Reference island, or *lu pongank*: Pikelot

Wind: northeast

Initial course: Tubul Uliul

Puluwat lies under:	**Alter course (AC) to/at:**
Tan Ul (indicating no current)	AC to Tubula Mailap at Etakidigina (1)
	Puluwat then starts to move south again.
	Hold course of Tubula Mailap for one *etak*, to point 2
	Then from:
	2 to 3 under Tubula Paiiur
	3 to 4 under Tubula Mailap
	4 to 5 under Tubula Paiiur
	5 to 6 under Tubula Mailap
	6 to 7 under Tubula Paiiur
	7 to 8 under Tubula Mailap

Tana Maragar (indicating current from northerly direction)	Hold a course of Tubula Mailap for 1.5 *etak*. AC to Tubula Paiiur for one *etak*. Then alternate between Tubula Mailap and Tubula Paiiur, altering course at each *etak*.
Tana Mun (stronger northerly current)	Hold Tubula Mailap for two *etak*, then Tubula Paiiur for one *etak*; repeat.
Tan Egulig (even stronger northerly current)	Hold Tubula Mailap for 2.5 *etak*, Tubula Paiiur for one *etak*; repeat.
Tana Wulego	Piailug says current never runs this strong.
Tana Paiifung (indicating current from southerly direction)	Tubul Uliul for two *etak*, Tubula Mailap for one *etak*, Tubula Paiiur for one *etak*, Tubula Mailap for one *etak*; continue switching between Tubula Paiiur and Tubula Mailap for one *etak* each.
Tana Mailap (strong current)	Tubul Uliul for 2.5 *etak*, Tubula Mailap for one *etak*, Tubula Paiiur for two *etak*, Tubula Mailap for one *etak*, Tubula Paiiur for .5 *etak*
Tana Paiiur (stronger southerly current)	Tubul Uliul for three *etak*, Tubula Mailap for one *etak*, Tubula Paiiur for two *etak*, Tubula Mailap for one *etak*, Tubula Paiiur for one *etak*
Tan Uliul (very strong southerly current)	Tubul Uliul for 3.5 *etak*, Tubula Mailap for one *etak*, Tubula Paiiur for two *etak*, Tubula Mailap for one *etak*, Tubula Paiiur for .5 *etak*
Tana Sarapul	Current never runs this strong.

Satawal-Pikelot

Reference island or *lu pongank*: West Fayu

Wind: northeast

Current: none

Initial course: Fuesemagut (or as close-hauled as possible)

Depart main channel. Tack around to Wenimung. Satawal bears Tubula Mailap.
At One Tooth (A)
At Etakidigina Satawal (B)

Keep tacking as to cross the *yalap* at the *etak* points (C, D, et al.)
At *etakidigina* Pikelot should bear Tan Egulig (Q)

Tack north, sailing under Fuesemagut

Tack east
Tack north again on the star path of Tubula Wulego

Wind: north

Per dashed lines on diagram

Piailug says this is normally an easy voyage as Pikelot is always "moving slowly" and to windward of the canoe.

Pikelot-Satawal

Reference island or *lu pongank*: West Fayu

These directions will put Satawal to the north of the canoe when sighted, allowing the navigator to reach up to Satawal instead of falling off and possibly having to jibe, a much more difficult maneuver on an outrigger canoe than on a Western sailing vessel.

Wind: northeast

Initial course: Tubulup

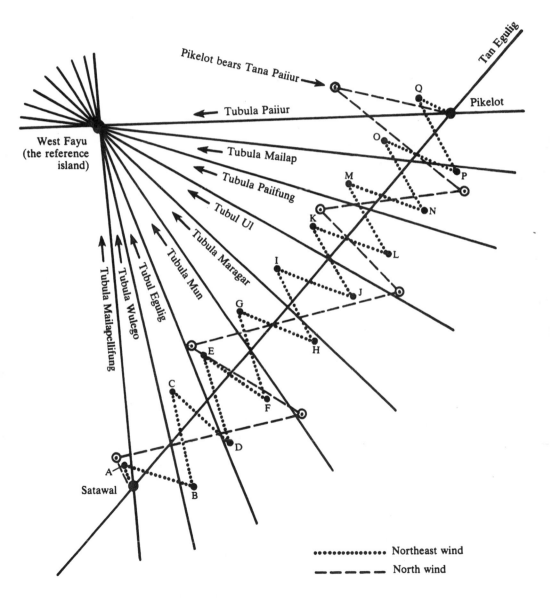

SAILING DIRECTIONS:
SATAWAL-PIKELOT

Tan Egulig

Pikelot bears Tana Paiiur →

Q

Pikelot

← Tubula Paiiur

West Fayu
(the reference
island)

← Tubula Mailap

O

← Tubula Paiifung

P

M

← Tubul Ul

N

Tubula Maragar

K

L

Tubula Mun

I

J

Tubul Egulig

G

Tubula Wulego

H

Tubula Mailapellifung

E

C

F

D

A

Satawal

B

•••••••••••• Northeast wind

— — — — North wind

Pikelot lies under:	Alter course to/at:
Tana Wule	Tubula Mesaru at *yaw luke*
Tan Egulig	Tubula Mesaru when West Fayu lies under Tubula Mun
Tana Mun	Tubula Mesaru at Etakidimaan Pikelot
Tana Maragar	Tubula Tumur at Etakidigina Pikelot
Tan Ul	Never
Tana Mailapellifung	Steer Tubulup until West Fayu bears Tubul Ul
Fuesemagut	Never

Note: If Satawal is not sighted the navigator assumes it is upwind—i.e., to the west—since these directions deliberately steer slightly to leeward of Satawal.

Wind: northwest

Initial course: Tubula Tumur

Pikelot lies under:	Alter course (AC) to/at:
Tana Mun (i.e., no current)	Tubula Mesaru at *yaw luke*
Tan Egulig	Tubula Tumur until West Fayu lies under Tubula Mun. Then change to Tubula Mesaru.
Tana Wule	Tubula Tumur to Etakidimaan Pikelot, then change to Tubula Mesaru

If wind is from northeast and current is from the east, sail an initial course of Tubula Tumur, then, if Pikelot lies under:

Tana Maragar	Change to Tubula Mesaru when West Fayu lies under Tubul Ul
Tan Ul	Never

If Satawal is not visible at *etakidigina*, AC to Tubulup. Satawal must be to leeward.

SATAWAL-LAMOTREK

Reference island or *lu pongank*: West Fayu

Wind: northeast

Initial course: Tubula Mailap

Satawal lies under:	Alter course to/at:
Tana Mailap (no current)	Tubula Paiifung at *yaw luke*
Tana Paiifung	Nematch Tubula Paiifung and Tubul Ul, at *yaw luke*
Tan Ul	Tubul Ul at *yaw luke*
Tana Maragar	Nematch Tubul Ul and Tubul Maragar at *yaw luke*
Tana Paiiur	Nematch Tubula Paiiur and Tubula Mailap at *yaw luke*
Tan Uliul	Tubula Paiiur at *yaw luke*
Tana Sarapul	Nematch Tubula Paiiur and Tubul Uliul at *yaw luke*

The rule: For each whole star bearing Satawal moves south at One Tooth, add one-half star bearing to the correction at *yaw luke*. All corrections are designed to place Lamotrek one-half star bearing to the north, enabling the navigator to reach up to the island instead of falling off.

LAMOTREK-SATAWAL

Wind: northeast

Leave Tauweliwa channel (see Appendix 10)

Sail close-hauled (steering Tana Paiiur or Tan Uliul) to clear island (A, page 284)	Tack north
At B, Lamotrek bears Tubula Tumur	Tack southeast. If there is no current, Lamotrek will move under Tubula Paiifung, the canoe will be at One Tooth and on the path to Satawal. If Lamotrek bears other than Tubula Paiifung, its bearing will indicate the direction of the current.
At C, Lamotrek bears Tubul Ul	Tack north
At D, Lamotrek-West Fayu path	Tack southeast
At E, Lamotrek-Satawal path, proceed as per dotted lines	Tack north

SAILING DIRECTIONS:
SATAWAL-LAMOTREK

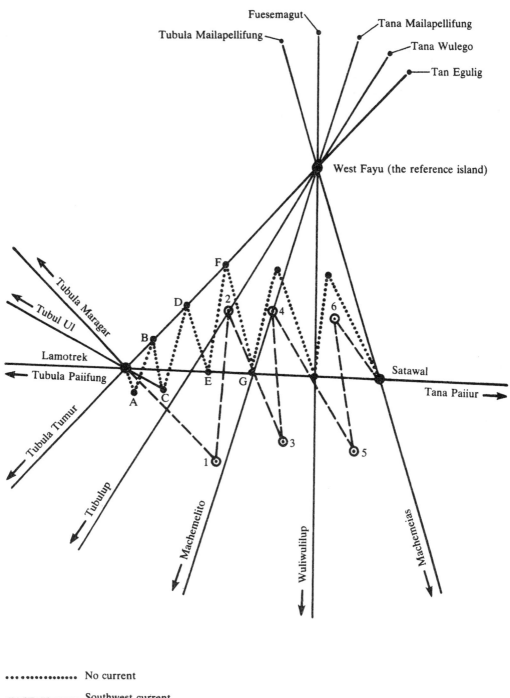

Fuesemagut

Tubula Mailapellifung

Tana Mailapellifung

Tana Wulego

Tan Egulig

West Fayu (the reference island)

Tubula Maragar

Tubul Ul

Lamotrek

Tubula Paiifung

Satawal

Tana Paiiur

Tubula Tumur

Tubulup

Machemelito

Wuliwulilup

Machemeias

F

D

2

4

6

B

E

G

A

C

1

3

5

·················· No current

— — — — — Southwest current

If there is no current, Piailug prefers to remain within the triangle formed by Lamotrek–West Fayu–Satawal.

Southerly current:

At 1, Lamotrek bears Tubula Maragar	Tack north
At 2, when intersecting the Tana Wulego–Tubulup path	Tack southeast

Continue tacking on the paths radiating through West Fayu, as per dashed lines.

10 APPENDIX

Fu Taur

This system specifies the various stars that the navigator can line up with certain features of islands in order to locate the channel at night. Most islands use Polaris as a range.

IFALUK

Place Fuesemagut halfway between the islets of Ella and Falalop

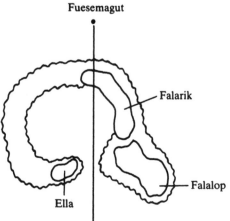

LAMOTREK

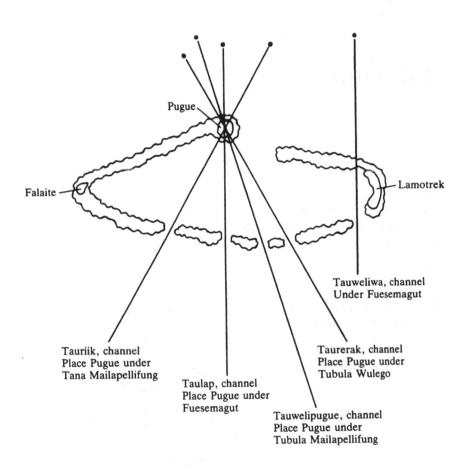

Pugue

Falaite

Lamotrek

Tauweliwa, channel
Under Fuesemagut

Tauriik, channel
Place Pugue under
Tana Mailapellifung

Taulap, channel
Place Pugue under
Fuesemagut

Taurerak, channel
Place Pugue under
Tubula Wulego

Tauwelipugue, channel
Place Pugue under
Tubula Mailapellifung

PULUWAT

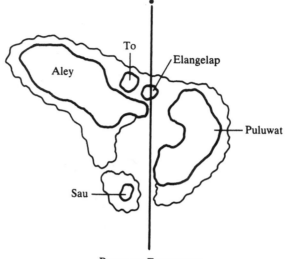

Range on Fuesemagut

WEST FAYU

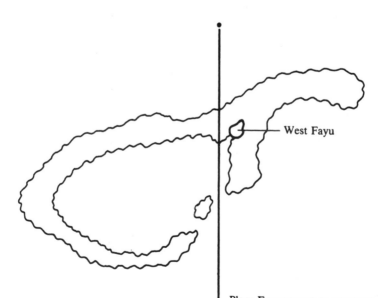

West Fayu

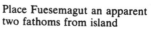

Place Fuesemagut an apparent
two fathoms from island

ELATO

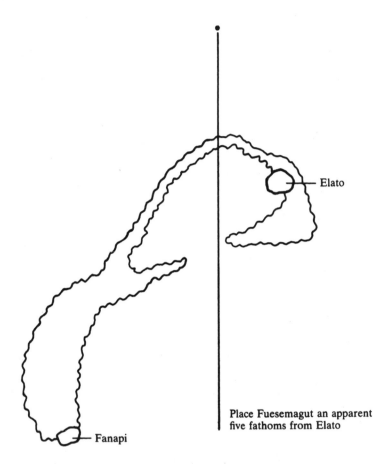

Elato

Place Fuesemagut an apparent
five fathoms from Elato

Fanapi

Toas

TRUK

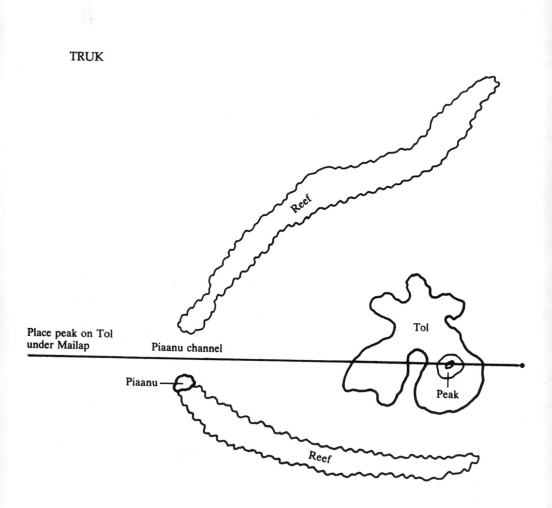

Reef

Place peak on Tol
under Mailap

Piaanu channel

Tol

Peak

Piaanu

Reef

Throughout this book I have made no attempt to apply any of the orthographies that exist for Carolinian languages, choosing instead to use simple phonetic spellings of Satawalese words and phrases. In Satawalese there is no distinction between *n* and *l* in many words, the final sound being a conjunction of the two sounds. Thus in Pulap, Nemanong, Masano, Lepotig, Wuliwulilup, for example, the *l*'s and *n*'s could be interchanged without mispronunciation. There is no plural form of nouns, multiplicity being indicated by a numeral modifier, such as "one *turrh*," "two *turrh*," "many *turrh*"; or "one *pwogos*," "two *pwogos*," etc.

afour   Species of small, bitter fruit carried on long voyages because it does not readily spoil

aiu   Jack crevelly

alet   Species of plant, unidentified

ama   Booby bird

amas   Literally "to face." A navigational exercise in which the navigator places a toy canoe in the center of the *paafu* circle and asks his students to name the stars over the bow, stern, outrigger, and lee platform.

amei   Stone fish weir

Anumwerici Literally the "spirit who wears flowers." Anumwerici makes himself manifest in the rainbow and is the patron spirit of the navigator. Also known as Yaluluweii, literally the "spirit of voyaging"

aoulong Portion of the reef upon which the waves break (see Appendix 2); also "chiefs" in *itang*

aparog Tradition for showing respect in which women bend at the waist before men, and men before chiefs

apwanna fu A system which pairs the following stars or constellations: Mun and Maan, Paiinemaanemeiifung and Mailap, Sepie and Eech, Ceuta and Illelligek, Piing and Sarapul, Na and Apisarapun, Poop and Cu, Aremoi and Alimatau, Roe and Maragar, Ul and Tumur, Uliul and Mesaru, and Poop in the upright position indicates Mun is rising. When Poop is at Machemelito, Mailap is rising.

arefu "Shape of star": term for the last night of which the waning moon is visible

aroom Navigational lesson in which the student names the primary navigational stars and their reciprocals—e.g., rising Altair and setting Altair, rising Vega and setting Antares

arreuw Traditionally, a man who knew navigation but who had not been through the *pwo* initiation ceremony. The term is no longer commonly used.

atirro To greet with solemn respect, especially a chief or great personage

ayu Mast

cha Blood, the color red

chu To meet

enas A medicinal ritual to protect young children and pregnant mothers from the harm of evil sea spirits

epar "To fix" or "to aim." Denotes the individual birds, fishes, whales, and reefs listed in the *pookof* system

epep Lee platform on sailing canoe

Etak A conceptual plotting system that enables the navigator to track his position at sea without charts, sextant, compass, or other modern aids to navigation. Also a unit of measurement.

etakidigina The "*etak* of sighting": the first and last *etak* of any voyage, inside which the island is visible

etakidimaan The "*etak* of birds": the second (and second to the last) *etak* in any voyage, delineated by the farthest range of certain seabirds, predominantly noddys and terns, which at dawn fly eighteen to twenty miles from their islands to fish for the day and at dusk return to their roosts

faimo   Gravel

fairon   Small black basaltic stone used in magical and medicinal rituals

fatonomuir   "Facing astern": a navigational technique by which the navigator measures the current displacing his vessel by backslighting toward his island of departure to observe the star under which the island has "moved"; abbreviated *muir*

fu taur   "Star channel": a navigational system delineating the star bearings of the channels through the reefs around certain islands, thereby allowing the navigator to find them at night (see Appendix 10)

imwelliyang   "Wind house": large cumulo-nimbus clouds thought to store wind. If they are present at dawn or dusk, the navigator expects the wind to blow from the direction in which they lie.

ina   There, that's it

inamo   There now, it's all right now

ira muan   "Man's timber" or gaff

ira rauput   "Woman's timber" or boom

itang   A collection of metaphorical verses or poems, the meaning of which is held secret, containing the wisdom and ethics of the culture. Some *itang* is used to resolve conflict and settle disputes; other *itang* verses are spoken at ceremonial occasions. *Itang* is also called "the talk of wisdom" and "the talk of light."

itimetau   The navigational system listing the names of the seaways between islands (see Appendix 3)

kapesani lang   "The talk of the skies": the lore of forecasting the weather by interpreting the shape and color of clouds at sunrise and sunset

kapesani lemetau   "The talk of the sea": the totality of navigational lore

kapesani serak   "The talk of sailing": a series of course corrections and current-compensation regimes enabling the navigator to correct for the displacement of current and leeway (see Appendix 9)

katoaragnap, katoepaipai, katogoose, katomai, katonu   "Calling skipjack tuna," "calling floating logs," "calling octopus," "calling breadfruit," and "calling coconuts." All are magic rituals to call these things to the island.

kkun   A delicious dish of pounded breadfruit covered with coconut milk

kruga   Sooty tern

kuling   Plover

lealulu   Shallow, narrow pool between the breakers and Satawal's beach

lefung   "The impatience": the winter months of strong northeasterly tradewinds, lasting from December through March

leraak "The year": the summer months of plenty, from April through November

lessor anim Trukese for "good morning"

long The trunks of coconut fronds upon which canoes are skidded to and from the water

lu pongank An island (or *epar*) off to one side of the course used in the *Etak* modeling process. *Lu* means "middle"; *pongank* means "crossing" or "athwart." Called the "reference island" in Western literature.

maan Bird, creature

maaneluke soamwoan "Bird outside the chief" or possibly "man outside the chief": a chief's next-youngest brother, who assists in governing

mas "Eye," "face"; also the "V"-shaped decoration on either end of a canoe

mau Hawksbill turtle, Piailug's nickname

maumau "Strong," in common speech; as one of the essential qualities of the *palu*, *maumau* implies strength animated by intelligence

meaify Literally "to feel": in navigation a technique used on nights when stars and swells are invisible to maintain the canoe's course by sensing its motion in the seaway. When the canoe's course changes, its motion will change as well.

merek keiky "Unfolding the mat": a student's first lessons in navigation— *paafu*, *aroom*, and *amas*—are sometimes taught on a mat upon which the stars are represented by a circle of coral lumps

mesanafanu "Face of the island": the populated side of an island, usually the west or southwest corner, which is sheltered from the tradewinds

meselipic Flu or cold

metau rhiperhip "Seas of kicking": short seaways on which a slight miscalculation of current or other mistake will result in the navigator's missing the objective

muen Sheet, or rope for controlling sail

muir Contraction of *fatonomuir*

mwan "Man," or right. The right arm is called the "man's" arm because it is stronger than the left, or "woman's," arm

nana "Plenty," abundance

oom Earth oven; food to be cooked is placed in a pit lined with hot rocks and covered with banana leaves.

paafu First lesson of navigation, which teaches the fifteen stars and constellations that, at rising and setting, mark thirty-two points around the horizon

Paiiroro Parowa A flock of thirty or forty *paiiroro* birds, unidentified but described as brown, long-beaked, with black on feathers, forty or fifty miles from Woleai. Parowa was a navigator who became very ill. As a gift to those who cared for him, he revealed this *epar*.

palu   Navigator fully initiated in *pwo*

peraf   Outrigger platform on sailing canoe

perhyan ayufan   "The tail of bluefin tuna," a navigational system, similar to *wofanu* but laid out in the shape of a fish's tail, which lists star courses from Moguchis, the north channel of Truk Lagoon, to various islands

pookof   A navigational system which gives star courses and ranges to distinct and identifiable birds, fishes, whales, and reefs arrayed around each island

poongen kilai   "Night of begin": seventeenth day of the moon's cycle, the beginning of a period of moonless evenings

poongen litu   "Night of going down": sixth day of the moon's cycle, when crabs are said to go down to the water to lay their eggs

poongen uur   "Night of pulling": night of the full moon, when the moon rises as the sun sets. The sun is said to "pull" the moon from the sea.

pukulaw   "Wave tying": a technique by which the navigator maintains a steady course at sea by using ocean swells

pwang   A body of skills that includes the repairing of canoes at sea, building houses, and a form of judo. *Pwang* is one of the six "arts," the others being *palu*, *pwin* (fishing), *safay* (medicine), *sennap* (canoe construction), and *pwe*.

pway   A flock of birds engaged in feeding

pwe   A method of divining the future by tying knots in palm fronds

pwerra   Fierceness; implies a warrior who is willing to cut and be cut in combat; "warrior" in common speech

pwipwimetau   "Brother seaways": a navigational system that pairs up similarly aligned seaways (see Appendix 4)

pwo   The initiation ceremony in which a navigational student becomes a full fledged *palu*

pwogos   A family compound or lineage village

raak   Year, season

raap   "Trunk," or base of a tree; also refers to a master of navigation. The student is the sprout.

rauput   "Woman," or left

reah   Retribution. Sent usually by Alulap, the "great spirit," upon hearing people gossip about a misdeed.

reipy   Wise, wisdom

re metau   "People of the sea," the collective term for the outer islanders used by the Yapese *roe*   Literally "dip net." A ceremony in which, for four days after a birth or death, the whole island fishes for the family; also the constellation Corona Borealis.

rongirup   See Appendix 2

rop   To cut fish or turtle into portions in preparation for division

rugger   Mahogany-type tree

ruung   A taboo area

saisaulig   The man who greets arriving canoes in order to learn their origins and intentions; literally "master of greetings"

saulig   To greet incoming canoes

saumai   "Master of breadfruit": calls breadfruit to the island by magic chants

sausafay   "Master of medicine": a practitioner of traditional medicine

saway   A parent-child relationship binding certain Yapese families to all the members of individual outer islands. While on Yap, all Satawalese are under the protection of Satawal's *saway* ("father"); they bring him gifts and in turn gather coconuts, taro, and breadfruit from his land.

sawie   Conch-shell trumpet

sennap   Master canoe builder

sooahsoo   A delicious dish of baked taro swirled with coconut milk

souwienet   "Master of dividing": fishes, turtles, and some other commodities are divided equally among the eight clans of Satawal by a master of dividing. Typically, each woman receives a share, then men and children.

taimeang   Part of Pookof Woleai, a school of small dolphins between Ifaluk and Elato

tam   Outrigger of sailing canoe; also may denote navigators and chiefs, as both control and stabilize that over which they have authority

tan   "Rising": prefix to indicate a star is rising. An *a* is suffixed to bridge two consonants, e.g., Tana Mailap.

teek   A type of long grass, unidentified

telap   Leader of each of the Clans of the People

thu   Men's loincloth. Formerly the term was not to be used in mixed company.

tololayu   "Clitoris of the mast": small nub carved in the masthead

tubul   "Setting": prefix to indicate star is setting, also with an *a* suffixed to bridge two consonants

turrh   Woman's skirt

umau   Traditional period of celebration and sexual license during the time when picking coconuts was taboo

uu   sail

uulegool   Part of Pookof Woleai: one green leaf of the *gool* tree (unidentified)

venuk   Benches on sailing canoe

warigerig   You are tiring yourself; thank you
wee   A school of fish rushing just beneath the surface of the water
wenimum   Polite greeting
wofanu   Navigational system delineating the star courses between the islands

yalap   "Great path," the direct course between two islands
Yaluluweii   See Anumwerici
Yanna tingie annie!   "The cunt flies to you!": an all-purpose expression used only in all-male company
yaopiyop   Navigational system of ranges to establish the initial course when beginning a voyage during the day. This system has fallen into disuse since the introduction of the magnetic compass.
yarama   Species of shrub, unidentified
yaw luke   "Middle path": the midpoint of a voyage. On some voyages this point is marked by a star path radiating through the reference island. On other voyages it is not.

Adam, 55, 67
Afour (fruit), 58, 188, 291
Age, Micronesians' concept of, 37–38
Agoroup, 110
Aiu, 30, 291
Alet, definition of, 291
Alimatau (star), 174, 239, 241, 270
Aloha (canoe), 66, 68, 70, 93, 136, 138, 140, 147, 180
Alulap, 104
Alung (star), 239, 241
Ama, 182, 291
Amalap, 55, 67, 70
Amalug, 55
Amas, 28, 291
Amei, 114, 291
Analungifir, 168
Anatiu clan, 58
Angora (Piailug's uncle), 50, 83, 118–20, 155
Aninga (canoe), 150–56, 178
Annupo (star), 24, 239, 242
Antonio (Piailug's son), 45, 74, 160
Anumwerici, 11, 39, 88, 118, 168
chants to, 197–204

definition of, 292
power of, 198
story of, 85–86
Aouani, 212
Aoulong, 102, 292
Ap (star), 239, 242
Aparog, 162, 292
Apiaoumuun lusessen, 87
Apinallay, 174
Apisarapul (star), 239, 242, 271
Apwanna fu, definition of, 292
Arefu, 177, 292
Aremoi (star), 239, 241, 271
Aroom, 28, 170, 292
Arreuw, 118, 292
Arrouw, 139n
Aruruwow, 250–251
Assaf, 67, 68, 136, 138–42, 147, 169, 170, 181, 187, 191
Asugulap (village), 43
Asuguo (canoe house), 56
Atarino (Piailug's grandchild), 149, 151
Atirro, 200, 292
Auhror, 19–20, 24, 92, 195
Auren Mangar (planet), 240, 242

Austerio (Piailug's son), 45
Ayu, 68, 292

Basket of spirits, 167
Battista (Piailug's son), 45, 216
Bêche-de-mer, trade in, 16–17
Birds, in *pookof*, 30–31
Bonefacio (Piailug's son), 34, 46, 109, 122,
  136, 138–40, 149, 177, 216–17, 232–34
  Piailug's hopes for, 161–62
Breadfruit, 57

Canoe
  construction, 53
  "eyes" of, 71
  parts of, Satawalese names for, 68
  steering, 136, 140
Canoe house(s), 25–26, 46, 56
  Piailug's, at Nemanong, 149
Carlita (Piailug's daughter), 44–45, 149,
  151, 152
Caroline Islands, 6, 16–18
  island caste system, 15–16
Celestial navigation, 7–8, 9. *See also*
  Navigation
Ceuta (month), 92, 270
Ceuta (star), 38, 174, 239, 242, 269
Cha, 208, 292
Chant(s)
  navigator's, 198–99, 203–4
  for student bidding farewell to master,
  233–234
Chiefs
  author's relationship with, 209
  Piailug's evaluation of, 232
  power of, 101–102
  role of, on Satawal, 59, 195
Child, death of, Satawalese customs sur-
  rounding, 106
Childbirth, Satawalese customs surround-
  ing, 106, 165–66. See also *Roe*
Christianity, effect on Satawalese culture,
  161, 199, 203
Chu, definition of, 292
Clans of the Chiefs, 58
Clans of the People, 58–59
Clouds, in weather forecasting, 175–76
Coconut
  as food resource, 57
  used as soap, 50, 156
Coffee, Satawalese value of, 52

Conch shells, Piailug's gift of, 147
Copra, 16, 57, 207
Council of Elders, 59, 195
Cu (month), 39, 270
Cu (star), 92, 107, 174, 239, 241, 270
Current
  Micronesian navigator's method of
  determining, 31–32, 76, 91
  Micronesian navigator's use of, 29–30

Dancing, Satawalese, 107, 127
Dark Stomach (spirit), 101
Dead-reckoning navigation, 75
Dolphins
  clan descended from, folk tale about,
  168–69
  in *pookof*, 30–31
Dolphin tattoo, on chiefs, 47, 117
Downwind passages, 114

Eddy, 170, 181, 186–87, 192, 214
Education, Western
  effect on Satawalese culture, 159–62
  in Micronesia, 75, 106–7, 131
Eech (month), 271
Eech (star), 239, 241, 271
Egulig (star), 27, 239, 241
Eguman (Uurupa's son), 48, 55, 67, 69,
  74, 92–93, 157
Eguwan (*epar*), 252
Eguwan (Piailug's uncle), 131, 188, 230
Eguwan (shark), 116
Emilia (Piailug's daughter), 45, 149,
  151–54, 157, 160, 165–66, 185, 194, 196
Enas, 165–66, 292
Eniwetok, 17
Epailuk, 167
Epan, 24–25
Epar, 115–16
  definition of term, 86*n*, 292
  myth of origin of, 86–87
Epwinegerik, 87*n*, 255
Equatorial Countercurrent, 31
Erai, 202
Etak, 77, 78, 80, 82, 112, 113
  definition of, 292
etak (unit of distance), 78*n*
Etakidigina, 80, 292
Etakidimaan, 80, 292
Etak of birds, 80, 82, 114, 183, 184
  definition of, 292

Etak of sighting, 80, 82
  subdivision of, 243–44
Eu Ponank, 255

Faimo, 116, 293
Faimoran, 256
Fainin (village), 57
Fairon, 167, 293
Fais, 16
Faitoyang, 259
Fanagoon (bathing place), 50, 192
Fanur, 85, 103, 119, 168
  meaning of name, 86
Fara, 118
Farailap, 28
Farepuey, 198
Faselos, 258
Fatonomuir, 29, 76, 112, 293
Fatul, 258
Federated States of Micronesia, 6, 15
  Compact of Free Association with U.S.,
  18, 210
Felix, 89
Fiesta, on Saipan, 119–20
Fighting stars, 38, 39, 135, 175, 268–71
Finney, Ben, 158
Fishes, in *pookof*, 30–31
Fishing, Satawalese practice of, 66,
  68–70, 143–45
Fishing taboos, 69
Flying-fish song, 98
Fuesemagut (star), 239, 242
Fu Raan (planet), 241, 242
Fu taur, 116, 286–90, 293

Gajdusek, Carlton, 12
Galingatuk (canoe house), 46, 56
Geriger, 159, 223, 227, 228
Germans, occupation of Satawal, 203
Ghosts, Satawalese concept of, 44, 88–89
  See also Spirit(s); Spirit world
Gifts, author's, to Satawalese, 60–61
Gilberts, 17
Gnathanodon speciosus, 253
Gu, 258
Guam, 17, 108–11
Halelegam, 15, 18–19
Halig (Piailug's son), 33, 45, 109, 111
Hippour, 111
Hokule'a, 11, 108–9, 126, 132, 158
Houses, on Satawal, 42

Howie (Piailug's son), 45, 149, 151, 177,
  181–82

Ifungunul (star), 239, 241
Igisapan, 254
Igosuuk, 259
Ikerip, 68
Ikimai, 45, 89, 169
Illelligek (star), 239, 241, 271
Illellpuumaan (spirit medium), 89
Imwelliyang, 175–76, 293
Imwoligat (village), 57
Ina, definition of, 293
Inaiman (Piailug's son), 35, 45, 74,
  151–52, 170–71, 206, 222
Inamo, definition of, 293
Ineffitimwar, 252
Innanomwar, 252, 254
Inner Passage, 16
Inosagur, 85
Insoruun (Piailug's niece), 149
Insouluke (Uurupa's wife), 52
Ira muan, 68, 293
Ira rauput, 68, 293
Itang, 97–106, 234
  to control rebellious man, 100
  to control threat of violence, 102
  definition of, 293
  to impel chiefs to resolve conflict,
  99–101
  meaning of, 104–5
  Piailug on, 128
  Piailug's attitude toward, 172, 234
  publication of, 238
  used by *palu* after being lost at sea,
  102–3
  Westerners' definitions of, 97n
Iti, 67, 70, 138, 145, 147–159, 180
Itimetau, 83, 245–46, 293
Iur, 201–3

Jack crevelly. See *Aiu*
Japanese, occupation of Satawal, 203
Jesse (Uurupa's nephew), 55–56, 59–60,
  65–67, 90, 94, 222, 228
Jesus (Piailug's son), 45
John, 181, 187, 189, 192
Josede (Piailug's son-in-law), 149–150,
  153, 157, 158, 160, 163, 166, 168, 170,
  194, 196–97, 205, 209, 215–17,
  228–29, 232–35

Joseph, 141, 159, 181, 184, 191, 192, 213, 214, 223, 227, 228
Josephina (Piailug's niece), 149, 157, 208

Kapesani lang, 73, 293
Kapesani lemetau ("talk of the sea"), 26, 293
Kapesani serak, 76, 112–13, 272–85, 293
Kata (Nemioto's mother), 151, 167
Katamang clan, 44, 54–56, 58
Katoaragnap, 121, 293
Katoepaipai, 121, 166–67, 293
Katogoose, 122, 293
Katomai, 201, 293
Katonu, 201, 293
Kkun, 71, 293
Kruga, 140
  definition of, 293
Kuling bird, 85*n*
  definition of, 293
Kusaie, 17, 29
Kutu, 256
Kwajalein Atoll, 5, 17

Laifanimung, 253
Lamotrek (island), 28, 34
Lananannan, 256
Land, value of, to Micronesians, 58
Laousourer, 199
Lapita people, 4
Lar, 257
Lealiwan, 89
Lealulu, 65, 293
Learhumoi, 256
Lefung, 37, 38, 39, 268, 293
Lelillio, 201, 201*n*
Lepotig (canoe house), 56
Leraak, 37, 92, 268, 294
Lessor anim, definition of, 294
Lewis, David, 111, 158
  We, the Navigators, 7–8, 12
Lewis, Evan, 202–3
Long, definition of, 294
Low, Sam, 12, 25
Lugarig, definition of, 56
Lugarig (chiefs' canoe house), 46, 56
Lugoisum, 87, 116, 253, 254
Lugunumaat, 260
Luito, 110
Lupomai, 150–51, 170
Lu pongank, 78, 80, 82, 83, 113, 180, 294

Maan (bird), 116, 294
Maan (month), 271
Maan (star), 21, 159, 239, 242, 270–71
Maaneluke soamwoan, 59, 294
Maanusuuk (Piailug's uncle), 96, 107, 118, 124–25, 128, 130, 146, 163–64, 218, 226, 234
  instructs author about *itang*, 97–106
Machemeias (star), 240
Madrich, 18
Magic
  bad, 202
  in navigation, 198
Mailap (month), 38–39, 270
Mailap (star), 27, 28, 159, 177, 240, 241, 269
Mailapellifung (star), 28, 240, 242
Mailuk, 258
Manerh, 256
Manirrik, 253, 255
Maragar (star), 27, 28, 175, 177, 240, 242, 270
Marcia (Piailug's daughter), 45, 149, 173
Maria (Assaf's daughter), 136, 138–39, 141
Marianas, 17–18, 110–11
Marigot (Piailug's daughter), 45
Marshall Islands, 5, 17–18
Mas, 72, 294
Masano, definition of, 56
Masano clan, 56, 58
Matto, 68, 138, 159
Mau (turtle), 117, 294
Maumau, 163, 294
Mauricio (Piailug's grandchild), 149, 151, 229
McCoy, Mike, 126
Meaify, 76, 294
Medicinal rituals, Satawalese, 165–67
Melosar, 202
Merek keiky, 28, 294
Mesailuke (Piailug's son), 34, 45, 74, 111, 165, 170, 171, 205, 211, 213, 214, 216, 217, 223
Mesal Arik (star), 240, 242
Mesalialu, 253
Mesanafanu, definition of, 56, 294
Mesarmeifung, 252
Mesarmeur, 252
Mesaru (star), 240, 242
Meselipic, 208, 294
Metau Pongank, 83

Metau rhiperhip, 115, 294
Micronesia, 4, 16–17
Microspirit (freighter), 23–24, 107, 131, 171
Moenefar clan, 59
Mongoisum (star), 21, 240–241
Morellifu, 268
Mose (star), 240–42
Motch (Piailug's cousin), 136, 139–42, 145, 147, 169
Muanirik, 19–21, 24–25, 33–35, 93, 169
Muir, 229, 294
Mun (month), 38, 269
Mun (star), 27, 159, 177, 240, 242
Mwan, definition of, 294
Mwaramai, 196–97, 209, 224, 227, 232
Mwaramwar, 258

Na (month), 107, 270
Na (star), 39, 82, 240, 241, 270
Naifailuke, 254
Naimorman (Piailug's daughter), 45
Nainearh, 198
Nakayama, Tosiwo, 6
Namonuito (island), 15, 16
Nana, definition of, 294
Nanyo Boekie Keisa Trading Company, 47
Napota, 54, 56, 67, 70, 169
Narun (spirit), 89
Nauwan, 150
Nauwenimar, 259
Nauwinimaan, 87
Navigation, 9
  blue-water, 75
  myth of origin of, 85–86
  schools of, 118
  teaching of, 91–92, 105–6
Navigation, Micronesian, 75–85
  as dying art, 91–92
  effect of Western culture on, 125
  vs. Western, 9, 31
Navigation, Western, 75, 76
  Satawalese curiosity about, 90
Navigator. See also *Palu*
  courage of, Piailug on, 127
  future of, Piailug's views on, 122–23, 155–56, 169, 176–77
  Lapita, 4
  secular vs. spiritual nature of, 129
  taboos of, 161–62
  training, 26
Navigators, The (film), 85

Naweeimai, 259
Neagumwuan, 253, 254
Neamirh, 54, 56
Neamirrh, 253, 255
Neamoun (Piailug's aunt), 118
Neanuaas (spirit of wisdom), 99–100
Nefaifai, 141, 145
Nemaigu, 258
Nemanong (village), 44, 56, 57, 126, 149–50
Nematch, 272
Nemoito (Piailug's wife), 44–46, 57, 109, 150, 152, 154, 160, 163, 173, 192, 196, 205, 208, 228–29
Nesattacu, 57
Neyarh clan, 58
Nitar, 198
North Pacific High, 31
Nosomar clan, 58

Obsidian, as trade commodity, 4
Oceania, ancient navigators in, 4
Olaipemwar, 198
Olaisettmwar, 198
Olaman, 54, 56, 67, 71
Olimaan, 258
Onalap, 97
Oneipwinik, 255
One Tooth, 113, 272
Oognalepar, 258
Oom, definition of, 294
Ootenap (canoe house), 46, 56, 68
Orraiferh, 258
Orraifu, 257
Orrailar, 257
Orrailem, 258
Orrailemwar, 258
Orrailepoap, 257
Orrailepoopen, 258
Orrainaiepweou, 259
Orrairepar, 106, 253, 258
Orraisaita, 258
Orraisu, 258
Orraitaakunumaar, 260
Orraitigilimaan, 116, 257
Orraitiinipu, 259
Orranik, 258
Orranipul (Piailug's father), 117–18

Paafu, 27–28, 75–76, 80, 295
Paiifung (star), 27–29, 240–41

Paiinemaanemefung (star), 159, 240, 242
Paiinemaanemeiur (star), 240, 241
Paiiroro Parowa, 169, 259, 295
Paiiur (star), 240–41
Palau, 17–18
Palu, 11–12. *See also* Navigator; Taboos, of the *palu*
  commitment of, 83
  definition of, 295
  distinction of, 126
  Piailug's attainment of status of, 118–19
  qualities of, Piailug on, 163
  role of, 105
  status of, 162
Palulap, 168
  fables of, 103
Parowa, 169, 259
Parrung ai Tumur (star), 242
Partner stars, 28
Paul (Uurupa's nephew), 55–57, 65, 67, 69, 90, 94, 97–99, 105, 107, 181, 217–18
Peleliu, 17
Pelifaimo, 116, 257
Perhyan ayufan, 139n, 295
Peter, 181, 187, 192
Piailug, 3, 107, 130–32, 160, 205
  attitude toward West, 125–26
  author's first meeting with, 24–25
  author's leavetaking of, 233–35
  author's relationship with, 32–33, 152, 172, 192, 218–19, 224, 226
  on bravery, 83–85
  building new canoe, 131–32
  character, 124–129, 145
  childhood, 117–19, 154–55
  children, 45
  on cultural change on Satawal, 161
  "eaten" by sea spirit, 89
  fighting skill of, 54
  Hawaii-Tahiti voyage, 126
  home, 44
  instruction in navigation, 154–55
  instruction of author, 26, 27, 111–23, 169, 173–77
  as navigator on voyages with author, 135–41, 180–93
  nickname, 11, 117
  offense on Assumption Day, 221
  pwo ceremony, 11

  relationship to other islanders, 209–11
  relationship with chiefs, 24, 35, 47–48, 222
  reputation, 126
  on Saipan, 119–21
  training in navigation, 27–28
  Uurupa's relationship with, 74
  on visit to Saipan, 108–22
  voyages of, 11, 111, 125
Pigale. *See* West Fayu
Piing (star), 174, 240–41
Pik clan, 56–58
Pikelot, 28
  epar of, 115
  geography of, 188
  voyage to, 179–193
Pis, 170, 256
Planets, Satawalese names, Western counterparts, 240–41
Poap, 257
Polynesian language and culture, 4
Polynesians, indigenous navigating tradition, 4–5
Ponape, 4, 6, 15, 17
Pookof, 30–31, 83, 85n, 115–16, 180, 252–60
  definition of term, 86n
  myth of origin of, 86–88
  variations of, 87n
Pookof Lamotrek, 254
Pookof Pikelot, 257–59
Pookof Pulap, 257
Pookof Pulusuk, 256–57
Pookof Puluwat, 255–56
Pookof Satawal, 252–54
Pookof West Fayu, 254–55
Pookof Woleai, 169, 258–59
Poongen kilai, 158, 295
Poongen litu, 157, 295
Poongen uur, 156, 295
Poop, 258
Poop (star), 240, 271
Potig, definition of, 56
Pukulaw, 76, 295
Pukulielie, 256
Pulap (island), 16, 28, 85
Pulusuk (island), 16, 28
Puluwat (island), 16, 28
Pun, 257
Punorrun (spirit), 89
Pwang, 54, 295

Pway, 69, 295
Pwe, 229, 295
Pwerra, 163, 295
Pwilenan, 258
Pwipwimetau, 83, 247–49, 295
Pwo, 85–86
Pwo ceremony, 11, 73, 74, 118, 155, 295
Pwogos, 56, 156

Raak, definition of, 296
Raangipi (Piailug's grandfather), 27–28, 118
Raap, 91, 296
Raglmar, Jesse, 6
Rapirugger (village), 57
Rau (old man), 54–56
Raulawup, 255
Rauput, definition of, 296
Reah, 104, 296
Reference island. See *Lu pongank*
Regaliang (Muanirik's brother), 68, 169, 181, 196
Reipy, 163, 296
Religion, Western, Satawalese practice of, 35–36, 90
Re metau ("people of the sea"), 58, 296
Repaghituun, 259
Repota, 259
Rewena (chief), 46–47, 111, 169, 171, 181, 191, 195, 209–14, 227
  author's offense against, 211, 213–15
  author's relationship with, 59–61
Rewena (*epar*), 255
Roe (after childbirth), 106, 158, 165, 296
Roe (month), 38, 269
Roe (star), 240, 242, 269, 296
Rongelap, 103, 168
Rongerig, 103, 168
Rop, definition of, 296
Ropitiu (canoe house), 46, 53, 56
Rovigno (Piailug's son-in-law), 136, 138, 140, 142, 147, 150–51, 170–71, 181, 184, 187, 191, 216
Rugger (canoe), 66, 68, 70, 93, 180, 183–84, 187
Rugger (tree), 53, 296
Rutapinau, 258
Ruung, 201*n*, 296

Saavedra, 16
Sagur, 200

Sagur (spirit and chief), 85
Sailing directions, 112, 272
Sailing magic, modern attitude toward, 121
Sailmaking, Satawalese, 66–67
Saiow, 223
Saipan, 17, 108–12
Saipweric, song of, 212–13
Saisaulig, 102, 296
Samoa, 4
Sandra (Piailug's daughter), 45
Sanny Ferto, 202
Sapu, 118
Sarapul (month), 38, 269
Sarapul (star), 240, 242
Satawal, 3, 6, 11, 16–17, 19–20
  author's arrival on, 35
  clans of, 57–59
  food resources on, 57–58
  housing on, 207
  matrilineal culture, 24, 57
  matrilocal culture, 57
  story of origin of, 196–97
  wofanu for. See *Wofanu*
  young men of, views on future, 216
Satawalese (language), 20
  orthography, 291
  translation of, 237–38
Satawalese (people), 16
Satellites, Satawalese interpretation of, 177
Saulig, definition of, 296
Saumai, definition of, 296
Saumek, 71
Saurhewon, 201–2, 204
Sausafay, definition of, 296
Sauwenima (spirit), 167
Saway, 16, 296
Sawie, 198, 296
Seasons, Micronesian, 37–39, 268
Sea spirits, 88, 165–66, 202
Sea turtles. *See* Turtles
Sea urchins, gathering of, 157
Seaways, 245–46
  names of, 83
  similarly aligned, 247–49
Sennap, 53, 296
Sepie, 258
Sepie (star), 38, 174, 177, 240, 242, 269
Sepie Mailan, 258
Sepie Mailuk, 258

Seulang (patron spirit of canoe builder), 103
She of Hiding (spirit), 102
She of the Meeting (spirit), 100
She of the Resolution (spirit), 100
She of Why (spirit), 102
Sidereal compass, 27
Sigafna (canoe house), 56
Slaughter of Saiow, 58
Sooahsoo, 220, 229, 296
Sorcerers, 162, 202
Soueriang, 259
Soupuungwa, 259
Sousat clan, 58
Souwen clan, 58
Souwienet, 126, 296
Spirit(s). See also Sea spirits
  appeals to, in itang, 99
  of gathering, 198
  in itang, 100, 101–2
  of middle heavens, 198
  Satawalese belief in, 89–90, 158, 194
  of unbent knees, 101
Spirit world, 166–68, 203, 206
Star channel, 116. See also Fu taur
Star courses, 261–67
  Micronesian navigators' use of, 28–29
Star months, 37–38, 269–71
Star names, 21, 24, 27
  Western counterparts, 239–42
Stars
  appearance of, 159
  rising positions, Micronesian navigators' use of, 27
  unnamed, navigation by, 76
  Western names, and Satawalese counterparts, 239–42
Sterna dougallii, 254
Sterna sumatrana, 256
Steven, 55
Suntory (canoe), 53–54, 65, 67, 68, 90, 93, 146
  men sailing on, 67
  rebuilding of, 55, 66
Suukarim, 255
Suuoh, 259
Swells, navigator's use of, 76

Ta, 257
Taak, 260

Taboos, 162–63. See also Fishing taboos
  of the palu, 74
  on picking coconuts, 215
Tagalar, 116
Tagu, 253
Tahiti, 4–5
Taimeang, 169, 259
  definition of, 296
Talk of sailing, 115. See also Kapesani serak
Tan, definition of, 27, 296
Tarawa, 17
Tattooing, on chiefs, 47. See also Dolphin tattoo
Taumuan, 165–68
Teek, definition of, 296
Tefrhowai (star), 240, 242
Teiifung, 91
Telap, 59, 195, 222, 296
Terei (Piailug's son-in-law), 67
Thomas, Stephen
  adoption into Piailug's family, 49
  father of, 5–6, 9–10, 129, 153
  first trip to Satawal, 3–36
  leaves Satawal for first time, 107
  voyage from Galápagos to Marquesas, 6–7
  voyage from Seattle to Hawaii (race), 7
  work in charter trade in Greece, 9–10
Thu, 35, 296
Thurang, 258
Thureng (chief), 21, 24, 195, 221, 230
  author's first meeting with, 18–20
Tiger (chiefs' canoe), 60, 66, 68, 70, 140, 146, 147, 157, 195
Tigiri, 149, 152, 166, 194, 196, 208
Tiin, 259
Tingar Uliul (star), 240, 241
Tiufatul, 258
Tololayu, 168, 296
Tom (Piailug's grandson), 181, 182, 184
Tom (Piailug's son), 45
Tonga, 4
Torres, Don Luis, 110
Truk, 4, 15, 28
  in World War II, 17
Tuba, 33, 178
  banning of, 195
Tubul, definition of, 27, 296
Tumur (month), 38, 269

Tumur (star), 240–41, 269
Tun, Petrus, 6
Tuna
  Satawalese fishing for, 69–70, 72
  schooling around floating logs, 166*n*
Tupia (navigator), 5
Turrh, 45, 58, 296
Turtles, hunting of, 51, 142, 145–46, 187,
  189, 209, 221
  Piailug's concern about, 176, 193
Turtle shell, use of, 189–90
Tuun, 259
Typhoons, 58

Ul (month), 270–71
Ul (star), 21, 27, 28, 39, 135, 174, 177,
  240–41, 270
Uliso (bird), 253–54
Uliso (chief), 47
Ulithi, 16, 207
  in World War II, 17
Uliul (month), 271
Uliul (star), 28, 39–40, 174–75, 177, 240,
  242
Umau, 127, 215, 297
Unghaur, 159
Upwind passages, 114, 276
Uru (Piailug's son), 45, 111
Uulegool, 169, 259, 297
Uurorran, 254
Uurupa (Piailug's brother), 33, 46, 51,
  59–60, 65–67, 69–70, 97–98, 112, 118,
  124, 131, 145, 150–51, 153, 157, 169,
  170, 179, 206, 207, 226, 230
  admiration for Piailug, 74
  author's first meeting with, 48–50
  early life of, 73–74
  instruction of author, 55–56, 73–75,
  78–92
  leaves for Yap, 93–95
  master canoe builder, 53
  voyages of, 74

Villages, Satawalese, names of, 56–57
Villalobos, 16
von Kotzebue, Otto, 110
Voyages, initiated by day, sailing direc-
  tions for, 115
Voyaging season, 92

Wareyang, 85, 103, 118, 168
  meaning of name, 86
Warigerig, definition of, 297
Waves. *See also* Swells
  navigator's use of, 76
  shape of, navigator's use of, 29
Weather, stars' rule over, 38
Weather forecasting, 190–91. See also
  Kapesani lang
  Micronesian method of, 21, 73, 175–76
  Piailug's ability at, 135
Weather signs, 169
Wee, 69, 259, 297
Weito (legendary navigator), 139
Wenallute, 258
Weneto (chief), 89, 157, 195, 206
Wenimum, definition of, 297
Weriai Tumur (planet), 241, 242
West Fayu, 28, 141–42, 188
  canoe voyage to, 135–41
Whale, Piailug's encounter with, 230
White Horse (canoe), 136, 138, 140
Wofanu, 28–29, 75, 78, 83, 86, 112, 115,
  116, 261–67
  definition of, 297
  Piailug's knowledge of, 28–29
  for Satawal, 29
Woleai, 33
Woleaian (language), 20
Woleatu (canoe house), 46, 56
Women, power of, on Satawal, 59. See
  also Satawal, matrilineal culture
Wonipik, 258
Wule (star), 240, 242
Wulego (star), 28, 240, 242
Wuligee, fishing on, 69

Yalap, 78, 297
Yaluluweii, 292
Yang ilito, 271
Yaniruun, 259
Yanna tingie annie!, 70, 297
Yaopiyop, 115, 297
Yap, 14–17
Yapese (language), 15
Yapese (people), 14–15
Yarama, definition of, 297
Yaw luke, 83, 272, 297
Years, Satawalese, 268
"Yeast", 209, 222
Yoliwa, 86, 116, 199, 253–54